SMALL BUSINESS AND ENTE

D0245892

MACMILLAN SMALL BUSINESS SERIES

Series Editors: Jim Dewhurst and Paul Burns

The books in this series are designed for use by students in higher education taking courses in small-business related courses at undergraduate and post-experience level. They are also particularly useful for those studying for professional examinations and for well-informed managers of small and growing businesses.

The books are comprehensive in scope and written by leading experts and researchers in this field. They deal with the subject in a sophisticated and rigorous way whilst still providing essential practical guidance.

PUBLISHED

Small Business Management (Third Edition) Jim Dewhurst and
  Paul Burns (eds)
Small Business in Europe Paul Burns and Jim Dewhurst (eds)
Small Business: The Independent Retailer Gary Davies and Kim Harris
Small Business: Production/Operations Management Terry Hill
Marketing for the Small Business Derek Waterworth
Small Business and Entrepreneurship (Second Edition) Paul Burns and
  Jim Dewhurst (eds)

Series Standing Order

If you would like to receive future titles in this series as they are published, you can make use of our standing order facility. To place a standing order please contact your book-seller or, in case of difficulty, write to us at the address below with your name and address and the name of the series. Please state with which title you wish to begin your standing order. (If you live outside the United Kingdom we may not have the rights for your area, in which case we will forward your order to the publisher concerned.)

Customer Services Department, Macmillan Distribution Ltd
Houndsmills, Basingstoke, Hampshire RG21 6XS, England

SMALL BUSINESS AND ENTREPRENEURSHIP

Second Edition

Edited by Paul Burns and Jim Dewhurst

First edition 1989
Reprinted five times
Second edition 1996

Published by
MACMILLAN PRESS LTD
Houndmills, Basingstoke, Hampshire RG21 6XS and London
Companies and representatives throughout the world

ISBN 0-333-64586-3 hardcover
ISBN 0-333-64587-1 paperback

A catalogue record for this book is available from the British Library.

10   9   8   7   6   5   4   3
05   04   03   02   01   00   99   98

Typeset by Acorn Bookwork, Salisbury, Wiltshire

Printed in Great Britain by Antony Rowe Ltd
Chippenham, Wiltshire

Contents

List of Tables		vii
List of Figures		ix
Preface to the Second Edition		xi
Notes on the Contributors		xiii

1	Introduction: The Significance of Small Firms *Paul Burns*	1
2	Start-up *Sue Birley*	20
3	Growth *Paul Burns and Jean Harrison*	40
4	Uncertainty, Innovation and Management *David Storey and Nigel Sykes*	73
5	The Entrepreneur *Jim Dewhurst*	94
6	Financing Small Firms *Martin Binks and Christine Ennew*	110
7	Venture Capital *Gordon Murray*	131
8	Franchising *Colin Barrow*	166
9	The Business Plan *Paul Burns*	180
10	Small Firms Policy in Europe *Jim Dewhurst*	198

Case Studies

The McArdle Syringe   221
Claridges Restaurant   232
John Jederman   255
Hightech Components   270
Consetec Ltd   288
Rollerdoors Ltd   300
Rough Rider Seating plc   304
Franchising: Evaluating the Profit Potential of a Franchise
    Opportunity   314
Short Engineering (a)   321
Short Engineering (b)   326

Index   331

List of tables

1.1 Average annual registration and deregistration rates by
    industry, 1980–90   8
1.2 Regional changes by type of organisation, 1980–90   9
1.3 Net percentage change in VAT registrations by county,
    1980–90   12
1.4 Net percentage change in the numbers of businesses
    registered for VAT by industry, within region, 1980–90   13
2.1 Influences on the entrepreneurial decision   22
3.1 Growth and state company characteristics   41
3.2 Competitive threats   57
3.3 Elements of strategy   57
3.4 The Churchill and Lewis growth model   63
3.5 Growth stage imperatives   65
3.6 Business imperatives as a firm grows   67
6.1 Financing characteristics   121
6.2 Ranking of main constraints in 1988, 1990, 1992 and 1994   123
6.3 Constraints for participative and non-participative firms   124
6.4 Service quality for participative and non-participative
    firms   125
6.5 Banking relationship for participative and
    non-participative firms (1)   125
6.6 Banking relationship for participative and
    non-participative firms (2)   126
7.1 Total European venture capital annual investment by
    stage of finance, 1992   137
7.2 Institutional sources of capital for UK independent
    funds, nominal and real (1985) values   139
7.3 UK venture capital activity in start-up and other early
    stage investments as a percentage of aggregate annual
    investment less MBO values   145

7.4   Venture capital firms' minimum IRR requirement by
      investment stage for technology and non-technology
      investments   156
8.1   Percentage of franchise chains and franchisees that
      ceased trading   167
8.2   The advantages of franchising   176
8.3   Personal franchisee characteristics required for success 177
9.1   Outline contents of business plan   190

List of figures

1.1   Trends in VAT registrations and deregistrations   7
1.2   Growth in the number of businesses, by type   8
1.3   Net change in number of VAT-registered businesses,
      1979–90, by industry   10
1.4   Distribution by type of business within industry   10
2.1   The credibility merry-go-round   29
2.2   Some sources of help   36
3.1   The elements of success   44
3.2   Porter's five forces   51
3.3   Long-run average cost curves   52
3.4   Competitive advantage   55
3.5   Product market matrix   59
3.6   The Greiner growth model   62
3.7   Work effectiveness during transition   64
3.8   The process of failure in the smaller firm   69
7.1   Annual value of venture capital investment, 1981–91   136
7.2   Percentage distribution of annual investment by
      stage of finance, Europe and UK, 1992   144
7.3   Growth of management buy-outs and buy-ins, 1980–91   151
7.4   Tyebjee and Bruno's decision process model of venture
      capital activity   153
7.5   'A competitive forces' analysis of the UK venture
      capital industry in 1993   159
9.1   The planning process   181

Preface to the second edition

This book is about small business, warts and all. It is about new businesses, growing businesses, businesses that go nowhere and businesses that fail. It is also about the owner-managers that run these firms. Most interesting of all, it is about entrepreneurs, that small group of owner-managers who try – and sometimes succeed – in growing their business and making a success of it.

It is aimed particularly at those students of business that are interested in the way the majority of firms actually work. It is suitable for all students taking courses on small business and entrepreneurship in universities and colleges, as well as those entrepreneurs interested in their own endeavours. It is primarily a 'why to do it' text and is designed to be used with its sister text, *Small Business Management* (now in its third edition), which is more of a 'how to do it' text. The book has developed out of MBA (Master of Business Administration) courses at Cranfield University School of Management, and Warwick Business School UK. MBA students seem fascinated by entrepreneurs and many come to a business school harbouring a deep-seated desire to set up their own business. Sadly, few ever do.

The sheer diversity and complexity of the issues facing the entrepreneur in business today is such that no one person can ever claim to be an expert in all the areas. This book brings together a large number of contributors, all experts in their respective fields. This second edition has many changes and many new contributors. There is a greater emphasis on the way firms develop and the problems small firms face in raising finance. Even chapters you may recognise from the last edition have been extensively rewritten. The structure of course that this book is designed to support involves some 'talk-at' sessions but also case analysis. This edition of the book has many new case studies, this time with questions to be addressed in class. Inevitably, however, any course on entrepreneurship must involve a talk by an entrepreneur on 'what it is really like'. Our experience is that this will be the highlight of the course. No matter how good the teacher, there is no substitute for the real thing – somebody who did it.

The book retains a chapter on the business plan, now revised and updated. Part of the course work on many small business courses involves the preparation or review of a business plan on an idea for a business start-up. Ideally students should be asked to prepare a plan on an idea of their own that they think has some commercial potential. Preparing the plan forces them to be creative and entrepreneurial. It also takes them beyond the ideas stage and forces them to crystallise their ideas, write them down on paper and show how they can be made to happen. This is not only creative, but also an excellent management discipline. It integrates all the functional areas of management that, sadly, all too often are taught separately. We normally insist that students present their plans to fellow students so that each can learn from the other's endeavours

In the final analysis, any course on entrepreneurship must challenge students to think entrepreneurially. It must make them realise how the needs of the owner-manager and the business are intertwined. It must make them address issues in a multidisciplinary way. But, most of all, it must be fun and interesting.

PAUL BURNS
JIM DEWHURST

Notes on the contributors

Colin Barrow is Head of Enterprise Group, Cranfield, and non-executive chairman, Midland Bank, Thames and Chiltern Venture Capital Fund. He is the author of a number of books and guides on franchising, small businesses, etc.

Martin Binks is Senior Lecturer in Economics at the University of Nottingham, specialising in entrepreneurship and the financing of SMEs. He is visiting professor to the Clairmont Graduate School in California, council member of the Small Business Research Trust and associate editor of *The Journal of Small Business Finance*.

Sue Birley is Professor of Management in the field of entrepreneurship at the Management School, Imperial College of Science, Technology & Medicine, and is chairman and co-founder of Newchurch & Company.

Paul Burns is Chairman of Design for Learning Ltd and Director of the 3i European Enterprise Centre. He was Professor of Small Business Development at Cranfield University and was founding President of the Institute for Small Business Affairs. Previous books include *Small Business Management* (1993) and *Business Finance – A Pictorial Guide* (1994).

Jim Dewhurst is a chartered accountant. His extensive commercial experience includes periods as company secretary and financial director. He currently lectures on the Open Studies Programme at the University of Warwick. He is the author of a number of books, the two most recent in this area being *Business Mathematics* and *Small Business Management*.

Christine Ennew is Professor of Marketing in the School of Management and Finance at the University of Nottingham. Her research interests lie in the area of financial services and particularly on the relationships between banks and small businesses. She is the author of a variety of marketing-related books and is the associate editor of the *International Journal of Bank Marketing*.

Jean Harrison is Managing Director of Design for Learning Ltd. She was deputy director of the Small Business Programme at Cranfield University. She is a former director of the Institute for Small Business Affairs, and has lectured and written extensively in the areas of small business and entrepreneurship.

Gordon Murray is Lecturer in Marketing and Strategic Management at Warwick Business School, University of Warwick. He has published widely in the area of venture capital finance in both practitioner and academic journals. Dr Murray is particularly interested in trans-Atlantic comparisons of early stage venture capital support. He is also a non-executive director of a venture-backed Anglo-American high technology start-up company.

David Storey has degrees from Hull, Oxford and Newcastle Universities. He is a Professor and the Director of the SME Centre, University of Warwick. He is the author of *Understanding the Small Business Sector* (1994).

Nigel Sykes joined the SME Centre, University of Warwick, in 1988 and is currently Senior Teaching Fellow. He was formerly Enterprise Agency Director and Community Programme Manager, Birmingham Chamber of Commerce.

CHAPTER 1

Introduction: the significance of small firms

Paul Burns

THE LOVE AFFAIR	1
WHAT CONSTITUTES A SMALL BUSINESS?	3
ARE SMALL FIRMS DIFFERENT FROM LARGE ONES?	4
THE ANATOMY OF SMALL FIRMS IN THE UK	6
THE FUTURE	15
CONCLUSIONS	17
EXERCISES	19
REFERENCES	19

The love affair

In the 1980s Britain was having a love affair with small business. You could not open a newspaper without reading about some business success story. In fact the love affair was not so much with small businesses as with their owner-managers or, more particularly, the small number of entrepreneurs who started up small firms, made them grow and perhaps became millionaires in the process. However, like many love affairs, this one was based upon a novelty that waned over time and in the 1990s Britain's approach to small business is far more low key and pragmatic. Government incentives to establish a new business have been cut back. Survival rather than growth has become a badge of success and the newspapers have turned elsewhere for their human interest stories.

1

Perhaps the love affair of the 1980s was indeed based upon a romanticised view of small firms. Most firms are born to die or stagnate. They do not grow to any size. It is estimated that over two-thirds of businesses consist of only one or two people and often the second person is the spouse. Three-quarters of the rest employ ten or fewer people. Almost 97 per cent of firms employ fewer than 20 people, over 99 per cent fewer than 100 and only 9,000 – less than a third of 1 per cent employ 200 or more. Britain is a country of very small firms and probably still has a smaller firms sector than most other countries although, because of the growth in the number of start-ups in the 1980s, the difference is much less than it used to be. The self-employment rate in the UK has grown at three times the European Community (EC) average in the 1980s. In 1989 it was 12 per cent (1979: 7 per cent), compared to the EC average of 13 per cent (1979: 11 per cent). Also, although Britain now has large numbers of very small firms, it has relatively low numbers in the slightly higher size brackets. The share of total employment of firms employing under 100 people in 1986 was 98.9 per cent in the UK, compared to the EC average of 99.4 per cent. The British seem not only disinclined to set up their own businesses, but also disinclined to grow them to any size.

It has been argued that, because owner-managers place a great value on independence, embarking on a high-growth strategy might lead them to feel their independence is threatened. Others have argued that they are also aware of the problems of growth and this itself acts as a disincentive. What seems true in most countries is that most firms grow only in the first few years after start-up and then stabilise to provide the owner-manager with an acceptable, independent life-style with sufficient income. At this stage the business provides sufficient sales to ensure survival, an adequate return on capital and an acceptable standard of living. Most owner-managers seem satisfied at this 'comfort level' of activity and do not actively grow their firms beyond it.

Nevertheless small firms account for a significant part of economic activity in the UK. While one small firm can make only a small contribution, collectively their contribution is enormous. After all, there are almost three million of them.

- In 1989, the 97 per cent of UK businesses that employed less than 20 people also accounted for 35 per cent of total employment outside of central and local government (1979: 27 per cent) (Employment Department, 1992).
- The same businesses contributed 17 per cent of national output.
- Between 1987 and 1989, firms employing fewer than ten people created about one million additional jobs, almost as many as

larger firms – even though the larger firms employed nearly four times as many people in 1987 (Daly *et al.*, 1991).

What constitutes a small business?

Small businesses are easier to describe than to define. The Bolton Report (1971) described a small business as follows:

- In economic terms, a small firm is one that has a relatively *small share of its market*.
- It is managed by its owners or part owners in a *personalised* way, and not through the medium of a formalised management structure.
- It is independent in the sense that it does not form part of a larger enterprise and that the owner/managers should be *free from outside control* in taking their principal decisions.

The characteristic of a small firm's share of the market is that it is not large enough to enable it to influence the prices or national quantities of goods sold to any significant extent. Personalised management is, perhaps, the most characteristic factor of all. It implies that the owner actively participates in all aspects of the management of the business, and in all major decision-making processes. There is little devolution or delegation of authority. One person is involved when anything material is concerned. Independence from outside control rules out those small subsidiaries which, though in many ways fairly autonomous, nevertheless have to refer major decisions (for example, on capital investment) to a higher authority. Of course there are other characteristics of small businesses that may be added to the list; perhaps the most obvious is the severe limitation of resources faced by small firms, both in terms of management and manpower, as well as money.

The same Bolton Committee made heavy weather of a statistical definition of small firms. Recognising that one single definition would not cover industries as divergent as manufacturing and service, the Committee used eight definitions for varying industry groups. These range from under 200 employees for manufacturing firms, to over £50,000 turnover for retailing, and up to five vehicles or less for road transport. But any definition which is based on turnover, or indeed any other measure of size expressed in financial terms, suffers from terrible inherent disadvantages in times of inflation.

Under the UK Companies Act 1989, medium-sized companies are exempt from certain requirements relating to compliance with accounting standards, and also to delivery to the companies registrar of individual accounts and other documents. Small companies are given a few additional exemptions. However we are concerned with medium businesses, and the conditions which must be met under the Act for these organisations to qualify are that two or more of the following requirements must be met:

— a turnover not exceeding £8 million,
— a balance sheet total not exceeding £3.8 million,
— a number of employees not exceeding 250.

Earlier the Companies Act 1985 had given similar conditions. The 1989 Act kept the number of employees at the same 250 figure, but the turnover and balance sheet total figures were increased by just under 40 per cent to take account of inflation. Using the same approach the corresponding figures for the mid-1990s would be of the following order:

— a turnover not exceeding some £12 million,
— a balance sheet total not exceeding £5 million,
— a number of employees not exceeding 250.

Earlier the EC, too, by implication defined small firms. The EC commission gave the following conditions to be met by a small firm wishing to qualify for state aid:

— a turnover not exceeding ECU 20 million (say £16 million),
— a net capital not exceeding ECU 10 million (say £8 million),
— a number of employees not exceeding 250.

The corresponding sterling figures for turnover and net capital above have been arrived at by using a conversion rate of £1 = ECU 1.25.

Most EC individual countries use a number-of-employees definition and allow up to 500 employees, rather than the 250 figure. Indeed the European Commission itself uses the 500 employees definition as almost standard. Risking a broad generalisation, one may say, however, that in Europe small firms are those with less than 200 employees and medium-sized firms are those with 200–500 employees. In the USA, all firms employing up to 500 employees are regarded as small. Often firms with under 20 employees are called micro businesses.

Are small firms different from large ones?

Small firms are not just scaled-down versions of large ones. They have some special characteristics that set them apart and make the process of management different from that of larger firms. These characteristics also make most small firms inherently riskier than larger firms. These characteristics include the following:

- One person – the owner-manager – has an overwhelming influence on the firm. Their views and values will influence all aspects of its activities. This means that business decisions will often become personal decisions and the logic of the balance sheet will not always apply. There is also the risk of overdependency upon one individual for the well-being of the firm.
- Most small firms are unlikely to be able to exert much influence on their market. They are price takers in the classic economic sense and are likely to face significant competition. This makes the risk of failure high and means that competitive strategy is of paramount importance. However some small firms combat this danger very effectively by differentiating their product or service and/or segmenting their market and developing a market niche for themselves.
- Small firms are likely to operate in a single market, or a limited range of markets, probably offering a limited range of products or services. This means that the scope of the firms' operations is limited and less of a strategic issue than in large firms. However it also means that, unlike larger firms, they find it more difficult to diversify their business risk.
- Small firms are likely to be over-reliant on a small number of customers. This means they are particularly vulnerable to losing any one customer and the effect on the firm of such a loss will be disproportionately large. This is another reason why they are riskier than large firms.
- Small firms are not public companies. This means they often have problems raising capital and this can significantly constrain their choice of strategies. Indeed, for many small firms seeking to grow, raising finance can become a major strategic issue and relationships with financing institutions such as banks can become a major resource issue.

Small firms are not homogeneous. Each is different and has special characteristics. Trying to generalise about three million organisations is clearly dangerous, but it is important to differentiate between two types of small firm. Firstly, there is the 'life-style' business that has been set up to provide the owner-manager with an acceptable income at a 'comfort level' of activity. Once that level of activity is reached, management becomes a routine, tactical activity. There is probably little thought about strategic management, unless things start to go wrong, and the most likely thing to go wrong is that the market changes without the owner-manager realising it. Most small firms fall into this first category.

Secondly, there is the 'entrepreneurial' business set up with the intention of growth. In this case the owner-manager is far closer to the classic concept of the entrepreneur, where innovation is a driving force in the way Schumpeter (1934) defines it (see Chapter 4). These firms present many of the classic change management problems. They are not easy to manage and extremely risky. Most will probably not survive without encountering at least one crisis that will threaten their survival. Effective strategic management is vital if the firm is to develop.

The anatomy of small firms in the UK

The growth in the number of small firms in recent years represents the effect of a very large number of 'birth' but also a large number of 'deaths' – a factor called churning. What constitutes a 'birth' or a 'death' is difficult to define in a way that is measurable. What is more, this churning is part of the dynamism of the small firm sector. It is evidence of the flexibility that makes small firms so responsive to market changes. Indeed most businesses that cease trading do not involve bankruptcy or liquidation, they simple cease trading and the owner perhaps retires or moves on to another activity.

Most statistics about small firms are derived from VAT statistics of registrations and deregistrations. The Department of Employment, Statistical Services Division (Moorfoot, Sheffield) has been monitoring this information since 1980. The net increase of 420,000 in the number of VAT registered businesses between 1979 and 1990 is the difference between 2.15 million new registrations and 1.73 deregistrations. This information is available in many forms, for example, total numbers of registrations and deregistrations:

- by year,
- by local authority district,
- by industry groups,
- for England, Wales and Scotland by county and region.

Data are also available online via the NOMIS project, Mountjoy Research Centre, based at the University of Durham.

VAT key facts

- As a proportion of the total number of businesses, the number of deregistrations has remained virtually unchanged in recent years.

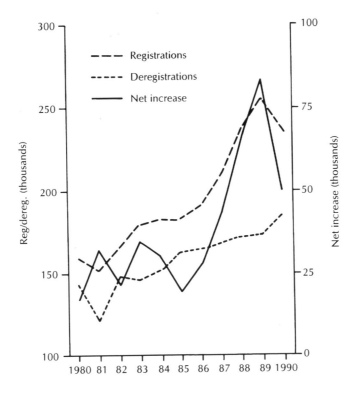

Figure 1.1   *Trends in VAT registrations and deregistrations*

- From the end of 1979 to the end of 1990, the numbers of small firms registered for VAT rose by approximately 420,000 (33 per cent).
- From June 1979 to June 1991 the numbers of self-employed rose by 65 per cent, from 1.9 million to 3.1 million.
- During 1990 the number of businesses registered for VAT rose by an estimated 50,000 (an average of nearly 1,000 a week).
- In 1990 the number of businesses rose in each region, and in all industries other than agriculture and retailing.

Table 1.1 shows a summary of industry-related information. It shows declines in agriculture and retailing businesses and increases for all other industry sectors. This information can be used to review the business sectors that are growing and declining, to compare local industry growth against national averages.

What types of small firms?

The VAT data also distinguish between sole traders, partnerships and limited companies. Since the end of 1979, there has been a 40

Table 1.1   Average annual registration and deregistration rates by industry, 1980–90 (per cent)

Industry	Registration rate	Deregistration rate	Turbulence (reg. + dereg.)	Net change
Agriculture	3.5	3.6	7.1	−0.1
Production	13.6	11.1	24.7	2.5
Construction	14.2	10.5	24.7	3.7
Transport	14.6	12.0	26.6	2.6
Wholesale	14.4	11.9	26.3	2.6
Retail	13.0	13.3	26.2	−0.3
Finance, etc.	16.0	9.2	25.2	6.8
Catering	15.3	14.5	29.8	0.8
Motor trades	12.9	11.2	24.0	1.7
All others	20.2	12.9	33.1	7.3
Total	**13.5**	**10.9**	**24.5**	**2.6**

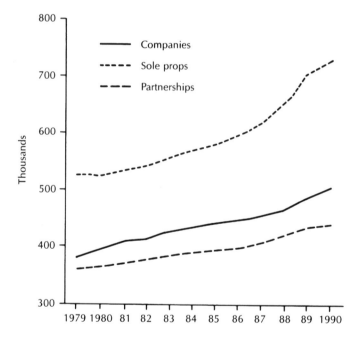

Figure 1.2   Growth in the number of businesses, by type

per cent increase in the number of sole traders, as opposed to a 24 per cent increase in the number of partnerships. In the early 1980s the fastest increase was in the number of companies. Figure 1.2 shows the growth in the number of businesses by type. The information is also available by region, as Table 1.2 shows.

Table 1.2 Regional changes by type of organisation, 1980–90 (thousands and per cent)

Region	Companies					Sole proprietorships					Partnerships				
	End 1979 stock	Reg.	Dereg.	Net	End 1990 stock	End 1979 stock	Reg.	Dereg.	Net	End 1990 stock	End 1979 stock	Reg.	Dereg.	Net	End 1990 stock
South East	170	326	265	35.7	230	156	352	259	59.7	249	86	163	129	39.4	120
East Anglia	13	20	12	38.4	17	23	39	30	35.4	32	15	20	16	26.9	19
South West	25	40	32	34.8	34	52	93	71	40.5	73	44	55	45	23.4	54
West Midlands	34	53	43	28.4	44	83	67	36.1	61.0	31	43	36	24.3	38.0	32
East Midlands	23	34	27	32.7	31	37	68	55	36.2	51	26	36	30	25.8	32
Yorkshire and Humberside	28	38	32	19.7	33	41	76	63	31.8	54	31	43	37	18.2	37
North West	38	61	51	27.4	48	51	95	82	24.1	63	36	51	47	12.0	41
North	11	17	13	35.9	15	21	38	32	26.6	26	19	22	19	12.1	22
Wales	12	19	15	35.2	16	31	48	39	28.4	39	27	26	22	14.5	31
Scotland	20	37	27	49.8	30	41	65	54	26.2	51	33	34	31	10.1	37
N. Ireland	6	6	5	15.8	7	28	26	19	24.0	35	9	8	6	22.6	11
UK	378	651	525	33.3	504	525	982	773	39.8	734	357	501	417	23.5	441

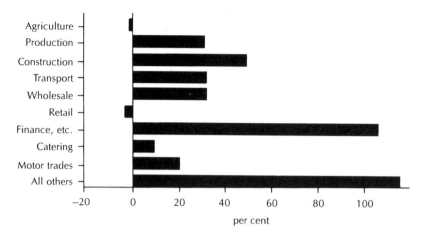

Figure 1.3   Net change in number of VAT-registered businesses, 1979–90, by industry

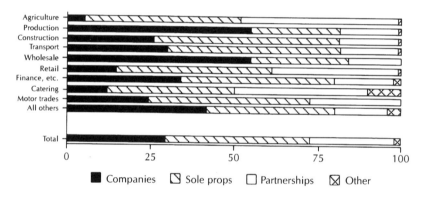

Figure 1.4   Distribution by type of business within industry

Location of small firms

The information in Figure 1.4 offers, in part, an explanation for the variations in growth and decline of some types of businesses within industries. Sole traders and partnerships are more common in agriculture and retailing and less common in the fastest growing sectors.

The number of businesses rose substantially between 1980 and 1990 in every region, ranging from an increase of 19 per cent in the north west to 46 per cent in the south east. Table 1.3 shows the net change in the number of VAT registered businesses by county. More striking, because of the wide variations, is the difference in the number of registrations by industry (Table 1.4). This ranges from 3 per cent in the retailing sector to over 100 per cent in the 'services' sector, including finance, property, professional services and 'other' services. This last sector covers a multitude of other business services, for example contract cleaning, and personal services like hairdressing and entertainment.

The 'services' sector is the fastest growing in the UK and nearly a third of all new businesses will contribute to its growth. A look at the regional variations in sector growth will show, however, that, despite the fact that the highest concentration of service industries is in the south east, there was surprisingly low growth in East Sussex and the Isle of Wight compared with the relatively high growth in Cheshire in the north west (see Tables 1.3 and 1.4). To some extent this variation is due to the mix of industries within the region, and in all regions there has been a shift towards the faster growing sectors, although the size of the potential gains from the shift in industry mix varies substantially.

All of this information is usually summarised and reported in very readable article form in the *Employment Gazette*, published by the Department of Employment.

What other information is available?

The Employment Department's Annual Labour Force Survey (LFS) also offers valuable information about the make-up of the small firms sector. Another commonly used measure of the size of the sector is the number of self-employed. Although self-employed people would not usually be seen as enterprise owners, the two are linked and are often used to support the findings of the research on VAT registrations and deregistrations. Both the number of self-employed people and the number of small businesses have increased substantially since 1979.

Perhaps the most valuable information which can be gleaned from the LFS is the variety of data it yields on the personal characteristics of the self-employed, including their age, education, gender, ethnic origin and family circumstances. This information can give us different insights into the constituents of small firms. For example:

- The proportion of employed women who are self-employed remains much lower than that for men: 6 per cent as opposed to 17 per cent.
- The number of self-employed women has increased by 109 per cent since 1979, double the rate of increase for men.
- The number of self-employed women who employ others rose by 49 per cent, in comparison with a 14 per cent increase for men.

Table 1.3 Net percentage change in VAT registration by county, 1980–90

County	%	County	%	County	%
Bedfordshire	57	Avon	43	Humberside	22
Berkshire	68	Cornwall	21	North Yorkshire	24
Buckinghamshire	73	Devon	22	South Yorkshire	26
East Sussex	24	Dorset	35	West Yorkshire	23
Essex	38	Gloucestershire	33	Yorkshire and	
Hampshire	59	Somerset	40	Humberside	_24_
Hertfordshire	57	Wiltshire	56		
Isle of Wight	17	South West	_33_	Cheshire	37
Kent	42			Greater Manchester	16
Greater London	40	Hereford and		Lancashire	14
Oxfordshire	57	Worcestershire	30	Merseyside	17
Surrey	62	Shropshire	31	North West	_19_
West Sussex	43	Staffordshire	31		
South East	_46_	Warwickshire	45	Clwyd	27
		West Midlands	_24_	Dyfed	16
Cleveland	32	West Midlands	_29_	Gwent	44
Cumbria	16			Gwynedd	12
Durham	24	Derbyshire	32	Mid-Glamorgan	35
Northumberland	21	Leicestershire	35	Powys	18
Tyne & Wear	_18_	Lincolnshire	20	South Glamorgan	22
North	_21_	Northamptonshire	56	West Glamorgan	21
		Nottinghamshire	23	Wales	23
		East Midlands	_32_		

County	%
Cambridgeshire	44
Norfolk	27
Suffolk	34
East Anglia	_34_
Borders	17
Central	36
Dumfries and Galloway	12
Fife	29
Grampian	21
Highlands	31
Lothian	28
Orkney, Shetland and	
Western Isles	35
Strathclyde	22
Tayside	18
Scotland	_23_
Northern Ireland	22
United Kingdom	33

Table 1.4 Net percentage change in the number of businesses registered for VAT by industry, within region, 1980–90

Region	Agriculture	Pro-duction	Con-struction	Transport	Wholesale	Retail	Finance, etc.	Catering	Motor Trades	Other Services	Total
South East	−4.6	18.7	63.1	34.1	33.7	−0.5	93.0	10.5	22.5	125.0	45.6
of which:											
Greater London	−16.2	−3.7	51.6	18.7	16.0	2.2	81.0	22.4	7.2	106.2	39.6
East Anglia	−10.1	58.2	56.5	40.2	52.3	−2.3	148.2	15.7	26.0	128.0	34.4
South West	−1.0	52.6	59.6	42.2	45.8	1.6	124.9	7.1	30.6	119.8	33.4
West Midlands	−3.5	33.0	40.3	26.4	35.7	−1.4	111.0	10.7	24.5	109.4	29.3
East Midlands	6.6	48.0	45.8	51.7	42.6	−1.0	136.7	12.1	24.6	120.7	31.9
Yorkshire and Humberside	−5.7	27.2	35.3	35.3	25.9	0.5	121.0	4.4	19.3	102.8	23.8
North West	−9.3	23.8	23.9	21.2	17.1	−10.1	102.0	0.2	10.5	100.8	18.6
North	−1.1	54.6	34.1	19.7	21.1	−7.3	121.7	15.7	7.7	88.2	21.0
Wales	2.9	66.9	53.7	31.0	28.6	−5.0	105.2	11.7	19.7	107.9	23.4
Scotland	3.7	34.8	41.1	17.6	19.1	−9.4	143.7	15.5	8.2	87.3	23.4
Northern Ireland	17.0	52.2	29.5	19.1	40.5	−1.8	90.7	13.1	11.9	74.6	21.8
United Kingdom	−0.8	31.3	49.4	32.0	32.1	−3.0	105.4	9.6	20.2	115.7	32.6

Information is also available on education patterns and attainment
– this could give clues about literacy, numeracy and ability to articulate – and ethnic minority businesses.

Life cycles and failure statistics

The net increase of 420,000 VAT registered businesses represents the
difference between 2.15 million registered and 1.73 million deregis-
tered businesses. It is clear that many small businesses have a very
short life span:

- about 10 per cent deregister within the first year;
- half deregister within five years;
- two-thirds deregister within ten years.

The most vulnerable period is between 12 and 30 months after registration. But what constitutes business failure? There is a lot of confusion about business failure rates, which is not helped by a lack of a
definition of a 'failure'. The overall trends in the number of businesses and trends in business failure are essentially separate questions – related, but not in a straightforward way. Rapid rises in
failure rates do not necessarily imply a drop in the overall business
population or an increase in the number of business closures overall.

Most businesses which cease trading do so far a variety of reasons.
These include the death or retirement of the proprietor, or a change
in their personal motivation. Some owners will close a seemingly
'successful' business because in their view it is a failure! One
business closes and another starts, but overall the balance remains
the same. The number of business starts is a significant factor. The
numbers of registrations and deregistrations show that the total
business population is capable of changing dramatically. This is
evidence of the flexibility that makes the small firm so responsive to
market changes.

There has been a lot of recent publicity about the high number of
insolvent businesses which, at some stage, will be included with
those going into receivership or liquidation. However most business
failures do not go through formal insolvency procedures and,
although the number of insolvencies is high, the number of companies going into liquidation has slowed considerably. Relative to the
total population, registrations have been running at 15 per cent
annually and deregistrations at 11 per cent. The total number of
insolvencies is in fact much lower than the number of VAT deregistrations. The anomaly is more likely to be explained by the number
of individual bankruptcies which are not necessarily business related.

The future

The pace of change in the commercial environment continues to accelerate because of changing markets, technology and social patterns. Product life cycles have shortened dramatically because of fashion and technology. Working methods and patterns too have altered dramatically, some might say not always for the better. The service sector has taken over as a major force in economic activity.

The 1990s opened in a dramatic way. The dismantling of the Iron Curtain and the reunification of Germany, the development of the East European economies and the resulting trade opportunities, the inevitable reduction in the defence industries – all are having their effect. The effects of the decimation of large areas of tropical rain forest and the growing signs of instability in the Third World and the Middle East are likely to be felt for many years to come. So far the 1990s have been a time of recession, high unemployment and fierce competition. But will this continue? Tom Peters (1987) refers to it as 'a world turned upside down' and as 'chaos'. Charles Handy (1989) describes it as 'the age of unreason', where there is no 'logic' or 'order' underlying the seemingly random occurrences in the business world. Others (Cannon, 1991) think they 'bear all the hall-marks of a major industrial change or revolution'. How will smaller firms respond to these challenges?

Global markets and fragmented market segments

Global markets have already arrived for many products such as Mac-Donald's, Coca Cola and some computer products (Microsoft operating systems are used by 90 per cent of worldwide personal computers). This reflects common product values and globalisation of life-styles. At the same time markets have become more dispersed as barriers to entry of national or local markets becomes fewer. Alongside this, there is the growing trend towards fragmented market segments, with niches becoming ever smaller, often by entrenching consumer views, for example, with regard to quality, customising or satisfaction. The number of potential niches seems to be growing incrementally.

The trend towards ever narrower market niches creates obvious opportunities for small firms that recognise these trends and are able to match an identified market need. Increasingly there is also the opportunity to market niche products or services nationally or even globally, for example using homeworkers, to allow a firm to reach a bigger market for its product or service and thereby achieve economies of scale.

Sandiford Computer Services Ltd is a small software company established in 1988. As a by-product of its main activity of developing process control software, it developed a unique software product that enabled engineers to develop plant schematics on personal computers and then transfer the display files specifically to a Honeywell TDC3000 distributed control system. The Honeywell is very expensive and is used to control process plant such as power stations. By removing the necessity for plant schematic development to take place while a plant is running, Saniford's system offers considerable savings to users as well as increasing plant safety. By 1992 Sandiford employed seven people full time and five people part time from its Bedford offices. Despite its size, the company now sells its software to over a dozen countries, including Japan and the USA. It sells this unique product exclusively to users of the Honeywell system, a clearly defined and easily identifiable market segment that Honeywell help them address. Sandiford have succeeded in finding a niche in a global market.

Both globalisation and the development of niche markets creates a demand for information – on products, customers, markets and competitors. The current development of information delivery systems (the information super-highways) will ensure that these trends continue. However networks, cooperation, partnerships, alliances and joint ventures are also likely to increase in firms of all sizes as an answer to this need for information. For example, some of the smaller UK accountants are already forming alliances, not only nationally, but also on the mainland of Europe in an attempt to offer a better service and gain competitive advantage.

The deconstruction of large firms

John Naisbitt (1994) feels that the future lies very much with small firms. His book is based upon the apparent paradox that 'the bigger the world economy, the more powerful its smallest players.' He sees much of the growing importance of smaller firms, and with them entrepreneurs, coming from larger firms which will have to restyle themselves into 'networks of entrepreneurs' if they are to survive into the next century.

> Downsizing, re-engineering, creative networking organisation, or the latest, the virtual corporation, whatever it is called, it comes down to the same thing. Corporations have to dismantle bureaucracies to survive. Economies of scale are giving way to economies of scope, finding the right size for synergy, market flexibility, and above all, speed. (Naisbitt, 1994)

Already 50 per cent of US exports are created by micro firms with less than 20 employees; the same is true of Germany. Only 7 per cent of US exports are created by companies with over 500 employees.

> To survive, big companies today – ABB, AT&T, GE, Grand Metropolitan, Coca-Cola, Benetton, Johnson & Johnson, British Petroleum, Honda, Alcoa, Xerox – are deconstructing themselves and creating new structures, many as networks of autonomous units. Deconstruction is now in fashion, because it is the best way to search for survival. (Naisbitt, 1994)

Asea Brown Boveri (ABB), the largest power engineering company in the world with sales of some $30 billion per annum, is in fact made up of some 1,200 separate companies each employing, on average, only 200 people. Even their Zurich headquarters has less than 200 employees.

The other side to this trend towards downsizing and deconstructing big companies is that they will increasingly concentrate on their core activities, where they have competitive advantage, and the subcontracting of non-core activities will increase. This enables them to reduce their fixed cost base and flatten their organisation structures, so ensuring quicker response times to changes in the market-place. This should result in the growth of small, specialist subcontractors, particularly in the manufacturing sector. 'Partnership sourcing', as practised by Japanese firms and Marks & Spencer, will increase, whereby a close relationship is built between the bigger company and the smaller subcontractor, with one helping the other to grow. Charles Handy (1989) predicted that there will be a growth of the 'shamrock organisation' in larger companies, the three leaves being core staff, temporary staff to ease them over peaks and troughs in work and smaller organisations supplying specialist services. He is being proved right.

Conclusions

Although some observers think that 'the new importance that small-scale economic activity has achieved in the UK is likely to be tested over the next decade' (Stanworth and Gray, 1991), many of the problems they face are global problems. In many way it would seem that small firms are in better shape to meet the challenges of the 1990s than many larger firms. For example:

- With their flat, flexible organisations they are more sensitive and responsive to market changes than large firms.

- With the owner-manager's network of contacts and information, they can often perceive a market opportunity that larger companies do not.
- Because the owner-manager depends for his livelihood on the success of the business, this can be a highly motivated organisation.
- Because of their small size, they are better able to form personal relationships with customers – an important service element – particularly if selling a relatively undifferentiated product.
- Economies of scale, the raison dêtre for many large firms, are becoming less important to many customers and at the same time easier to achieve on a global scale by small firms.

What is more, the number of small firms is likely to increase, not only because of the 'pull' factors of market opportunities, but also because of the 'push' factors of social change such as increasing unemployment and early retirement. Indeed, an increasing number of people are likely to have more than one job, often dipping into self-employment as a part-time activity. It is estimated by the Inland Revenue that over 600,000 people already have more than one job. People already realise that there is no such thing as a 'job for life', so keeping all the options open by having a part-time self-employed occupation is likely to prove increasingly attractive. Indeed many activities will encourage it, as homeworking and teleworking become increasingly popular. (It is estimated that about 2.5 million people will work from home by 1995.) And if that occupation develops into a lucrative market opportunity, self-employment may offer more independent security than employment. As Charles Handy (1994) put it:

> It is the end of the age of the mass organisation, the age when we could all confidently expect to be employed for most of our lives if we so wanted, and over 90% so wanted ... What we do, what we belong to, why we do it, where we do it – these may all be different and could be better ... Change comes from small initiatives which work, initiatives which, imitated, become fashion. We cannot wait for great visions from great people, for they are in short supply at the end of history. It is up to us to light our own small fires in the darkness.

So, as the millennium approaches, is it right that we should end our romanticised love affair with small firms? Of course they are here to stay. They are also likely to increase in importance. More and more of us are becoming part of them. Many of the new small firms in the next decade will come from the large firms of today. Many of the new entrepreneurs will be ex-managers from large firms. For these reasons alone small firms will be integrated more and more into the mainstream of economic activity, not looked down upon but rather regarded as part of our everyday life. Perhaps the love affair may be over, but the marriage is just beginning, and that needs to be worked on.

Exercises

1. List the pros and cons of running your own business.
2. Write an essay on how the management of a small firm differs from that of a large one.
3. Using the most up-to-date statistics from the Department of Employment, write a report highlighting the latest trends in small firms statistics.
4. List the political, economic, social and technological threats and opportunities facing small firms in the UK in the 21st century.
5. Write an essay on how you see developments in information technology affecting small firms in the 21st century.
6. Write an essay on how you think small firms will develop in the 21st century.

References

Bolton Report (1971), *Report on the Commission of Enquiry on Small Firms*, Cmnd 4811, HMSO.

Cannon, T. (1991), *Enterprise: Creation, Development and Growth*, Butterworth-Heineman.

Daly, M., M, Campbell, G. Robson and C. Gallagher (1991), 'Job Creation 1987–89', *Employment Gazette*, February.

Employment Department (1992), *Small Firms in Britain*, HMSO.

Handy, C. (1989), *The Age of Unreason*, Hutchinson.

Handy, C. (1994), *The Empty Raincoat*, Hutchinson.

Peters, T. (1987), *Thriving on Chaos*, Pan.

Naisbitt, J. (1994), *Global Paradox*, BCA.

Stanworth, J. and C. Gray (eds) (1991), *Bolton 20 Years On: The Small Firm in the 1990s*, Paul Chapman.

CHAPTER 2

Start-up

Sue Birley

INTRODUCTION	20
THE ENTREPRENEUR	21
ENTREPRENEUR OR SMALL BUSINESSMAN?	24
ENCOURAGING START-UPS	25
THE RESOURCES MERRY-GO-ROUND	27
THE ENTREPRENEURIAL NETWORK	30
STUMBLING BLOCKS	32
PICKING WINNERS	37
EXERCISES	37
REFERENCES	38

Introduction

Starting a business is not an event, but a process which may take many years to evolve and come to fruition. Very few people are born entrepreneurs and very few new businesses are unique. Yet it is estimated that around 200,000 new firms are created each year in the UK. While many do not survive beyond the first few difficult, formative years, many do continue to grow and provide a livelihood for both owners and employees, although few of these grow to be the large firms of the future, or, indeed, beyond the ownership of the original founders. Interestingly, since the early 1980s, this has been despite the wider availability of venture and development capital, and the launching of the various junior securities markets.

The study of 'start-up' is concerned with two issues: first, the process by which an individual arrives at the decision to try to develop a business out of an idea, and second, the process of assembling the resources necessary to begin trading.

The entrepreneur

Early studies of the origins of the entrepreneur concentrated almost entirely upon their motivations. It was assumed that entrepreneurial flair, the ability to take risks and the desire to create a business were inherent in the individual – he or she was born with them. This motivation was described by Schumpeter (1942) as an 'innovative' drive, by McLelland (1961) as a 'need for achievement', and was measured by Rotter (1966) as 'locus of control'. However, McLelland also showed that, while these motivations were essential for the successful creation of business, they were not genetically bound. In his experiments, those groups which received his achievement motivation education demonstrated a larger supply of entrepreneurs than his control group which had not received the training. Thus evolved the idea that entrepreneurs were made rather than born; that lifetime experiences were just as important as genetic influences.

Cooper (1981) provides the most comprehensive and useful framework for explaining the various factors which may contribute to the 'entrepreneur's decision'. He classified them into three groups:

1. The entrepreneur, including the many aspects of his background which affect his motivations, his perceptions, and his skills and knowledge.
2. The organisation for which the entrepreneur had previously been working, whose characteristics influence the location and the nature of new firms, as well as the likelihood of spin-offs.
3. Various environmental factors external to the individual and his organisation, which make the climate more or less favourable to the starting of a new firm.

Cooper defined these three groups as Antecedent Influences, the Incubator Organisation and Environmental Factors (see Table 2.1). Despite this, little is known about the actual characteristics described by Cooper. The answer to the question on the lips, and in the minds, of every investor – 'How can we pick winners?' – remains elusive. While the motivations of entrepreneurs have been studied extensively, there is, as yet, only limited knowledge about the lifetime characteristics. Moreover, much is culturally bound, being grounded in the USA.

Family

Nevertheless, the limited data which are available tend to support the popular view that many entrepreneurs come either from a family

Table 2.1   Influences on the entrepreneurial decision

Antecedent influences
  Genetic factors
  Family influences
  Educational choices
  Previous career experience

Incubator organisation
  Geographic location
  Nature of skills and knowledge acquired
  Contact with possible fellow founders
  Motivation to stay with or leave organisation
  Experience in 'small business' setting

Environmental factors
  Economic conditions
  Accessibility and availability of venture capital
  Example of entrepreneurial action
  Opportunities for interim consulting
  Availability of personnel and supporting services
  Accessibility of customers

---

firm or from families with some form of business background. This result is intuitively acceptable since such strong grounding in the business ownership ethic at an early stage is a useful and powerful driving force for children as they begin to choose future careers. However this is not to say that all children from family firms choose business ownership as a future career, just as not all actors' children become actors, but rather that those who do choose self-employment tend to have had some involvement in a small or family business during their formative years. Indeed many future inheritors of a family business eschew the apparently attractive future which awaits them for employment with some other, often large, organisation where their progress is determined by their skill and training rather than by family relationships (Birley, 1986).

Background

The traditional view of the entrepreneur is an uneducated, unskilled poor immigrant, often with an ethnic background, who finds himself 'socially marginal' (Stanworth and Curran, 1976) and who, therefore, seeks upward social mobility. While it is true that certain social groups have provided classic examples of this phenomenon – the Jews, American settlers, Asians in Britain – it is not true that this is sustained in the current economic climate. For example, conclusions regarding education have changed since the early studies by Collins *et al.* (1964), which showed that the entrepreneur was badly educated: recent studies have found them just as well educated as the population in general (see Kent *et al.*, 1982; Gartner, 1984) and in some cases better than their peers running the larger, blue-chip firms (Birley and Norburn, 1987). It must be noted, however, that the particular *content* of the education does not appear to be an important factor. Thus, Birley and Norburn (1987) found no connection between the type of degree awarded and the nature of the product/ market of the new firms. Despite this, there is, as yet, no evidence that those students in MBA programmes who chose small business or start-up electives are any more likely to be successful in running their own firm than their colleagues choosing other specialities to study!

Age

Regarding age, there is general agreement that the typical entrepreneur starts his firm in his thirties. While it would appear that this is a period of very high risk, when the individual is likely to be at his most financially stretched, it is also clear that this is the age when a strong base of business experience has been developed, when personal confidence is rising, and when frustration with the bureaucratic system begins to develop. Moreover, it is not surprising that this is also a time when many reach a personal crisis in their lives – the issues of 'Who am I?' 'What have I done with my life?' and so on are very powerful and positive motivators.

Experience

Common sense suggests that, as with all lifetime experiences, prior work experience will have an effect on the nature of a new venture. In other words, the type of 'incubator' organisation in which the founder was employed immediately prior to start-up may well be a significant influence both upon the decision to start a new business and upon its characteristics. Certainly there is clear evidence that most start close to home, often within their current 'travel to work area' (TTWA); very few are sufficiently attracted by the various incentives offered elsewhere, although some are. Indeed, as early as 1970, Cooper (1970) claimed that 'regional entrepreneurship depends upon incubator organisations which hire, train and motivate the prospective entrepreneur'. In theory, therefore, the location of the incubator provides an opportunity to develop not only local contacts and market knowledge but also managerial skills and market knowledge. In practice, this is not always the case. A number of studies have found that, while many start in the same industry as their previous employer, an equal number start in entirely different product/ markets. Indeed Birley and Norburn (1987) reported: 'no particular pattern was observed in the employment experience of the "high flying" entrepreneurs' which they studied. What is clear from the research, however, is that historically the majority or owner-managers emanate from the private sector. In order words, in the past, business has begat business. Not so in the future, as will be discussed later.

Entrepreneur or small businessman?

If the thesis that entrepreneurs are made rather than born is accepted, then lifetime experiences must also mould the *nature* of the entrepreneurial decision, and the size and type of business eventually created. Researchers have sought to explain the variety of businesses created in terms of sub-classifications of motivation – not all those who choose to leave employment do so in order to create the IBM of tomorrow. Many, indeed most, have much more modest aims. Various models have been suggested. Stanworth and Curran (1976) differentiate the 'artisan', who seeks intrinsic satisfaction, from the 'manager', who seeks recognition for managerial excellence, from the 'classic entrepreneur', who is profit-oriented. Similarly Dunkleberg and Cooper (1982) segment into the 'growth orientated', the 'independence orientated', and the 'craftsmen orientated'. Perhaps more simply, Carland *et al.* (1984) focus upon the essential factor of growth in distinguishing the small business venture from the entrepreneurial venture, and the 'small business owner' from the 'entrepreneur':

> A *Small Business Venture* is any business that is independently owned and operated, not dominant in its field, and does not engage in any new marketing or innovative practices.
>
> An *Entrepreneurial Venture* is one that engages in at least one of Schumpeter's four categories of behaviour: that is, the principal goals of an entrepreneurial venture are profitability and growth and the business is characterised by innovative strategic practices.
>
> A *Small Business Owner* is an individual who establishes and manages a business for the principal purpose of furthering personal goals. The business must be the primary source of income and will consume the majority of one's time and resources. The owner perceives the business as an extension of his or her personality, intricately bound with family needs and desires.
>
> An *Entrepreneur* is an individual who establishes and manages a business for the principal purpose of profit and growth. The entrepre-

neur is characterised principally by innovative behaviour and will employ strategic management practices in the business.

The inherent simplicity of these classifications is appealing, yet they are based upon two important assumptions: that it is possible to dichotomise the whole of the sector by simple motivations and personal drives which, since they do not change, allow us to predict the size and nature of the eventual firm. Recent research, conducted in a variety of countries and cultures, does not support this view. The results from the study conducted in the UK illustrates the point. When owner-managers were asked about their reasons for starting their business (Birley and Westhead, 1993), seven components were identified:

1. *A need for approval*, strongly linked with McLelland's theories on need for achievement and with Maslow's (1954) need for self-actualisation.
2. *A need for independence*, similar to Hofstede's (1980) scale of individualism.
3. *A need for personal development*.
4. *Welfare considerations*, strongly linked to Hofstede's collectivism index; starting a business is seen as a way for the founder to contribute to the welfare of the group of which he is part.
5. *Perceived instrumentality of wealth*: in her analysis of the Italian data, Dubini (1988) calls this the 'materialism' element.
6. *Tax reduction and indirect benefits*: this reflects the owner-manager's wish to retain any personal wealth earned.
7. *Following role models*, including those both external and internal to the family group.

These make intuitive sense. More important than this, however, is that they are not mutually exclusive. As we expected, it was possible for entrepreneurs to articulate more than one reason for starting their business. Fine. But does that help us to predict success, to pick winners? Unfortunately not. There was no apparent relationship between the reasons which owner-managers espoused and the subsequent size or performance of their business.

Encouraging start-ups

So far this chapter has suggested that the decision to start a new firm, and the development of the associated product idea, take many years to incubate. The corollary to this is the fact that the supply of entrepreneurs is not a fixed quantity, but can be influenced by external factors. On a national level, the role of national culture, acceptable norms of behaviour and traditional family relationships clearly influence individuals attitudes. Moreover the availability of attractive role models such as Richard Branson (Virgin) or Stephen Jobs (Apple), and the much publicised success of the management buy-out, have made significant contributions to shaping national attitudes to entrepreneurial behaviour. However, beyond this, the current economic climate is also an important factor in influencing the number of people who finally decide to move from either unemployment or employment to self-employment. Thus the mere fact that many large firms have substantially reduced their employee base, and that management at all levels can no longer look to the large firm as a source of long-term security, has meant that many have sought a new form of security – that of self-reliance through the ownership of their own firm.

This move towards enterprise is not confined to the private sector. The privatisation of parts of the public sector, the creation of agencies and trusts, general practitioner fund holders, the separation of purchaser and provider, the requirement for market-testing of services have all contributed to the creation of a new breed of 'social businesses' – those organisations with both a social and a commercial imperative (Birley, Manning and Corble, 1992). In developing their new strategies, many have adopted the (public sector) venturing procedures of their colleagues in the private sector through spin-outs, management buy-outs and the creation of entirely new businesses (Manning and Birley, 1990). Thus enterprise and entrepreneurship are now alive and well throughout all parts of the UK. Moreover, since the collapse of the Berlin Wall and the demise of the command economies, this trend is apparent throughout Europe, although with very different commercial and cultural bases. Consequently it is not clear at the time of writing how difficult the path will be or how long it will take to reach stability and relative economic prosperity. As with most judgements in this field of enterprise, the usual rule of thumb probably applies – at least twice as long as anticipated.

The 'triggers' to the start-up decision

The factors described above determine the total supply of new firms, but what are the factors which *trigger* the particular decision at a particular time? Listed below are some which I have observed on a number of occasions, and personally experienced on a few. They are not mutually exclusive.

1. *The 'it works' syndrome*: a product which has been worked on for many years, either as a hobby or at work, finally gells.

2. *The 'eureka' syndrome*: perhaps the most exciting and satisfying – an idea completely out of the blue, but which is often simply a new way of packaging old products or ideas.

3. *The 'if only' syndrome*: 'If only I could buy products in smaller packages' (Anita Roddick); 'If only I could call a reliable service for emergencies' (DynoRod!).

4. *The 'high comfort level' syndrome*: constant encouragement and support from family and friends.

5. *The 'friendly push' syndrome*: the individual has constantly talked about an idea, and suddenly the path is made clear. Resources are made available by a benevolent employer in the form of, for example, premises or orders; friends and family begin to disbelieve the intent, and the individual is finally forced to make a decision one way or other; entrepreneurship courses are offered as a way of testing the idea and formulating a strategy for market entry.

6. *The 'misfit' syndrome*: the fact that the person does not fit as an employee finally dawns upon him. He is unhappy, does not get promotion, fights authority, always believes that he could do the job better than those around him. This is the classic view of an entrepreneur – a troublemaker within a large organisation. However it does not always follow that misfits will always start businesses, nor that those who do will eventually prove to be successful.

7. *The 'unfriendly push' syndrome*: unemployment or enforced redundancy.

8. *The 'no alternative' syndrome*: this is usually brought about by physical disability or illness, rendering the person unable to obtain regular employment or to continue a career.

9. *The 'grey to white' syndrome*: many people 'moonlight', selling products or services on the fringes of the black economy while in full employment: for example, the amateur antique dealer, the trainee accountant who does the book for a group of friends, the hairdresser who has private clients in the evenings. Sometimes, however, the magnitude of the demand, and thus the income, can force the individual from the fringes into full-time self-employment.

Unfortunately, while these triggers clearly describe the process which many entrepreneurs go through as they move from the passive consideration of an idea to actively pursuing it, they cannot be used for forecasting either the potential start-up or the potential success.

The resources merry-go-round

Just as the process of reaching the decision to 'have a go' can be protracted, so is the process of actually assembling the resources necessary to commence trading. The entrepreneur begins with an idea for a product or a service out of which he wishes to create a business. Unfortunately the process is not simple. Many different forms of business can be created to capitalise upon just one idea. For example:

- parts or all of the manufacture and marketing can be subcontracted, licensed or franchised;
- a joint venture can be set up with either a manufacturing or a marketing company;
- the business can include more than one part of the value added chain (the manufacturer of Kitty Litter in the USA also owned the raw material source; Laura Ashley is a manufacturing *and* retail organisation);
- various choices of distribution channel are available – for example, mail-order catalogues, retailers, wholesalers, agents, a direct sales force.
- assets can be leased, hired, bought or borrowed!

The choices made, and the resultant shape and size of the business which is eventually created, will be influenced by a combination of two factors.

The entrepreneur's own 'concept of the business'

Very few people who start their own firm are able to be creative about its form. Most have very fixed ideas about the 'proper' shape of the business, much of which is derived from personal experience of the norms of other, similar businesses, but particularly of their immediate previous employment. However, whatever the entrepreneur's background, there is often a tendency to purchase assets early in the life of the firm rather than to lease or hire. While this is not always advisable, since it is often better to retain as much flexibility as possible in the early life of the business, it is often the only way to ensure future borrowings – tangible asset backing is almost always sought by funding agencies.

This picture of the embryo business which the entrepreneur holds in his mind can be constraining for others. There is nothing more frustrating to an investor who finds an idea which he considers to have great potential than to discover that the entrepreneur merely wants to run a small workshop at the bottom of his garden, and to sell to a few friends and acquaintances. Many potentially large businesses have been stillborn at this very early stage.

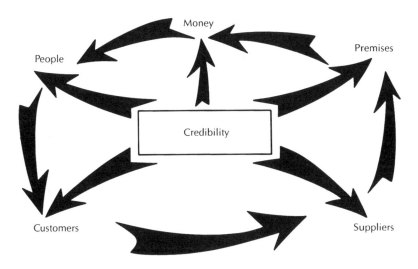

Figure 2.1 The credibility merry-go-round

The dictates of the market-place

Although very difficult to forecast, the perceived size of the potential demand, particularly in the development phase, will determine the nature of the resources assembled.

Perhaps the most important of all, however, is the entrepreneur's ability to ride successfully the resource merry-go-round (Birley and Norburn, 1984) (see Figure 2.1). In the final analysis, creating a business is a matter of assembling resources from all potential 'investors': people, premises, equipment, customers, suppliers, money. Unfortunately only very rich entrepreneurs are able to assemble an ideal shopping list and to make swift and satisfactory purchases. Indeed, if this were the case, many more badly conceived and executed businesses would be born than is currently the case. The *process* of assembling the resources is critical.

The entrepreneur can mount the merry-go-round at any point. Let us imagine that he goes first to the bank, probably with an ill-thought-through proposal and very little documentation, but a very clear idea of how much money he 'needs'. He is sent away with a flea in his ear, and told to come back when he has evidence of an order. The banker is asking for evidence from the market-place that the product is credible. Approaching potential customers, the entrepreneur is asked questions about, for example, reliability, availability, price, marketing support, product insurance and, perhaps more embarrassing, he is asked to produce both product *and* previous satisfied customers. Unable to produce product without equipment and premises, he approaches potential suppliers, only to be told that suppliers of equipment will require cash (he has no trading record with them) and landlords require bank guarantees – and the loop is closed. The picture looks bleak. How, then, do any new businesses emerge?

The entrepreneurial network

Vesper (1979) warned us not to overlook the 'experience factor' as a source of new venture ideas. He underlines the point: 'Instead of searching randomly, as many popularised entrepreneurship books seem to suggest, the entrepreneur should closely examine his or her own education, work experience, and hobbies as idea sources. The large majority of the entrepreneurs studied primarily used their own expertise rather than that of others.' This point is of funda-mental importance. The 'experience factor' is of value not only in selecting new venture ideas, but also in providing a framework for evaluating their viability, for stepping off the credibility roundabout and establishing the business. Credibility is established through personal contact and knowledge of the skills, motivation and past performance of the individual; the bankers call this the 'track record'. Since for an embryo firm there is no trading track record, investors must look to their previous relationship with the indivi-dual, whether it be commercial or personal. Thus, for example, a previous employer may agree to be the first customer, a friend may allow use of spare office space, or a relative may be prepared to lend money with little real hope of a return in the short or even medium term (in the UK, this is known as the 'Aunt Agatha Syndrome').

This use of the existing contact network is a way of providing credibility, and thus comfort, to those organisations which are being asked to invest in the business by, for example, supplying raw mate-rials on credit.

Social networks

Clearly, therefore, a strong informal or social network is essential for the successful launch of the firm. Aldrich and Zimmer (1986) state: 'The approach we take ... focuses upon entrepreneurship as embedded social context, channelled and facilitated or constrained and inhibited by people's position in social networks.' The following was found when studying start-ups in St Joseph County, Indiana (Birley, 1985):

Informal contacts, mainly business contacts, are seen overall to be the most helpful in assembling the elements of the business.
Family and friends are the most useful where local issues were concerned, as with the seeking of location and employees.
The formal sources come to the fore when the elements of the firms are set and the entrepreneur is seeking to raise finance. It is hardly surprising, therefore, that the institution mentioned most of the time was the bank.
All other formal, declared sources of help, including the SBA [Small Business Administration], were mentioned on very few occasions.

These findings have subsequently found support in collaborative studies in a number of countries. Indeed, as Aldrich *et al.* (1991) note, in this sense there can be said to be a 'generic entrepreneur'. Aldrich and Zimmer (1986) also note that these social networks have an influence not only on the individual entrepreneurial decision, but also upon the total supply:

> Voluntary associations, trade associations, public agencies, other social units increase the probability of people making connections with one another ... The complex pattern of social organization described by Everett Rogers and Judith Larson in their book *Silicon Valley Fever* illustrates the synergistic effects of brokers, central meeting points – such as well known 'watering holes' and restaurants – and family and friendship networks that supported the high start-up rate in the Silicon Valley.

Artificial networks

Unfortunately, despite the meteoric growth of Enterprise Agencies and Business Links in the UK, and Small Business Development Centers in the USA, both of which are formed to provide advice and assistance for the new and small firm, these networks are not built overnight. Let me illustrate the point with reference to Northern Ireland, where formal support for enterprise began in 1971 with the formation of the Local Enterprise Development Unit (LEDU), followed in 1973 by the first Local Enterprise Agency (LEA). By 1993, 33 LEAs were in operation, supported by six LEDU regional offices. Despite this, in a recent study with colleagues in Northern Ireland (Birley Cromie and Callaghan, 1992), we found owner-managers to have smaller direct and indirect personal contact networks than the international comparison groups. More important, we found 'one of the most noticeable gaps ... is any mention of the members of the "artificial" networks, those agencies which were set up to facilitate the development of a healthy new and small firms sector and which were the primary source of firm for this study'. In a subsequent study, we noted that, 'if entrepreneurial supporters are to surmount this apparent weakness ... it is incumbent upon them to excel at personal networking' (Cromie *et al.*, 1993). Yet 20 years after the formation of the first agency we still conclude that 'the community entrepreneurs appear to have a useful web of associates ... who are in touch with their environment ... However, the network is still young. A fully integrated, holistic approach to enterprise creation and development has yet to evolve' (Birley, Cromie and Callaghan 1991).

Stumbling blocks

A new business entering a hostile environment is a delicate entity. Many embryo businesses fail to raise the necessary resources to commence full-time trading, and many new businesses fail in the first two or three years. The common received wisdom is that this is due to the unwillingness of the investing community, whether clearing banks, venture capital companies or financial funds, to put up seed capital. The response from these organisations is that there is plenty of money eagerly seeking good investment ideas, but that there are very few around. There is an element of truth in both of these. Unfortunately entrepreneurs often approach investors too soon, and financial investors too often dismiss good ideas because they are presented without a formal business plan. It is not the purpose of this chapter to debate this issue, but merely to outline a number of the most common stumbling blocks along the way from an idea to a viable business.

The question as to whether the business will work must be approached from three separate, but interlinked, dimensions: the product, the package and the people.

The product

WILL IT WORK?

The step from the workshop bench to commercial production of a product can be very large. The ability of the entrepreneur to 'bodge' when things go slightly wrong is important in the early design stages, but this is not an appropriate skill in a factory. Customers expect uniform quality and reliable performance for the products which they buy. Indeed they expect the firm to provide some form of product indemnity. Thus there are three issues which the entrepreneur must consider:

1. Can the required skill be transferred to others at a reasonable cost?

2. What product indemnity is necessary, and what will be the cost of insuring the firm against claims.
3. What service support is needed in the case where repairs are necessary?

While these questions are important for all firms – for example, liability insurance is an often ignored issue in service firms – they are particularly important for those firms with a complex manufacturing process.

HOW WELL IS THE ENTREPRENEUR PROTECTED?

Patents, copyright and registered trade names are all ways of affording some protection against predators. But too often entrepreneurs fail to protect themselves adequately. The most common argument against registering patent goes as follows: 'They are too expensive, they give my competitors too much information, and I couldn't afford to sue even if they did break patent.' While this may be true in certain cases and, indeed, getting the product to market as fast as possible may be the best protection possible, the important point is that establishing *ownership* of the product or idea is of fundamental importance in maintaining a competitive advantage. Too many entrepreneurs avoid the issue.

The package

Many ingredients are necessary in the translating of an idea into a viable business and it is the 'baking' – the packaging of resources and the strategy adopted – that determines future viability. Certain issues, however, are common.

IS THERE A GENUINE NEED?

The identification of market potential is fraught with difficulties, and this is more so for new business, even in those cases where the product itself may be well established. The relationship between price, product characteristics and market share is difficult to capture in a dynamic market environment and to translate into forecasts of revenue. However the most important question for all potential investors is whether the entrepreneur knows and understands his market-place, and whether he has collected data which are appropriate to evaluating the viability of the business. Thus expensive market research studies are often unnecessary in situations where the total market is large and established, and the entrepreneur is concerned to obtain a minute proportion of a local market. Conversely a new, high-technology, expensive product which has few potential customers will require a detailed study of the market-place. In both cases, however, the entrepreneur should be concerned to ascertain whether his product will sell, and for this purpose there is no substitute for orders. Indeed potential investors will be *most* impressed by such tangible evidence that the product is credible to customers.

WHAT IS THE MARKET ENTRY STRATEGY?

In the early days, the entrepreneur is attempting to establish the credibility of himself and his firm through the medium of his product. 'Product' in this case refers to the entire range of the marketing mix – products characteristics, price, promotion and place, or channels of distribution. Therefore a market entry strategy which is flexible, and which allows for adaptation to customer reactions, is extremely important.

WHAT IS THE BEST BUSINESS FORMAT?

Unfortunately the best business format may not fit the needs of the entrepreneur. Setting up a new manufacturing plant in a market dominated by large firms, both at the manufacturing point, and more importantly, at the distribution point, may well be courting disaster. On the other hand, a joint venture or a licence agreement with one of the firms could increase the chances of a successful launch quite substantially. It is often necessary, therefore, to separate the personal and the commercial reasons for the choice of a particular strategy.

HOW LONG WILL IT TAKE?

At the risk of appearing flippant, the answer to this question, too, is usually 'Twice as long as you think!' It may be the most important thing in the entrepreneur's life, but the same cannot be said of others. Moreover this applies to both resources and sales. For example, lawyers can take an interminable time to negotiate leases; suppliers are not always reliable (after all, the entrepreneur is unlikely to be an important customer); printing cannot take place until the firm is registered for Value Added Tax – which takes time. However perhaps the most underestimated factor in most start-ups is the time taken for the market-place to react to a new product. Cash flows can very quickly go severely awry, not because there is no demand, but because it takes, say six months longer than anticipated to build up sales; six months during which employees and suppliers have to be paid.

WHAT ARE THE VARIOUS LEGAL FORMS OF BUSINESS?

Basically, there are four:

1. Sole proprietorship.
2. Partnership.
3. Incorporation or limited liability.
4. Co-operative or common ownership.

The main differences are twofold, the first concerning the nature of the taxation. In a sole proprietorship or a partnership, the law does not distinguish between the individual and the firm. Therefore tax will be paid at the personal tax rates of the owners. An incorporated firm is seen as a separate entity which therefore pays corporation tax.

The second difference concerns the nature of the liability. In theory, in a limited liability firm any debts which the firm incurs are limited to the assets of the firm. This is not the case for the other entities. However this has been severely eroded by recent company and insolvency legislation; and the bank manager, landlord, and possibly suppliers, may demand personal guarantees before they will agree to trade with the new firm, thus 'bypassing' the limited.

WHAT DO I DO WHEN THINGS GO WRONG?

Things will almost certainly go wrong. Few entrepreneurs can forecast all possible problems and, even when they can, they are not always able to provide adequate contingency plans. However a successful entrepreneur will not only know his business sufficiently well to be aware of the most sensitive areas, but he or she will also learn from mistakes. Moreover it is no use trying to hide them from financial investors. Few investors, whether they be the local clearing bank or a venture capital fund, expect the business plan to turn into exact reality, but they do expect to be kept informed. They most certainly do not like surprises.

HELP!

There is a great deal of help around. The traditional sources of advice and assistance for any firm come from professional relationships – the accountant, the bank, the lawyer, the customer or the supplier. However each of these sources is likely to view the firm from a particular, technical bias; until recently, few professional advisers were able to give general commercial advice. Moreover the type of advice, assistance and information which a new firm requires can be time-consuming and cover a wide spectrum. As a conse-

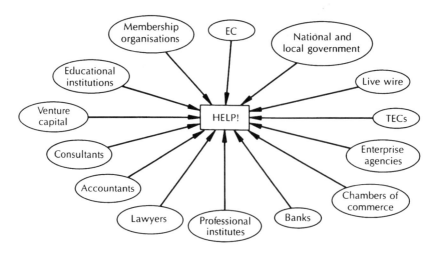

Figure 2.2   Some sources of help

quence it is expensive to provide to a customer who may well be unwilling or unable to pay a commercial rate. Therefore, in recent years in both Europe and the USA, there has evolved a range of advice, assistance and education focused particularly on new firms and financed, at least in part, by the government. A diagrammatic representation of a selection of the sources of help available to the entrepreneur is seen in Figure 2.2.

The people

We end where we began: small firms, new firms involve people: their goals, needs and skills are inextricably intertwined with those of the firm.

ARE PARTNERS NECESSARY?

This is the wrong question. The important question is whether the firm has the necessary combination of managerial and technical skills, and whether the people involved are wholly committed. They do not necessarily all have to own equity. Indeed, while the 'greedometer' can start running fairly early in the life of the firm, involving others can create severe problems in the future. A partnership is all too like a marriage, which many enter into with insufficient thought. There are two essential ingredients to a successful partnership.

1. *Clear power*: the managerial roles of each of the partners should be clear and understood, particularly for those activities which are outside their traditional skills. Thus, if one partner is responsible for selling, and one for manufacturing, cash control should not be allowed to fall between the two.
2. *Common goals*: few partners discuss their future needs and goals. Yet this is often the eventual cause of substantial friction. The 'seven year itch' is alive and well in this arena also! For example, if one partner merely wishes to provide a comfortable life-style for himself and his family, while the other wishes to develop a large firm, there will be disagreements as to the level of reinvestment in the firm in the future.

Beyond this, however, is mutual respect and the ability to resolve conflict. Too many assume that a cosy professional or personal relationship will survive the rigours of launching a firm. Often it does not. Therefore one document is essential at the formation of a partnership in establishing guidelines for the future: the 'divorce agreement', a legal partnership agreement which also incorporates a formula for dissolution.

Picking winners

Anyone can pick winners, but not all the time. Moreover, it is neither easy nor totally scientific. While it is always possible to evaluate the various elements of the product and the package, and thus narrow the bounds of risk, in the end it is a question of judgement. Does the entrepreneur have the necessary skills, greed, hunger, determination, stamina and energy to see it through? Do you?

Exercises

1. Write a report evaluating your own ability to run a small firm.
2. List the ideas you have for a new business. Against each idea list the things you need to do to evaluate the market potential of the idea, the resources you would need to exploit it and the critical factors that will make the idea a commercial success. Evaluate the commercial potential of each idea.
3. List the fears you have about setting up your own business. Against each one consider what would need to change to persuade you to overcome those fears.
4. Write a mini case study detailing the issues faced by a recent start-up business that you know.

5. Write an essay evaluating the sources of and ease of obtaining start-up finance in the UK. If you have information on other European countries, compare the UK situation to theirs.

References

Aldrich, H. and C. Zimmer (1986), 'Entrepreneurship through Social Networks', in D. Sexton and R. Smilor (eds) *The Art and Science of Entrepreneurship*, Ballinger.

Aldrich, H., S. Birley, P. Dubini, A. Greve, B. Johannisson, P.R Reese and T. Sakano (1991), 'The Generic Entrepreneur? Insights from a Multinational Research Project', *Babson Entrepreneurship Research Conference*, March, Pittsburgh.

Birley, S. (1985), 'The Role of Networks in the Entrepreneurial Process', *Journal of Business Venturing*, vol. 1, no. 1.

Birley, S. (1986), 'Succession in the Family Firm: The Inheritors' View', *Journal of Small Business Management*, vol. 24, no. 3, July.

Birley, S. and D. Norburn (1984), 'Small Versus Large Companies: The Entrepreneurial Conundrum', *Journal of Business Strategy*, vol. 6, no.1, Summer.

Birley, S. and D. Norburn (1987), 'Owners and Managers: The Venture 100 versus the Fortune 500', *Journal of Business Venturing*, vol. 2, no. 4, pp.351–62.

Birley, S. and P. Westhead (1993), 'A Taxonomy of Business Start-up Reasons and Their Impact on Firm Growth and Size', *Journal of Business Venturing*,

Birley, S., S. Cromie and A. Myers (1990), *Entrepreneurship Networks in Northern Ireland*, Department of Economic Development and LEDU.

Birley, S., S. Cromie and A. Myers (1990), *Entrepreneurship Networks in Northern Ireland*, Northern Ireland Small Business Institute, University of Ulster.

Birley, S., K. Manning and N. Corble (1992), 'Social Businesses: The Restructuring of the Public Sector in the UK', *European Business Journal*, vol. 4, issue 4, pp.27–35.

Carland J.W., F. Hoy, W.R. Boulton and J.A.C. Carland (1984), 'Differentiating Entrepreneurs from Small Business Owners: A Conceptualization', *Academy of Management Review*, vol. 9, no. 2, pp.354–9.

Cooper, A.C. (1970), 'The Palo Alto Experience', *Industrial Research*, vol. 1, pp.58–60.

Cooper, A.C. (1981), 'Strategic Management: New Ventures and Small Business', *Long Range Planning*, vol. 14, no. 5, pp.39–45.

Collins, O.F., D.G. Moore and D.B. Unwalla (1964), *The Enterprising Man*, Michigan State University Press.

Cromie, S., S. Birley and I. Callaghan (1993), 'Community Brokers: Their Role in the Formation and Development of Business Ventures', *Entrepreneurship and Regional Development*, vol. 5, no. 3, July–September, pp.247–64.

Dubini, P. (1988), 'The Influence of Motivations and Environment on Business Start-ups: Some Hints for Public Policies', *Journal of Business Venturing*, 4, pp.11–26.

Dunkleberg, W.C. and A.C. Cooper (1982), 'Entrepreneurial Typologies', in K.H. Vesper (ed.), *Frontiers of Entrepreneurship Research*, Centre for Entrepreneurial Studies.

Gartner, W.B. (1984), 'Problems in Business Start-up: The Relationships Types of New Ventures', *Entrepreneurship Research*, Centre for Entrepreneurial Studies.

Hofstede, G. (1980), *Culture's Consequences: International Differences in Work Related Values*, Sage.

Kent, C.A., D.L. Secton, P.M. Van Auken and D. Young (1982), 'Lifetime Experiences of Managers and Entrepreneurs: A Comparative Analysis', paper presented at the 42nd Annual Conference of the Academy of Management New York, August.

Manning, K. and S. Birley (1990), 'Public Sector Venturing: The Creation of a New Breed', *European Business Journal*, vol. 2, issue 1, pp.3–8.

Maslow, A. (1954), *Motivation and Personality*, Harper & Row.

McLelland, D. (1961), *The Achieving Society*, Van Nostrand.

Rotter, J.B. (1966), 'Generalized Expectancies for Internal Versus External Control of Reinforcement', *Psychological Monographs, vol. 80, no. 609.*

Schumpeter, J.A. (1942), *Capitalism, Socialism and Democracy*, Harper and Brothers.

Stanworth, M.J.K. and J. Curran (1976), 'Growth and the Small Firm – An Alternative View', *Journal of Management Studies*, vol. 13, no. 2, May, pp.95–110.

Vesper, K. (1979), 'New Venture Ideas', *Harvard Business Review*.

CHAPTER 3

Growth

Paul Burns and Jean Harrison

INTRODUCTION	40
CHARACTERISTICS OF GROWTH COMPANIES	41
THE IMPORTANCE OF THE OWNER-MANAGER	45
STRATEGIES FOR GROWTH	49
MANAGING GROWTH	60
PATHS TO FAILURE	66
CONCLUSIONS	70
EXERCISES	71
REFERENCES	71

Introduction

It has already been pointed out that most small firms do not grow to any size. They are 'life-style businesses' that provide the owner-manager with an acceptable income but, more important, a comfortable life-style. However even they must develop in their early stages to a certain size if they are to survive. Of more interest are 'growth businesses', but even these often grow to a certain size and then falter or stagnate. Break points frequently occur at around five employees and 20 employees. Going beyond 20 employees often means the way the business is organised has to change.

The problems start when the business threatens to become a separate entity in its own right. At this point the owners start to feel that their business is out of their control. Typically, they can no longer do everything with one or two key support staff; communications are failing and mistakes are happening too frequently for comfort. The demands on the owner's time are unbearable and so the next stage is to formalise a management team and delegate responsibility and authority.

The owner is the only person who can decide whether to go for growth, and all that it entails, or to establish comfortable limits. For

Table 3.1   *Growth and static company characteristics*

	Growth companies	Static companies
Objective	Maximise profits Increase sales	Less emphasis on profits More on independence
Organisational structure	'Tree' structure Development of 'teams' 'Clover leaf' (full-time, part-time and temporary) employee structure emerging	'Tree' in well-established firms
Style of management	Autocratic to start Consultation emerging	Paternal
Structure of internal accounting	Strong movement to profit centres	Less emphasis on centres
Historical data	Strong on cash flow Trend to monthly forecasts	Very little
Key variables	Cash flow Profitability Sales	More emphasis on supplier relationships

Source: Ray, G. H. and P. J. Hutchinson (1983), *The Financing and Financial Control of Small Enterprise Development*, Gower.

the majority of business owners, the decision is about how to keep success at a maximum while maintaining the size of the company for their own comfort. The entrepreneurial owner will already have a plan for dealing with this situation, and growth can be rapid. If the owner did not go into business with the express purpose of growing a successful company, but the success of the business is encouraging, he may also be considering growth as an inevitable part of that success. His motivations and aspirations may not be different, but his views on scale and succession may have changed.

Characteristics of growth companies

A study of 'supergrowth' companies – those companies that grew rapidly to a stock market quotation – by Ray and Hutchinson (1983) underlines some of the important differences between growth and 'life-style' or 'static' businesses. The results are summarised in Table 3.1. It is noticeable that the supergrowth companies were considerably more focused in their objectives, with a strong emphasis on forecasting financial data on a regular and timely basis – particularly cash flow, but also profit and sales. Also apparent is a very different style of management. These conclusions are underlined by a number of other research findings. A 1989 report from the London Business School identified six common factors associated with successful growth businesses:

1. An experienced owner-manager with a good knowledge of the market and industry: venture capitalists know that management buy-outs are less risky than start-ups. This is partly because they are then backing a number of managers, each with a good knowledge of their industry.
2. Close contact with customers and a commitment to quality of product and/or service: higher profit margins were achieved by competing on service rather than price or, perhaps more surprisingly, uniqueness of product.
3. Innovation and flexibility in marketing and technology: this gives them a differential advantage over their competitors.
4. A focus on profit not sales, with good management systems controlling costs: there is the old adage that 'Turnover is vanity, profit is sanity'. (To which the accountant added, 'Cash flow is reality.')
5. Attention to good employee relations, often backed by a bonus scheme: there is a large body of research which now indicates that the major weakness of British business is not a lack of functional skills but basic man-management and that the firms that grow are the ones that get this right.
6. Operating in a growing market: spotting opportunities is something entrepreneurs are good at, but perhaps luck does play a part.

The 3i European Enterprise Centre has also conducted a number of surveys into smaller firms across Europe (1991, 1993 and 1994). One survey into high performance (high profit) firms in Britain and France found that they tended to have high levels of internal organisation. They produced regular plans which contained objectives, strategies and budgets involving a management team. They also produced regular, timely financial reports which were compared to budgets at regular meetings of the team. These results were broadly supported by subsequent research across five countries into companies with high profit and turnover growth. In this, the high growth companies were found to set clear objectives, up to three years ahead, whilst the low growth or declining companies were found to be constantly adapting their plans to changes in the market-place.

Other research supports the importance of planning and control for growing businesses as the emphasis changes from tactical to strategic and the pace of change accelerates.

The key points about management are summarised in Box 3.1.

Box 3.1 Key points about management

- The owner must understand the economics of the business's products and services and how they can be used to best advantage.
- The owner must understand which opportunities to pursue and which to leave.
- The owner must understand the customers and their needs.
- The firm needs to pursue its differential advantage over competitors.
- Planning needs to be developed to be systematic.
- Management controls must produce information to monitor the business effectively.
- The resources of the business need to be directed towards satisfying the customer.
- Successful business management is 10 per cent inspiration and 90 per cent perspiration.

Not all businesses are presented with opportunities for growth and, because of the uniqueness of every firm, there is no single formula that can guarantee successful growth. However it is possible broadly to define the elements of success for any business. These are shown in Figure 3.1. Essentially success depends upon the personal qualities of the owner-manager and their product/service idea or offering. These two elements are fundamental. Effective management, in all its different forms, can help focus on the needs of the customer. However on its own it will not guarantee success.

The importance of the product/service can be overstated, although many smaller firms make a good living out of 'me too' products. These are products that already exist in the market-place but which are presented in a more attractive and effective way. The trick for the small firm is to do things better than, or differently from, competitors. In this respect the management discipline of marketing is vital. Box 3.2 summarises these key points.

All of the key points above are a question of good management. Brian Warnes, author of *The Genghis Khan Guide to Management* (1986), a popular and very practical view of 'how to' management hints, asserts, 'There is no such thing as bad luck in business ... only

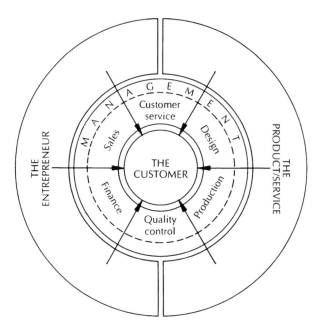

Figure 3.1   The elements of success

bad management.' Stock exchange collapses, earthquakes and terror-ist attacks aside, he has a point. Unfortunately a business owner has many functional roles to take on and many can fool themselves into believing that they can do it all.

Many owners of fast-growing businesses have difficulty coping with the multiplicity of internal and external demands placed on them. Few have the ability to cope with developing a strategic (business) plan, introducing new products, developing new markets and maintaining good links with banks.

Box 3.2   Key points about the product/service

- The product must be right for the market.
- It must be available when the market wants it ('ahead of your time' is often a failure).
- The business must understand their customers and their needs.
- The business must ensure the quality and reliability of the product.

The importance of the owner-manager

The personal characteristics required to launch a business success-fully are not those required for growth and, even more frequently, not those required to manage it once it has grown to any size. The role of the owner-manager needs to change as the business develops, but all too often they are not able to make the transition. However there do seem to be fundamental differences in the characteristics of those owner-managers that launch growth businesses and those that set up life-style businesses. These differences go to the heart of trying to describe what constitutes an 'entrepreneur'.

Collectively business owners do appear to have certain typical character traits, although the mix and emphasis of these characteristics will inevitably be different for each individual. Innovation is often taken as a key characteristic of the 'true' entrepreneur. However there is some difficulty in defining 'innovation', which also confuses the issue. Innovation tends to be linked with technological products that are completely new. Desk-top computers took the market by storm while IBM declined to invest in this move because 'people would not use them'. People, like Apple's Steve Jobs, who develop these exciting new ideas, are seen as typical entrepreneurs. However, an innovation can also be a new way of presenting or using an old product, a new way of marketing, or of structuring a company. For example, when the Open University began its distance learning programmes it was described as an innovation in education, despite the fact that correspondence courses had been in existence for some time. The marketing strategy of McDonald's was heralded as an innovation in marketing a product (fast food) that had been sold by many other competitors, including British 'fish and chip' shops.

In fact, few businesses can be described as innovative in the literal sense – completely new – and therefore the majority of owners may not be entrepreneurial in the dynamic, glamorous interpretation of the word. They may be entrepreneurial, however, in the way they use their resources to grow their businesses. Therefore using innovation alone to identify growth firms, or the entrepreneurial behaviour supposedly attached to them, can be misleading and does not necessarily indicate success, or potential growth, in the business.

Start-up

The key difference between the owner-manager and the entrepreneur probably derives from their motivations for going into business. There is no single reason that people give for either opting for self-employment or starting a business. Equally their original motivations, unless absolutely clear, do not dictate the subsequent size, or success, of that business. Many owners have no wish to grow their company to be a future IBM or Virgin. However, if a business shows potential for being successful, few owners will hinder growth until their personal resources are really stretched. At this point the owner reaches a watershed. They have to decide to curtail growth so that the business can be controlled mainly by them, or begin to put in place professional management practices to cope with the growth and to encourage more.

Most people usually base their business upon skills, experience or qualifications that they have already gained from a previous job, or through a hobby. Other people spot gaps in the market: opportunities that are not being taken by existing businesses. The entrepreneur has been distinguished from the business owner as being a person who is likely to spot opportunities and be innovative in the way they take them up. Initially, however, there appears to be little difference in the motivations of each 'group'.

The reasons for starting a business are usually a mix of the following:

- the need for independence,
- the need for personal development,
- the need for material wealth,
- the need for recognition,
- the need to support a family or to contribute to the support,
- the need to benefit financially from their own skills and experience,
- following role models.

Debate still continues as to whether or not a cultural environment, linked with positive attitudes towards self-employment, increases the likelihood of a person setting up a business. The changes in material and structural aspects of a region may automatically lead to increases in the numbers of start-ups which, in turn, bring about a change in the culture. No one, yet, claims to know. There do appear to be factors in a person's background that might influence them to set up in business. Boxes 3.3 and 3.4 show how the profile of those starting their own business has changed between 1991 and 1995.

Characteristics of the owner-manager

Owner-managers have been typified as innovative risk takers always seeking out opportunities. They are often seen as self confident all-

---

Box 3.3   Start-up profile, 1991

Gender	male
Age	middle-aged or beyond formal retirement age
Background	one or both parents already in a small business
Marital status	married
Education	carried out some form of apprenticeship (or, if not, have no formal qualifications)

Source: Stanworth and Gray (1991).

Box 3.4   Start-up profile, 1995

Gender	male
Age	thirties
Background	business-owner parents; sets up in home area with local contacts
Marital status	married (50 per cent chance of break-up in two years, whether successful or not)
Education	better educated than large company counterparts; likely to have a degree and skills already gained

Source: Various research reports.

rounders who have a need for achievement. But how much of this is true? There have been many attempts to differentiate between 'types' of owner-managers in order to better understand the factors that make up a successful, growth business. Unfortunately there is no corresponding 'type' of business. For example, one study showed that a reasonably large manufacturing company could be run by any one of the three 'types' of owners shown below:

1. The craftsman, artisan or owner-manager: these are owners who practise a trade, craft or occupation. They make the product or provide the service and enjoy doing it.
2. The opportunist, promoter or 'entrepreneur': this owner's main intention is the pursuit of personal wealth through doing 'deals'. They can create, grow and sell businesses without remorse.
3. The administrator, manager or trustee: this owner's primary aim is to build an organisation. They attempt to maintain controlled growth, and structure the company as a 'small,' big business.

Psychologists have identified five characteristics that are typical for all 'types' of owner managers:

1. *The need for achievement* 'Achievement' for the individual owner means different things depending what type they are: for example, the satisfaction of producing a beautiful work of art, employing their hundredth person, or the magic one million pounds. Owner-managers typically have a high need for achievement.
2. *Locus of control* If you believe that you can exercise control over your environment and ultimately your destiny, you have an internal locus of control. If, however, you believe in fate, you have an external locus of control and you are less likely to take the risk of starting a business. Owner-managers typically have an internal locus of control, which is the same for many senior managers in large firms (Brockhouse, 1982; Caird, 1990).
3. *Risk taking* Risk taking has long been associated with entrepreneurs, although business owners rarely pursue a business opportunity if there seems a low chance of success. Most decisions are taken on an incremental basis in an attempt to minimise risk. Those who do not want their businesses to grow will rarely put themselves in a position where a decision involves risk. Owner-managers are measured risk takers (Brockhouse, 1980).
4. *The need for independence* This is most often seen as 'the need to be your own boss' and is the trait that is most often cited, and supported, by researchers and advisors alike. However independence means different things to different people, such as control-

---

Box 3.5   *Characteristics of entrepreneurial owners*

- opportunistic
- adventurous
- 'ideas' people
- restless
- high-profile image makers
- proactive
- innovative

---

ling your own destiny, doing things differently or being in a situation where you can fulfil your potential. It has often been said that, once you run your own firm, you cannot work for anybody else (Collins and Moore, 1970).

5. *Innovative behaviour*   Many have singled this out as the true mark of the entrepreneur, as opposed to business owners generally. However few businesses are truly innovative in that they can claim to have something that is completely new. Most do things slightly differently or combine a number of different factors in a different way (Kanter, 1983).

Recent research (Chell *et al.*, 1991) looked at the characteristics of owner-managers who run growth businesses. The results produced the set of attributes for the entrepreneurial owner which are shown in Box 3.5. The research also classified three other types of owner. At the opposite end of the spectrum, the 'caretaker type' displayed none of these characteristics. The other two types, the 'quasi-entrepreneur' and 'administrator', exhibited a mix of the characteristics, with differences in emphasis.

One 'real' entrepreneur once remarked that 'the man who starts his own business generally does so because he is a difficult employee'. The characteristics and motivations discussed in the last few pages can be looked at from this less glamorous but more pragmatic viewpoint.

Strategies for growth

The second element needed for success is good management. That means that the owner-manager and their team can identify the nature of the firm's competitive advantage and pursue it effectively. One characteristic that singles out growth businesses from life-style businesses is the fact that they think strategically: that is, they think about the direction and scope of the business over the longer term. However the basis for any growth strategy is a thorough under-standing of where the firm is today – an internal analysis covering its strengths and weaknesses – and an external analysis of the oppor-tunities and threats that it faces. This is usually called a SWOT (Strengths, Weaknesses, Opportunities and Threats) analysis. The analysis involves looking at customers, competitors and markets, then matching them to the product/service offering (the marketing mix) to understand the nature of the firm's competitive advantage.

The industry

Of fundamental importance for small firms is an understanding of the nature of competition, and therefore the profitability of firms, in their industry and the economies of scale they face. Typically small firms can affect neither. In his book on competitive advantage, Michael Porter (1985) provides a structural analysis of industries which he claims goes some way towards explaining profitability. The aim of any competitive strategy, he says, 'is to cope with and, if possible change, the rules in favour of the company'. Unfortunately a small firm is unlikely to be able to change those rules, so it pays to understand them. Porter claims that five forces determine competi-tiveness. These are shown in Figure 3.2 and described below:

1. The power of *buyers*: this is determined by buyer versus firm size and concentration, the volumes purchased, buyer information and switching costs, and their ability to backward integrate. Thus a small firm selling what are, for it, large volumes to a big company buyer, but where these volumes represent small volumes to them, is *a priori*, in a weak competitive position. The power of the mar-keting mix and its ability to differentiate the product and insulate it from price sensitivity will also have an effect.
2. The power of *suppliers*: this is also determined by the relative size of firms and the other factors mentioned above. Thus the small firm buying from a large company is relatively disadvantaged.
3. The threat of *new entrants*: barriers to entry keep out new entrants to an industry. These can arise because of legal protection (patents and so on), economies of scale, proprietary product dif-ferences, brand identity, access to distribution, government policy, switching costs, capital costs and so forth. For example, a firm whose product is protected by patent or copyright may feel that it is relatively safe from competition.
4. The threat of *substitutes*: this revolves around their relative price performance, switching costs and the propensity of the customer

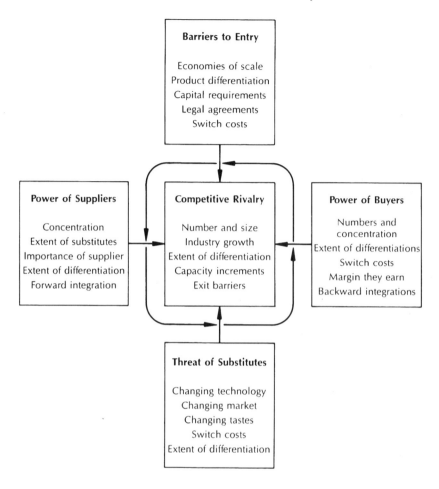

Figure 3.2 Porter's five forces

to switch. Thus, for example, a small firm selling a poorly differentiated product in a low-price, fashion market should find it difficult to compete.

5. The intensity of *rivalry*: the rivalry of an industry will depend on its newness and growth, its attractiveness in terms of profit and value added, intermittent overcapacity, product differentiation, brand identity, switching costs, concentration, diversity of competition and exit costs.

These five forces determine industry profitability and in turn are a function of industry structure – the underlying economic and technical characteristics of the industry. These can change over time but the analysis does emphasise the need to select industries carefully in

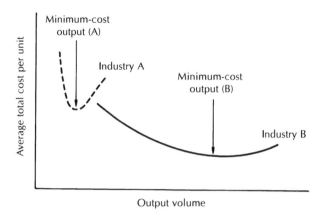

Figure 3.3   Long-run average cost curves

the first place. It also provides a framework for predicting, *a priori*, the success or otherwise of the small firm. For example, a small firm competing with many other small firms to sell a relatively undifferentiated product to a few large customers in an industry with few barriers to entry is unlikely to do well without some radical shifts in its marketing strategies. How many small firms face just such a situation?

The average size of businesses varies from industry to industry. For example, the average size of a chemical firm is very large, whereas the average size of a retail firm is relatively small. The fundamental reason for this is the extent to which economies of scale affect an industry; that is, how the total cost per unit produces changes as more units are produced. Generally this can be expected to decline up to some point – for example, as an expensive piece of machinery is used more fully. However beyond this point unit costs may start to increase – for example, as economies of scale of production become increasingly offset by rising distribution costs. The potential for economies of scale is often greatest in capital-intensive industries like chemicals. This is shown diagrammatically in Figure 3.3. Total costs include production, selling and distribution costs and are therefore dependent upon the state of technology, the size of the market and the location of potential customers. The unit cost for industry *A* turns up at a relatively low level of output, implying the optimal size of firm is relatively small, in contrast to industry *B* where there are considerable economies of scale. Porter calls these 'fragmented' industries, where economies of scale just do not exist and large firms cannot, therefore, dominate the industry.

As Dewhurst and Burns (1983) have pointed out, small businesses will not be able to survive, in the long run, in an industry where economies of scale exist and are important. This bold statement must, of course, be explained, since we all know of examples where small firms have survived and prospered in industries where economies of scale exist. There are two major reasons for this:

1. The market or product is new and economies of scale are being developed. Firms have not yet had time to grow to their optimal size. In this case, small firms must grow and aim to become large firms early in their life cycle simply to ensure their survival. These are the 'big bang' companies and they tend to be the glamorous ones that make the news headlines. However obtaining market dominance is a high-risk strategy and this road to high growth has many casualties on the way.
2. While economies of scale of production exist, the *market* for the product is limited, either in total or geographically, and the theoretical optimal size is not achievable. This happens particularly in highly specialised industries. But specialisation can be product- or market-based. Indeed having a differentiated, specialist product or service often goes hand-in-hand with having a well-selected market segment. This is called 'following a "niche" strategy'.

An example of the effects of economies of scale is the microcomputer industry. Born in the late 1970s with unknown demand for its products and no established producers, it has grown rapidly. However the industry offers substantial economies of scale, particularly in R&D for hardware and software. Consequently the market has consolidated, with many small firms going out of business. The survivors have been one of two types of firm. First, there are firms like the Apple Corporation, which recognised that the industry would eventually be dominated by a few large firms offering low cost or premium quality products. Apple realised that economies of scale were achievable and would become increasingly important to customers as the basic microcomputer became more and more a commodity. Apple grew rapidly, grabbing market share worldwide, so that it was in a good position to compete with the big company entrants such as IBM. Secondly there are the firms like Sun Microsystems which specialised in CAD/CAM equipment and aimed at even smaller specific market segments. Sun Microsystems established an effective market niche for itself and headed off any direct competition with big companies. Customers valued their expertise and economies of scale were less important. As often happens, it has been the middle-sized firm which has pursued neither strategy which has suffered in this industry.

Eventually even the big company can feel threatened by a large number of extremely effective niche companies. The computer industry as a whole has now fragmented into many different segments and no company other than IBM now tries to compete in every segment, including Japan's Fujitsu, Hitachi and NEC. Every other firm concentrates on the area where it can be best. Apple, Sun Microsystems, Intel, Compaq and Microsoft have all thrived in recent years despite brutal price wars. Companies with broader product lines based on large machines, such as DEC, Bull, Siemens-Nixdorf and Japan's computer makers have seen their profits collapse. This process is nowhere more evident than in IBM. Its profits have evaporated and it has had to completely reorganise to face the competition from effective niche marketers.

There is a strong element of luck in the 'big bang' strategy or, put more scientifically, it is a high-risk strategy. Often firms only realise that it is the strategy they must adopt as the market or technology for the product or service develops. This is because the company needs to establish:

1. that the technology offers the economies of scale (and often cost curves can change dramatically over time:;
2. that these economies are in some way important to the customers (through lower price or other advantages);
3. that they are achievable, given the market size.

Small firms, then, would be ill-advised to take the risk and enter a market where economies of scale are important. By far the lowest risk strategy to follow is one of differentiation. This entails finding out what elements in the marketing mix make the firm uniquely different from the competition. It involves specialising in customers or products, not methods of production. It emphasises the non-price elements of the marketing mix, such as quality, and stresses the inherent strengths of many small firms in innovation, flexibility and personalised service.

Generic strategies

Developing an effective competitive strategy is vital for the smaller firm. To help in this we shall consider a number of generic strategies. Generic strategies are the bases on which the firm might seek to achieve lasting advantage, but they are generalised strategies which need tailoring to the situation of individuals. Michael Porter (1985) argued that there are only three fundamental ways of achieving sus-

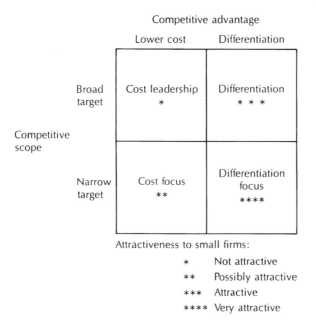

Figure 3.4   Competitive advantage

tainable competitive advantage. These are shown in Figure 3.4. They
are:

1. *Cost leadership*, where the firm sets out to be the low cost
   producer in the industry. This assumes that costs can be reduced,
   for example through economies of scale, and this is important to
   the customer. The risks are that cost leadership cannot be sustained, competitors might imitate and technology changes or any
   other basis for the cost leadership might be eroded. This is an
   inherently unattractive alternative for most smaller firms as they
   can rarely achieve the economies of scale of large firms and
   seldom have the capital to invest constantly in new technology.
   What is more, it is likely that sustainable cost leadership can only
   be achieved by means of 'substantial relative market share advantage' because this provides the firm with cost advantage through
   economies of scale, market power and experience curve effects.
   This means that any firm pursuing this strategy will have to fight
   competitors hard to sustain its advantage.
2. *Differentiation*, where the firm sets out 'to be unique in the
   industry along some dimensions that are widely valued by customers'. This is called developing a unique selling proposition
   (USP). The firm sets out to establish itself as unique and different

from its competitors in some ways. It can then charge a premium price. The risks associated with this are that the differentiation cannot be sustained as competitors imitate or the USP becomes less important to customers. If the premium charged is too high, customers may decide not to purchase. This is an attractive strategy for smaller firms, particularly when combined with the third generic strategy.

3. *Focus*, where the firm focuses on a narrow target market segment combined with either of the other strategies. If the firm adopts a strategy of 'focused differentiation' it is said to pursue a niche strategy. This is a very attractive option for smaller firms. Focus can also be used with cost leadership, where concentrating on certain market segments offers some cost advantage. The risks with this strategy are that it can be imitated, the segment becomes unattractive for some reason, smaller segments start to appear, or the basis for segmentation disappears as the differences between segments disappear.

In a survey of some 1,500 smaller companies across Europe, the 3i European Enterprise Centre (1994) found that those companies that had seen their sales and/or profit grow in the 1990s were those who had 'better or different products or services', and this led to weak-to-normal levels of competition. Those that had seen sales, but particularly profits, decline competed on price and encountered fierce competition. Another survey into 3,500 of Britain's 'Superleague companies' concluded that most of these high-growth companies served niche markets (3i, 1993). In other words, the successful firms follow a strategy of differentiation, probably focused on target market segments.

One family company that has been very successful in differentiating its products and selling to a small, but lucrative market segment is the Huntingdon-based Quad Electroaccoustics. Its silvery grey, bizarrely sculptured audio equipment looks like no others. When Japanese 'competitors' bring out new models every year, Quads stay the same and last forever. Its original electrostatic loudspeaker was in production for 28 years; its successor, the £2,500 ESL-63, is now in its thirteenth year of production and many believe it still to be the best in the world. In 1994, Quad's 125 employees will generate pre-tax profits of £350,000 on sales of £3.5 million, with 70 per cent of those sales being exported, especially to Europe and Japan.

Porters' generic strategies form a valuable framework for developing the further elements of strategy and, eventually, the tactics that a firm might adopt in pursuing them. Table 3.2 shows some of the threats that firms pursuing these strategies are likely to face. These relate simply to the generic strategies discussed above. The indivi-

Table 3.2   Competitive threats

Cost leadership	Differentiation
Changing cost structures	Loss of differential advantage
New bases for cost economics	Competitors imitate
Technology changes	New entrants
Price competition	Basis for differentiation becomes less important to buyers
Proximity in differentiation is lost	Cost proximity is lost
Lower costs possible through focus	Life cycle shifts
	Greater differentiation possible through focus

Focus
Niche structure of differences erodes
New entrants imitate or sub-segment
Customers start to value offering by broadly targeted competitors

Table 3.3   Elements of strategy

Cost leadership	Differentiation
Tight cost control	Reinforce differential advantage
Invest in cost reduction	Build brand image
Go for volume to achieve economies	Build on specialist skills
Keeping abreast of changes in technology	Respond aggressively to competitors or new entrants
Invest in barriers to entry	Invest in barriers to entry
	Monitor changes in market

Focus
Monitor changes in market segment
Be aware of market limits to maintain niche
Invest in barriers to entry

dual firm will face many more threats, related to its particular circumstances. Table 3.3 shows some of the more detailed elements of strategy that the firm will need to pursue in order to counter these threats and achieve a general objective of maximising profit. Of course, there are likely to be others, based upon the objectives that the company has set and the particular circumstances that it faces.

It is vital that a firm understands the basis of its competitive advantage. For a firm pursuing a differentiation strategy this means understanding the basis for its differential advantage. This can be based in law (a licence, copyright, patent and so on), upon elements of the product (quality, design and so on), the service offered or intangible things like image. For a shop it may be based on location (the only shop on the estate). The more elements that the firm can claim set it apart from the competition the better. However, these elements must be a real benefit and add value to the customer. If the firm has elements of differentiation then it should aggressively promote them, usually through a strong brand identity.

Niche strategy

Developing a market niche by differentiating a business from its competitors is a strategy that offers smaller firms a better chance of sustainable growth. Even large companies can feel threatened by niche companies. Their 'specialism' can be product- or market-based, and clear differentiation often goes with well-aimed segmentation. The key to segmentation is the ability to identify the unique benefits that a product or service offers to potential customers. Differentiation involves:

- finding out what elements in the marketing mix are 'unique' to the business;
- specialising in customers or products rather than methods of production;
- emphasising the non-price elements of the mix, such as quality;
- stressing the inherent strength of a small firm, such as innovation flexibility or personalised service.

Establishing a market niche is most effective when aimed at a narrowly defined market segment. Sometimes this can involve concentrating on gaps in the market-place left by larger companies. One problem of a niche market is its very narrowness, which limits it, but, what might be limited for larger companies offers smaller firms a range of opportunities. Entrepreneurs often run businesses in different niches, finding growth through diversification. However the environment does change; markets grow or shrink; technology changes and customers move around. As the picture changes, so do opportunities, and what might offer a good niche in one decade may turn into a free-for-all in another.

Those small firms that survive are able to sustain a higher margin because they do not compete primarily on price. One such company, that arguably could make even higher margins by charging a higher price for its products, is the Morgan Motor Company. Founded in 1909, it is the world's oldest privately owned car manufacturer. Every Morgan is hand-built and looks like it came from the 1930s. Each car is different, with a choice of 35,000 body colours and leather upholstery to match. It takes seven weeks to build a car and

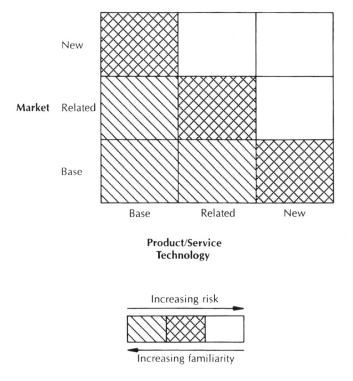

Figure 3.5   Product market matrix

customers are invited to the factory to see the process. Morgan sells only 480 cars a year, half overseas, and demand exceeds supply, cushioning the company from the vagaries of demand. In 1992 it made pre-tax profits of £994,000 on sales of £7.8 million.

Diversification

In its search for further growth, a business has four options, illustrated in the product market matrix in Figure 3.5.

1. It can stay with its base product or service, and its existing market, and simply try to penetrate the market further. This involves selling more of the same product to the same market. This is dealing very much with the familiar and is normally the lowest risk option, although the point will come when further penetration is not possible or economic.

2. It can develop related or new products for its existing market. For example, an off-licence might start to sell soft drinks or cigarettes. This is called product development.
3. It can develop related or new markets for its existing products. The off-licence might open a new branch in a nearby area of the town, or it might try selling directly to restaurants. This is called market development.
4. It might try moving into related or new markets with related or new products. The off-licence might try selling cigarettes directly to restaurants. Since this strategy involves unfamiliar products and unfamiliar markets it is high-risk.

The strategies discussed above are called 'horizontal' strategies. Two further strategies for growth are open to the small firm: first, 'backward vertical integration', where the firm becomes its own supplier of some basic raw materials or services, second, 'forward vertical integration', where the firm becomes its own distributor or retailer. Both strategies entail new product or service technologies and new customers and are therefore relatively risky.

Synergy is often used as a justification for diversification, particularly through acquisition or merger. Synergy is concerned with assessing how much extra benefit can be obtained from providing linkages within the value chain between activities which have been previously unconnected or where the connection has been of a different type. It has been demonstrated that firms which diversify by building on their core business do better than those who diversify in an unrelated way. However research indicates that diversification generally is difficult to justify. Nevertheless one of the companies that has adopted a strategy of diversification most successfully is Lonrho, and its strategy has been one of unrelated diversification. Its interests range from hotels in Mexico to freight forwarders in Canada, from motor distribution in Africa to oil and gas production in the USA.

Research indicates that successful firms follow a strategy of incremental, mainly internal growth. They move carefully into new markets with existing products or sell new products to existing customers. The strategy of diversification is high-risk and only to be adopted after careful consideration. Smaller firms must consider carefully whether this is really appropriate to their needs. If it is to be followed, the safest routes are through joint ventures or strategic alliances. There is no evidence that commercial acquisitions or takeovers (other than in a distress sale) add value to the firm.

Managing growth

Managing growth means managing change. The more rapid the growth, the more difficult it is to manage. As the firm grows, the application of the functional disciplines of marketing, accounting and people management changes and, with them, the role of the owner-manager. A number of growth models have been developed which seek to describe how these changes happen over time. The two most widely accepted models are the Greiner (1972) and the Churchill and Lewis (1983) models. Each offers a framework for considering the development of a business in five stages.

The Greiner model

Each of the stages of the Greiner model (Figure 3.6) has a particular management style, faces a given management problem and is characterised by a crisis which has to be overcome before the business can move on. Growth relates to the industry in which the company operates. In fast-growing industries, growth periods are relatively short; in slower growth industries they tend to be longer. In a rapidly growing market, a company would need to take on extra staff at a faster pace, and an appropriate organisation structure would be needed.

Greiner's model shows each evolutionary phase dominated by a particular management style used to achieve growth. Each revolutionary period presents a management problem to overcome. Only phases 1 to 3 really apply to smaller firms. However the model demonstrates how the management style adopted by the owner-manager must change if they are to pass successfully through the different phases.

The Churchill and Lewis model

The Churchill and Lewis model (Table 3.4) is the one most often used as a link with marketing, people and financial management issues. The five stages are identified as follows:

1. *Existence*: strategy is to stay alive, and the company needs to find customers and deliver products/services. The organisation is simple. The owner does everything. Planning is minimal/non-existent.
2. *Survival*: strategy is to establish the customer base and product portfolio. The company has to demonstrate that it has sufficient products and customers to be a viable business. It has to control its revenues and expenses to maintain cash flow. The organisation is still simple and planning is, at best, cash flow forecasting. The owner is still 'the business'.
3. *Success*: the company is big enough and has sufficient customers and sales to establish itself with confidence. The owner has

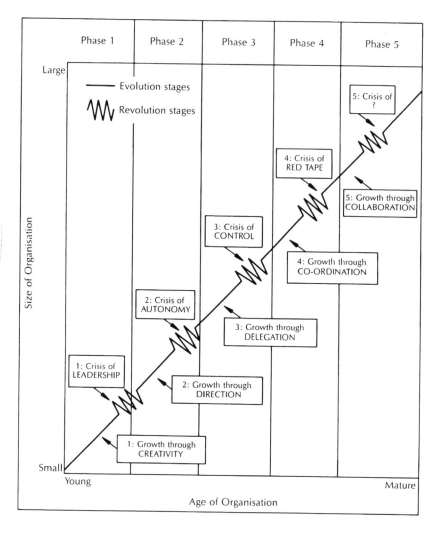

Figure 3.6   The Greiner growth model

acquired functional managers and basic marketing, financial and operations systems. Planning is in the form of operational budgets. This company has two strategic options. The first option is disengagement. If it can maintain its market niche and/or, adapt to changing circumstances, the company can stay like this for a long time. If not, it will either fold or drop back to the survival stage. The second is growth. If the owner consolidates the company, clarifies his vision and ensures that resources are diverted into growth, strategic planning is introduced to achieve that vision. The business, however, must remain profitable.

Table 3.4 The Churchill and Lewis growth model

	Stage 1 Existence	Stage 2 Survival	Stage 3(D) Success (disengagement)	Stage 3(G) Success (growth)	Stage 4 Take-off	Stage 5 Resource maturity
Management style	Direct supervision	Supervised supervision	Functional	Functional	Divisional	Line and staff
Organisation	Simple	Growing	Growing	Growing	Growing	Sophisticated
Extent of formal systems	Minimal to non-existent	Minimal	Basic	Developing	Maturing	Extensive
Major strategy	Existence	Survival	Maintaining profitable status quo	Get resources for growth	Growth	Return on investment

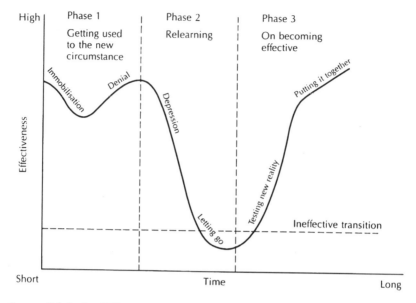

Source: Kakabadse 1983, p.150.

Figure 3.7   Work effectiveness during transition

4. *Take-off*: this stage is critical but, provided the owner can ensure satisfactory finance and management, the company can become very large.
5. *Maturity*: the business now begins to develop the characteristics of a stable, larger company with professional management and formal information systems which inform planning.

As the company passes through each stage, the business owner also faces a roller coaster of human problems. The classic change/denial curve (Figure 3.7) illustrates these changes very well and can offer insights into the attitude of the owner at each stage. The owner needs to learn to become more effective in a new role and to adopt new attitudes and skills. As with any change, this can take time.

PHASE 1

The unfamiliarity of the owner with their new role makes them feel anxious about their contribution and so their effectiveness drops slightly. Within a short time, having become used to the role using previously successful skills, and finding support to help them, their effectiveness improves and they do not believe that they have to change.

PHASE 2

Real demands are now being made and the individual is put under stress as they realise that they do have to develop new skills to keep up with the job. Although they will learn how to do the job, a period of anxiety makes them less effective because they can no longer rely on their old skills and they may believe that they can no longer do the job. In fact this 'low' indicates that the person is realising that they have to change and then, at some point, they abandon the past and accept the future.

PHASE 3

This testing period can be as frustrating as it can be rewarding. Mistakes can recreate the 'low', but, as the newly-learnt skills are brought into play effectively, the owner's performance improves and they achieve a higher level of effectiveness than at the beginning stage. They now have a set of new skills alongside their 'old'. However, this transition is not inevitable: some people fail to acquire new skills or cannot pull themselves out of the 'low'.

Churchill and Lewis also developed a simple summary of the key factors which affect the success or failure of a business in the different stages of its life. This is reproduced in Table 3.5. Four of the factors relate to the business owner and four to the business. The important point is the move from operational to strategic ability as the business grows. Even when the business is established in the final stage, the ability of the owner to think ahead is still critical to the development of the business. The business is therefore still tied to the owner's

Table 3.5   Growth stage imperatives

	Stage 1 Existence	Stage 2 Survival	Stage 3 Success	Stage 4 Take-off	Stage 5 Resource maturity
Owner's goal	***	*	***	***	**
Owner's operational ability	***	***	**	**	*
Owner's management ability	*	**	**	***	**
Owner's strategic ability	*	**	***	***	***
Financial resources	***	***	**	***	**
Personnel resources	*	*	**	***	**
Systems resources	*	**	***	***	**
Business resources	***	***	**	**	*

Note: ***critical; **important but manageable; *modestly irrelevant.

aspirations for the business. This summary provides a broad framework within which to assess the progress of the business.

Problems with growth models

The problem with growth models is simply that most firms do not experience growth. Even those that do rarely experience the process in quite the way the models predict. Often firms reach a plateau in their development at certain stages in the model. Indeed most firms do not survive the recurrent crises they face. However there is a well documented process of growth to crisis to consolidation that many surviving firms follow, although the actual sequence of issues or imperatives predicted by the models is not supported by empirical research. This is particularly true of Greiner's model. In many ways these models are best used as:

- predictors of problems that the firm is likely to face as it grows; and
- imperatives that the firms ought to have if it wishes to grow at different stages of development.

In this respect the Churchill and Lewis model is particularly useful. It allows us to focus on the business imperatives if the firm wants to develop and grow. These imperatives are summarised in Table 3.6. This shows clearly the move from operational/tactical to strategic as the business grows. It also shows how the imperatives in all four areas do change as the business grows. If you can identify which phase a firm is in, you will be able to understand the major issues that it needs to address, not only in that stage, but also in the next stage of its development.

Business owners start out able to control their business by physically being around, participating in the operational activity and personally discussing progress with their employees. As the scale of activity increases, they have to rely on collecting information in different ways at appropriate times, and the successful business owner learns this early. Information comes in many forms but is generally related to the business functions: management, marketing and financial control. The new business faces rapid change both externally and internally.

Paths to failure

It is easy to see from the stage theories of growth how firms fail because of the interaction of the personal characteristics of the

Table 3.6 Business imperatives as a firm grows

Orientation:	Existence	Survival	Success	Take-off
	Tactical	Tactical	Strategic	Strategic
Management	Owner is the business and has to be a 'jack of all trades'	Owner is still the business	Staff start to be recruited	Staff roles clearly defined
	Spider's-web organisation	Still spider's-web organisation	Organisation starts to become formalised	Decentralisation starts to take place
	Informal, flexible systems	Some delegation, supervision and control	Staff encouraged and motivated to grow into job	Greater co-ordination and control of staff
			Delegation, supervision and control	Emergence of professional management
	Opportunity-driven		Strategic planning	Operational and strategic planning
Marketing	Get customers	Generate repeat sales	Generate repeat sales and find new customers	Select new customers and generate repeat sales
	Undertake market research	Develop unique selling proposition (USP) and select market segmentation	Develop competitive advantage based upon USP and target markets	Aggressively attack competition
	Develop relationships and networks	Use relationships and networks	Use relationships and networks	Use relationships and networks

Table 3.6 Continued

Orientation:	Existence	Survival	Success	Take-off
	Tactical	Tactical	Strategic	Strategic
Accounting	Cash flow	Cash flow	Cash flow	Cash flow
		Accounting controls	Accounting controls	Accounting controls
		Break-even and margin of safety	Break-even and margin of safety	Break-even and margin of safety
			Balance sheet engineering	Balance sheet engineering
Finance	Own funds	Own funds	First phase venture capital	Venture capital
	Creditors, HP, leasing	Creditors, HP, leasing factoring	Creditors, HP, leasing factoring	Creditors, HP, leasing factoring
	Bank loans	Bank loans	Bank loans	Bank loans

Figure 3.8   The process of failure in the smaller firm

owner-manager with the managerial problems they face in their business. However they do not tell the whole story, as most firms do not grow to any size and still many manage to fail.

The personal characteristics of the owner-manager are particularly important factors early in the life of a business when failure rates are so high. In a survey of the literature, Berryman (1983) lists such personal problems as inability to delegate, reluctance to seek help, excessive optimism, unawareness of the environment, inability to adapt to change and thinness of management talent as reasons for failure. He lists some 25 different deficiencies, grouped under the general headings of accounting deficiencies, marketing deficiencies, lack of adequate finance and other areas such as excessive drawings, deficiencies in accounting and managerial knowledge and advice, as well as personal problems. Accounting problems are mentioned most frequently in the survey. All too many owner-managers rely on their auditors to produce out-of-date accounts on which to base their decisions. However many of the deficiencies are really just symptoms of deeper underlying causes.

Figure 3.8 gives a framework for looking at the process of failure in the smaller firm. The personal characteristics of the owner-manager interact with managerial defects to produce weaknesses in the firm. However the crisis that triggers the decline into failure is often brought about by some outside factor such as an unexpected change in the market-place, customer tastes, competition or distribution channels. These may lead to bad decisions being made by the owner-manager, such as a decision to overtrade or overgear. These, in turn, result in symptoms of failure such as running short of cash or declining profitability.

Larson and Clute's (1979) empirical research is one of the pieces surveyed by Berryman. The personal characteristics and managerial deficiencies they say lead to failure are:

Personal characteristics
- Exaggerated opinion of business competency based upon knowledge of some skill.
- Limited formal education.
- Inflexible to change and not innovative.

- Uses own personal taste and opinion as the standard to follow.
- Decisions based on intuition, emotion and non-objective factors.
- Past, not future, orientation.
- Little reading in literature associated with business.
- Resistant to advice from qualified sources but, paradoxically, accepts it from the least qualified.

Managerial deficiencies
- Cannot identify target market or customers.
- Cannot delineate trading area.
- Cannot delegate.
- Believes advertising is an expense, not an investment.
- Only rudimentary knowledge of pricing strategy.
- Immature understanding of distribution channels.
- No planning.
- Cannot motivate.
- Believes the problem is somebody else's fault and a loan would solve everything.

This insight into the process of failure is valuable, not only because it may help avoid the event, but also because it reinforces many of the lessons of success, and too few small firms are successful. However the reality is that most firms will not follow these strategies; most firms will not grow; most firms are born to die or stagnate.

Conclusions

The skills needed to manage successfully the growth of a firm are diverse. It is not an easy task. Indeed it places great pressures and strains on owner-managers and requires them to change their role as the firm develops. Is it any wonder that so many of them decide not even to try it?

However, while every firm is different and the process of growth is complex, it is possible to build up a picture of the stages of growth, the problems that the firm will face and the elements needed for success. Growth follows a predictable pattern of growth, crisis and then consolidation. The role of marketing changes from simply getting customers to developing competitive advantage based upon an understanding of the target markets to be attacked and the differentiated product/service offering they need. Small firms are good at networking and developing relationships. The importance of accounting information develops from a reliance on simple cash flow to a focus on profit and, in particular, break-even analysis. The role of the owner-manager must change from being autocratic in the early stages, with a spider's-web organisation structure, to a more consultative style, with formal structures and highly motivated teams. Owner-managers must learn to delegate.

It is even possible to paint a picture of growth businesses. They operate at a strategic rather than tactical level. They have a good knowledge of their markets and industry, close contact with customers and a commitment to quality, particularly of service. They seek out differential advantage, often selecting narrow market segments and creating for themselves a market niche. They are innovative (often in a marketing sense) and flexible, managing people well and encouraging teams to develop. They focus on cash flow and profit rather than turnover. They tend to operate in growing markets and grow incrementally, often through internal growth rather than acquisitions.

While it may be possible to identify the ingredients of success, it is far more difficult to define the precise importance of the different elements. Indeed, in any smaller firm, there is the overwhelming influence of the owner-manager and the vagaries of the market. However so much is now known about the process of growth that it is, at least, possible to say which firms have a better chance of achieving growth. More importantly, it is possible to recommend the best way for that growth to be managed.

Exercises

1. For a small firm with which your are familiar, describe and evaluate the strategy they are following.
2. For a small firm with which you are familiar, describe and evaluate the personal characteristics of the owner-manager.
3. Using Porter's five forces analysis, evaluate the key competitive pressures within an industry of your choice.
4. Undertake a SWOT analysis on a small business of your choice.
5. Porter argues that a business must have a clear generic strategy. assess the extent to which this is true for a small business of your choice.
6. Write an essay evaluating the universal applicability of Porter's generic strategies.
7. Write an essay evaluating the applicability of growth models.
8. Using whatever information is publicly available, undertake a strategic evaluation of Morgan Cars or another company of your choice.

References

3i European Enterprise Centre (1991), *Report 1: High Performance SMEs: A Two Country Study*, September.

3i European Enterprise Centre (1993), *Report 9: Britain's Superleague Companies*, August.

3i European Enterprise Centre (1994), *Report 12: Winners and Losers in the 1990s*, April.

Berryman, J. (1983), 'Small Business Failure and Bankruptcy: A Survey of the Literature', *European Small Business Journal*, Vol. 1, no. 4.

Brockhouse, R.H. (1980), 'Risk Taking Propensity of Entrepreneurs', *Academy of Management Journal*, vol. 23, no. 3.

Brockhouse, R.H. (1982), 'The Psychology of the Entrepreneur', in C.A. Kent, D.L. Sexton and K.H. Vesper (eds), *Encyclopedia of Entrepreneurship*, Prentice-Hall.

Caird, S. (1990), 'What does it mean to be enterprising?', *British Journal of Management*, vol.1, no. 3.

Chell, E., J.M. Haworth and S.A. Brearlet (1991), *The Entrepreneurial Personality: Concepts, Cases and Catagories*, Routledge.

Churchill, N.C. and V.L. Lewis (1983), 'The Five Stages of Small Business Growth', *Harvard Business Review* May/June.

Collins, O.F. and D.G. Moore (1970), *The Organisation Makers*, Appleton-Century-Crofts.

Dewhurst, J. and P. Burns (1983), *Small Business: Finance and Control*, Macmillan.

Greiner, L.E. (1972), 'Evolution and Revolution as Organisations Grow', *Harvard Business Review*, July/August.

Kakabadse, A. (1983), *The Politics of Management*, Gower.

Kanter, R.M. (1983), *The Change Masters*, Simon & Schuster.

Larson, C. and R. Clute (1979), 'The Failure Syndrome', *American Journal of Small Business*, vol. iv, no. 2, October.

Porter, M. (1985), *Competitive Advantage: Creating and Sustaining Superior Performance*, The Free Press.

Ray, G.H. and P.J. Hutchinson (1983), *The Financing and Financial Control of Small Enterprise Development*, Gower.

Stanworth, J. and C. Gray (eds) (1991), *Bolton 20 Years On: The Small Firm in the 1990s*, Paul Chapman, ch. 7.

Warnes, B. (1986), *The Genghis Khan Guide to Business*, Osmosis.

CHAPTER 4

Uncertainty, innovation and management

David Storey and Nigel Sykes

INTRODUCTION	73
A THEORETICAL FRAMEWORK	74
UNCERTAINTY	75
INNOVATION	80
MANAGEMENT	85
CONCLUSIONS	90
EXERCISES	91
REFERENCES	92

Introduction

'The differences in the administrative structure of the very small and the very large firms are so great that in many ways it is hard to see that the two species are of the same genus ... we cannot define a caterpillar and then use the same definition for a butterfly' (Penrose, 1959).

The quality of management is central to the performance of any firm, where performance is defined either in terms of growth in sales, assets, profits or employment, or even in terms of survival. In many respects the relationship between managerial quality and firm performance is likely to be even stronger in small than in large firms. In smaller firms the decisions made by owners will be implemented more quickly and are less likely to be diluted by subordinates than decisions made by top management in larger firms. On the other hand, the decisions made by the small firm owner, however well considered, will have more uncertain outcomes in the market-place, primarily because of the lack of market power of the small firm.

This chapter looks at the relationship between management and small firm performance both theoretically and empirically. As Penrose points out, a small firm is not simply a scaled-down version of a large firm. Using the Penrose analogy, we cannot assume that a caterpillar is a small butterfly. Instead we need to identify those characteristics of a small firm, other than pure size, which most clearly distinguish it from a large firm and theorise on their implications for the key dimensions of management.

A theoretical framework

In attempting to theorise about these factors it is convenient initially to discuss them separately, but it will become apparent that they are strongly interrelated. In the discussion there is also an overlap between the small firm and the concept of entrepreneurship. Here an entrepreneur is as defined by Casson (1982): as 'someone who specialises in making judgemental decisions about the co-ordination of scarce resources'. Nevertheless, entrepreneurship, as Penrose observes, is 'a slippery concept ... not easy to work into formal analysis because it is so closely associated with the temperament or personal qualities of individuals'.

Small firms and entrepreneurship

Despite these problems, the link between the small firm and entrepreneurship is clear at an intuitive level. The small firm is less concerned with formal systems and its decision-making processes will be more judgemental, involve fewer individuals and can therefore be quicker. It can be much more responsive to changes in the market-place but, conversely, is much less able to influence such developments. Hence the small firm is likely to adjust more quickly than the large firm to situations of market disequilibrium and, in these senses, embodies the characteristics of the classic entrepreneur.

Even so, not all small firms exercise entrepreneurship. Firstly many small firms come into existence only because their owners incorrectly observe market signals. It may be that their owners deem there to be a market for a totally new product where one does not exist. More frequently owners incorrectly assume there to be a currently unsatisfied demand, at a given price level, for an existing product or service. New firm founders also may incorrectly assess their own ability to manage and organise an enterprise, so that, even if the market exists, the particular firm in question is unable to satisfy it. It seems doubtful whether the inability either to correctly identify market signals or to be able to manage a business in such a way as to satisfy the market truly constitutes entrepreneurship, even though this is a major cause of new small firms being founded. It may therefore be necessary to amend the Casson definition of an entrepreneur along the lines of 'making judgemental decisions leading to improvements in the co-ordination of scarce resources'.

Secondly a large number of small firms are providing a 'standard' good or service provided by many other firms. Again it seems difficult to consider this an act of entrepreneurship on the part of the business owners, so that under the revised definition of entrepreneurship such individuals or groups of individuals would not be classified as entrepreneurs.

Given these provisos, this chapter will, at least initially, regard small firms and entrepreneurship as broadly overlapping sets. It will then devote itself to highlighting those dimensions, other than pure scale, along which small and large firms differ, and the implications of this for management.

Dimensions of entrepreneurship

While different writers have placed differential emphasis upon them, the literature on entrepreneurship emphasises three elements: uncertainty, innovation and management. It is appropriate to discuss each element in the context of smaller firms.

Uncertainty

The central feature of entrepreneurship is uncertainty. This is the heart of the non-size distinction between small and large firms. According to Knight (1921) individuals face the choice of offering themselves in the labour market for a fixed and certain wage, or becoming an entrepreneur who buys inputs at a fixed price but who sells outputs at an uncertain price in the hope of obtaining and adequate margin. According to the Casson definition this individual is making judgemental decisions, in the sense that they are assuming that they are either better informed, or have greater insight, than others unable to observe this opportunity.

It also seems clear that the uncertainty faced by a large firm will be considerably less than that faced by a small firm which, in turn, is likely to face less uncertainty than the individual entrepreneur. It has been shown that firm failure rates are inversely related to size, there being at least a sixfold difference between the smallest and largest size groups (Ganguly, 1985). This additional uncertainty over the likely continuity of smaller firms is also reflected in the interest rates at which financial institutions make funds available to the corporate sector (NEDC, 1986).

There are three different forms of uncertainty which the entrepreneur faces:

- market uncertainty,
- customer uncertainty,
- aspirational uncertainty.

We shall examine each separately.

Market uncertainty

Market uncertainty is the uncertainty facing a firm associated with an inability to influence price within a market by changing the quantity of output which it produces. Uncertainty facing the small firm itself stems from several factors. First it may be simply a reflection of the small firm's lack of market power. The large firm is much more likely to be able to influence price because its market share is likely to be higher. Even if its share in a particular market is small, the large firm can constitute a much more credible threat to firms in that market than a smaller firm through its ability to enter a market and, once inside, to compete on the grounds of low price, advertising and so on, and achieve low returns for some years. This is the so-called 'deep pocket' argument (Utton, 1984). The absence of market power for smaller firms, on the other hand, means that they are inevitably price takers in the classic tradition.

There is considerable empirical support for the view that large firms are more profitable than small. If market share is the key to profitability then, since it has been shown that profitability and market share are positively associated, and since size of firm and market share are also associated, it follows that large firms are likely to be more practicable than small. Hence while higher profits will risk the treat of entry into markets, they also provide the basis for repelling threats through the erection of product differentiation-type barriers. Baumol (1967) argues that large capitalised firms have the option of competing with small firms, but that small firms cannot easily choose to compete with large.

Finally, in relation to market uncertainty, it has to be recognised that many small firms operate in conditions of classic perfect competition, particularly in the area of personal services. The element of 'churning', that is high birth and deaths of firms (Birch, 1979; Beesley and Hamilton, 1984) characterises these markets since firms find it difficult to construct entry barriers, even to the extent of introducing any element of product differentiation to the consumer.

Customer uncertainty

A second source of uncertainty for smaller firms is their often limited customer and product base. A number of studies of smaller firms (for a review, see Storey, 1982) have shown that many smaller firms have no more than a handful of key customers, and a number have only a single customer. Davies and Kelly (1972) show that more than one-third of all small manufacturers sell more than 25 per cent of their output to one customer. In that situation, any difficulties which befall the larger company which is acting as customer may lead to the demise of the smaller company. Similarly many small firms produce only a single product or service, so that again the narrow nature of product/service base will, *ceteris paribus*, cause greater uncertainty than where a diversified range is provided.

The most extreme form is where small firms act as subcontractors to larger firms, and so not only exercise no price control but also may have all other elements of the production process and management controls tightly specified. Here the large firm customer not only sets the price and quantities at which the commodity is to be supplied, but also determines the nature of the inputs, the production method used and even the quality control checks which are to be implemented. While this does mean that, in one sense, some production and marketing uncertainties are reduced for the small firm subcontractor, it also means that the latter can become totally dependent upon a single customer.

Subcontractors are likely to achieve generally lower margins because of their weak bargaining position in which the purchaser is aware of all costs. It is therefore difficult to build up sufficient retained profit either to finance new development or to overcome difficult periods where orders are in short supply. Hence, if the large customer decides to look elsewhere for a source of supply, the subcontractor has fewer resources which it can use for searching to diversify its customer base.

Aspirational uncertainties

A third source of uncertainty which characterises small firms is a reflection of the diverse aspirations, motivations and abilities of the owners of such businesses. It has been shown in several studies (reviewed in Curran, 1986) that the owners of small businesses are not necessarily motivated by the need to grow and, indeed, many deliberately set out to avoid growth. For example, some business owners who have worked in large firms have established their own firms in order to rid themselves of the need to satisfy large company objectives such as achieving growth or increasing market share. The problem which arises, however, is that the owners of these types of firms frequently also fail to implement even the most basic management practices, such as an appropriate financial information system. It is perhaps for these reasons that studies in the USA by Phillips and Kirchhoff (1988) have shown that the small firms most likely to cease trading are those which also experience low growth.

The aspirations of small business owners are both a function of, and moulded by, the uncertainties of economic life. In attempting to understand these aspirations it is vital to recall the strong links that exist between the firm and the family. Indeed the two overlap in many respects. We have argued elsewhere that several important propositions follow from this observation. First, even in the small firm sector, it is by no means always the case that the individual entrepreneur owns a single business. Instead we have shown that, while single business ownership is common, it is by no means uniform throughout the small firm sector: the owners of successful small businesses often own several firms (Storey *et al.*, 1987) which were generally established after the successful firm.

The reason for this again reflects the nature of the uncertainty facing the small entrepreneur and the links with family income. Take the case of the entrepreneur who establishes a successful company, but who becomes aware that there are opportunities for developing in an associated market. Given the high uncertainties of establishing new companies, the entrepreneur is unlikely to jeopardise the continued development of the initial company, and the income which can be derived from it, by including the new development within its ownership. Instead the entrepreneur is more likely to create a second company which, if it does not succeed, can be liquidated without constituting a burden on the initial company. In the event of success, of course, the two companies may be combined at a later stage or continue to operate separately. Essentially because of uncertainty, therefore, successful small entrepreneurs frequently develop a portfolio of companies from which they and their families derive income. Growth may then be reflected, not just in the performance of a single company, but within the portfolio in general.

The derivation of both income and ownership is a very powerful motivation for small firm entrepreneurs in an uncertain environment. In many cases this is reflected in a resolute determination by entrepreneurs to maintain ownership of the portfolio of businesses within the family. It can also mean that the entrepreneur is prepared to forgo growth which could be facilitated by the injection of external equity in order to maintain ownership within family hands (Boswell, 1973). In other cases growth can be inhibited, again not necessarily by market opportunities, but because of the short-term views of directors utilising company income earmarked for investment purposes for their own personal consumption. Again this reflects the view that in a small firm corporate profitability and the income of the directors and family are closely intertwined (Watson 1990, 1991).

To understand the motivations of the entrepreneur and the strategy of the company requires the nature of family circumstances in a highly uncertain environment to be appreciated. This clearly differs from the case of larger companies where dividend policy is carefully assessed to satisfy the external requirements of the share-holders and the management, and where the options are publicly analysed in the market for shares.

The implications of uncertainty

For all these reasons the daily conduct of economic life is likely to be considerably more uncertain in a small firm than in a large firm. The entrepreneur has a short-term key objective to determine whether there is sufficient cash to pay the wages at the end of the week. In the slightly longer term a decision has to be made on the amount of money to be retained within the business and the amount which can be removed for personal consumption. For this reason the time horizon for key decisions can be extremely short, particularly in young businesses where business failure rates are more than 15 per cent annually (Daly, 1987).

The prime implication of the greater uncertainty facing the smaller firm is that short-run considerations inevitably take priority over longer-term issues. Given these priorities, it is easy to understand the relatively low emphasis given to the training of both management and the workforce in smaller companies. Even where such training is undertaken, the form of that training tends to be heavily focused upon 'on-the-job' training, with little formality (Marshall *et al.*, 1993). For the owner there is a reluctance to undertake any form of training which will mean being absent from the business whilst it is open (Townroe and Mallalieu, 1994). This reflects the uncertainty facing the business in the sense that numerous decisions are made by the owner during the day, any one of which, if made incorrectly, could lead to the demise of the firm. The minute-to-minute uncertainty facing the firm therefore means the owner cannot feel confident about being absent.

A second outcome of this uncertainty is that financial institutions, most notably the banks, require a risk premium for making loans to the small firm sector (Cressy, 1993). Given that the banks are unable to determine with accuracy those small firms which are most at risk, some firms will incur charges which are higher than their risk to the bank. These higher charges can then become a burden upon the firm, leading possibly to its demise. Since even the bank is likely to prefer the firm to be operating to closing it down, there is clearly an incentive on the part of both the firm and the bank to assess risk correctly. However the risk assessment costs to the bank are high compared with the losses incurred even in the event of a default, especially when the bank can require the imposition of a floating charge on the assets of the business (Cowling *et al.*, 1991).

The major factor encouraging banks to assess accurately the risks associated with lending to individual small businesses is competition amongst the banks. This is due to decreasing profit opportunities in the two major lending areas: overseas governments, where default rates have been high, and lending to large companies, where international competition has shaved profit margins. The implication is that, while there are uncertainties in lending to the small firm sector, there are also opportunities where it is possible to recognise low-risk opportunities, since these firms may experience significant growth leading to an increased demand for the whole range of banking services.

The short-term time horizon of entrepreneurs, together with the risk premium charged by the banks on borrowed money, also influences the nature of capital equipment in which the small firm invests. The small firm is likely to use a more labour-intensive production process than large firms both because labour is more flexible – that is, it can more easily be dispensed with, and because of the relatively high cost of capital. Even where investment in capital equipment is made, the nature of the equipment is likely to differ. Greater emphasis is likely to be placed upon flexibility, defined as the ability to undertake a wide range of tasks, and upon cost. Hence many small firms utilise second-hand capital equipment which is often many years old (Binks and Jennings, 1986).

In short this combination of market uncertainty, customer uncertainty and aspirational uncertainty is at the heart of the non-size distinction between small and large firms.

Innovation

It is the work of Schumpeter (1934) that most strongly relates entrepreneurship to innovation. For Schumpeter, 'the entrepreneur initiates change and generates new opportunities. Until imitators force prices and costs into conformity, the innovator is able to reap profits and disturb equilibrium' (O'Farrell, 1986). Schumpeter specifies five types of innovation:

1. the introduction of a new good (or improvement of an existing one),
2. the introduction of a new process,
3. the opening of a new market (especially exporting),
4. the identification of a new source of supply of raw materials, and
5. the creation of a new type of industrial organisation.

In practice few small firms could be classified as innovative according to the strict interpretation of these criteria. Their role is generally much less glamorous than that envisaged by Schumpeter.

New goods

There are considerable problems in determining what constitutes a new good. Is a small clothing firm which makes ladies' skirts, and which shifts to making blouses, producing a new product? The economist would probably not agree that it was a new product, since the cross-price elasticity is unlikely to be close to zero. The entrepreneur, however, might strongly disagree. But at what point has the firm produced a new product? When it moves to making outer garments such as coats, or does the firm have to move to making furniture covering or car seat covering?

Observation of small firms suggests that few introduce fundamentally new products, according to the 'car seat' example above, whereas many will vary the character of their output, as in the moving from skirts to blouses example (North *et al.*, 1994). While very few new firms will introduce a fundamentally new product into their own range of output, almost no firms will introduce a product which is new to the economy as a whole. Instead the more familiar role for small firms is to occupy what Penrose describes as the interstices of the economy. The characteristic of these firms is that they rarely compete directly with large firms even though, from a statistical classification point of view, they may be deemed to be in the same industry.

These firms will occasionally, but very rarely, introduce a fundamentally new product/service. These instances are extensively documented (see, for example, the discussion by Rothwell, 1986, of the development of the semiconductor industry in California as a classic new product initially introduced by the small firm sector, although subsequently developed by the large firm sector. A contrary view of the role of small firms in new industries is provided by Shearman and Burrell (1988) in their discussion of the medical laser sector).

Product/service differentiation

While the introduction of fundamentally new products is the exception for smaller firms, many will produce a differentiated product or service. The smaller firm, operating in these interstices, will produce a product which differs from that generally available from larger firms, in some minor but nevertheless observable respect. Hence, when owners of small firms are asked to discuss the nature of the competition which they face, they are likely to regard their rivals as being other smaller firms occupying these or adjacent interstices, rather than the large firms which dominate the main market.

Storey *et al.* (1989) examined the views of competition held by a group of fast-growing small firms and compared these with the views of a group of slower-growing or 'match' firms. The owners of the faster-growing small firm were much more likely to regard their comparative advantage as being in areas such as innovativeness, service and overall quality. The 'match' firms were much more likely to emphasise factors such as price/credit facilities, indicating the provision of more homogeneous products and services.

In many respects these differences between fast growth and 'match' firms relate to the concept of interstices outlined above. Frequently the small firms which were experiencing fast growth, but which were competing with other small firms primarily on the basis of non-price competition, occupied an interstice within the main market. Conversely the small firms competing with a large firm on the basis of price competition were more likely to be part of the 'main' market. *Ceteris paribus*, it would be expected that the 'match' firms' survival prospects were lower and their growth prospects weaker than for the fast growth firms.

It is therefore necessary to make a distinction between the small firms which produce a standard product/service and those which occupy the interstices of the market. The latter may not be innovative in the Schumpeterian sense of producing a new product, yet they provide an element of differentiation within the market-place for which there is a demand from consumers. This differentiation may take a number of forms. Firstly in some cases there is, and in other cases there is not, a real difference in the products on offer in the market-place. Taking the first case where there is no difference, it may be that one firm sees its advantage in terms of its ability to move quickly into exploiting a market opportunity, even where it knows that this will always be followed by competitors. In this case the firm's comparative advantage is in terms of its speed of response rather than in providing a different product/service. Illustrations of this include some smaller firms in the fashion sectors discussed earlier.

A second area where there is no difference between the products on offer from two firms, but where one firm may exploit its expertise, is in the area of marketing. Some firms clearly have a much greater awareness of their markets than others. One firm may have superior market intelligence to that available to most firms, in the sense of a greater awareness of what its competitors are doing, what their strengths and weaknesses are, and how these can best be exploited. It may also have particularly strong links with customers, having a clear understanding of their preferences.

A third area where, although apparently offering the same product/service, the small firm might, in fact, have a comparative advantage could be in the provision of something extra. Take the case of office and factory cleaning services. Here the small firm cleaners may clean the floors no better than the large firm cleaners – indeed they may even use the same workers. However it may be that a small firm will have a comparative advantage over a large national company because its customers know that, in an emergency such as a flood, fire or burglary, the owner of the cleaning company can be contacted at home at any time and the service provided. It may be more difficult to ensure the same type of 24 hour, seven days a week guarantee that the cleaning business owner will personally oversee the clients' needs where the service is provided by a large firm. Hence there may be a willingness on the part of some customers to go to the small firm in return for being able to feel confident that these difficult situations will be dealt with quickly and efficiently.

It is this willingness which is exploited by the small cleaning company. Hence, although the service on offer from both the large and the small firm is that of cleaning services, it could be argued that the two services do differ and that the markets are segmented, with the smaller firm occupying an interstice within the main market. This suggests that, even though the product/services being offered by two firms are apparently identical, different small firms may still occupy different interstices within the market. More familiar market interstices will be those where there are clear differences between the product/service offered by one small firm from that offered by another, even though they appear to be in the same sector. For example, one firm may specialise in quality, a second may specialise in products of high durability, whilst a third may specialise in the ability to meet the customers' requirements in terms of speed.

The first example may be a small firm which manufactures hiking gear, where workmanship of the highest quality has to be combined with design elegance. Here even the large firms will not be major producers, so far as the clothing and footwear sectors are concerned. There has been a massive increase in outdoor pursuits, and in the demand for equipment; the majority has been supplied by relatively large companies. Even so, the specialised interstices, involving small production batches and specialised designs, have remained and the small firms within them have prospered. The increase number of hikers, with generally well above average incomes, means that more people have become aware of the specialised interstices of the market, with certain labels developing almost 'cult' status. Such status can be exploited, because of their rarity value, to ensure high profitability for the smaller company, partly by restricting output.

A second firm may specialise in producing a product of the highest standards of reliability, possibly for military or security purposes, even where the product that the firm produces is fairly 'standard', such as a lock or a microchip.

The third type of firm could be one which produces material for display stands at exhibitions. It may see its comparative advantage in being able to respond immediately to customer demands, rather than in ensuring that the work is of the highest technical quality. In this market it is much more important for the customer, for example, to be able to exhibit at the Munich Trade Fair at two days' notice than to ensure that all the signwriting on its stand is immaculate. After all, the stand will be taken down in three or five days and, providing the presentation is not embarrassing, the exhibition company will be judged on its ability to meet the time limit, rather than upon the quality of its lettering.

The implications of innovation

These arguments relate to the issue of competitive strategy discussed by Porter (1980). He suggests that, while small firms may generally be less profitable than larger firms, their ability to identify and occupy niches can lead to an elimination of profitability differentials. Empirical support for this in the USA is provided by Bradburd and Ross (1989) who show that, in heterogeneous industries, large firms no longer have significant profitability advantages over smaller firms.

Many products and services are multidimensional, or it is in the firms' interests to present them as such. Instead of there being a single market for product or service X, there are likely to be series of segmented markets. Different customers will place different emphasis upon these dimensions and there may be interstices X1, X2, X3 and son on. Smaller firms, and particularly the more rapidly growing small firms, are likely to occupy and exploit these interstices.

In the medium term the smaller firm occupying a highly profitable interstice is likely to experience entry either from another small firm or from a larger firm – in other words competition. The original incumbent may either beat off the competition, identify another niche and move into it, share the market with the entrant or be pushed out completely. Alternatively it could decide that exclusive reliance upon this niche is risky for all the above reasons and could seek to identify alternative market-places. It is important to recognise that interstices, as well as individual small firms, may therefore be temporary. In this context it is very difficult to utilise familiar phrasing such as 'innovation' or 'introduction of new products' and be confident that, when comparing across interstices, these refer to the same developments. It is doubly difficult to be confident when the same terms are being used for both small and large firms. Here is yet another illustration that, using the classic Penrose analogy, the caterpillar is not a small butterfly.

Management

The purest forms of entrepreneurship, in which individuals buy at a low price and sell at a higher price because of market imperfections, most notably those associated with imperfect knowledge, does not require even the ownership of resources. Casson, in his definition of entrepreneurship, for example, talks about 'someone', and specifically excludes 'a team ... committee ... or organisation'. Hence entrepreneurship need not take place inside a legally constituted business organisation, and indeed the purer definitions of entrepreneurship specifically exclude this possibility. There is also no requirement for the entrepreneur to manage a business organisation and the individuals employed by that organisation. Even so, it is the case that a responsibility for organising the work of others is generally a condition for entrepreneurship to be exercised.

In the same way that we have tried to provide the small firm perspective upon the key entrepreneurship concepts of innovation and uncertainty, we also have to encapsulate those elements of management which best characterise the smaller firm. In so doing we have to take account of the above discussion of uncertainty and innovation.

The owner-manager

To achieve this we must clearly identify those managerial dimensions which most clearly characterise the smaller enterprise. The first re-emphasises the point made at the start of the chapter, which is that good management must be the key to the growth and development of a smaller firm. By this we mean that managerial tasks in smaller firms are concentrated in the hands of very few people, and possibly even a single person. The power to implement a decision, once made, lies with that individual and is less likely to be frustrated or diluted by the action or inaction of other managers. In this sense, therefore, the small firm owner/manager can be more certain that their decisions will result in a change in the direction of the business.

Within the business therefore the small firm owner-manager is more powerful, being subject to fewer checks and balances than a large firm counterpart. Conversely the external effects of any given managerial decision, in terms of its effects on the market-place, are, as we have noted earlier, much more uncertain.

Management evolution

The second dimension, along which those characteristics of management unique to smaller firms can be examined, is that of evolution. It has to be recognised that the nature, style and functions of management change considerably as a small company grows and evolves.

The previous chapter discussed the so-called 'stage theories' of business growth and in particular how the role and style of management change as the business grows. The central point of these models is that, as the business develops, new managerial skills are required, together with new levels of sophistication in existing skills. These can be achieved in three main ways:

1. The owners themselves can develop new skills. Thus the business founder who may, prior to the start-up of the firm, have a background in marketing may continue to have full responsibility for developing this function. Alternatively the individual may find that, since the creation of the business, they have developed new areas of interest such as finance or research and development. These we call 'diversified owner-managers'.
2. New individuals with proven managerial skills may be brought in from outside the firm. These will be professional managers who normally do not have an ownership interest in the firm. In some cases, however, the need for very specific managerial talent leads to a sharing of the equity with that individual. These are considered to be 'external' managers.
3. There may be individuals, who are not currently exercising a managerial function, but who are promoted into managerial

posts. These are individuals who have worked in the business for some time and whose functions and responsibilities have grown in parallel with the business. They may be considered the 'organic' management.

All three methods may be used by the same firm, or it may rely exclusively upon a single procedure. The extent to which the firm grows may be influenced by the extent to which its managerial resources are supplemented by 'external' or 'organic' managers.

The factors which influence the combination of 'external' and 'organic' managers chosen will vary from one firm to another. They may vary from one managerial function to another and they may also reflect the different 'styles' which pervade the business.

From entrepreneurs to teams

The role of the management team in the development of a smaller business is both complicated and dynamic. It is one that is not immediately suitable to empirical analysis since the development of the management team will facilitate the growth of the business, and yet the growth of the business will induce changes in the management team.

To Penrose, 'the capabilities of the existing managerial personnel of the firm necessarily set a limit to the expansion of that firm in any given period of time, for it is self-evident that such management cannot be hired in the market place'. She argues that not only does the existing team limit the number that can be hired, but also that previous plans determine the rate at which new personnel can be absorbed into the firm. Indeed she appears to suggest that, given an existing managerial structure, there is an optimum rate at which new management can be added: too fast and there will be administrative chaos, too slow and market opportunities will be lost.

Casson analyses this matter with respect to what he defines as the 'internal' and 'external' labour market. He begins with the assumption that labour is of variable quality as regards both integrity and ability, and that the problem of quality control is of greater significance in the recruitment of delegate decision makers – managers – than in the recruitment of other forms of labour.

For the entrepreneur these uncertainties, together with those discussed earlier, may lead some to a preference for promoting family members to decision-making posts. This serves also to echo the point made earlier of the role of small firms in providing family income and the difficulties of disassociating family and corporate income. Some firms enter the external market primarily for lower quality labour. While such strategies can be effective in the early days of a firms development, Casson points out that this pool of 'internal' labour is unlikely to provide the range of skills required and that entrepreneurs must develop their own skills in the recruitment of labour. It seems a reasonable hypothesis, given Casson's theorising, that the new firm will make a gradual movement from the internal labour market to the external as it grows. In the early days the firm/ entrepreneur is likely to favour the internal market which, in its most extreme form, will be family-only management. When that pool of resources is fully exploited, and that may be immediately, the firm will favour the next most 'organic' source, an individual with whom it is currently working, but where that individual is not a manager. This is because the 'risk' associated with that individual is low because the entrepreneur has experience of him or her in a work context. Similarly, if the entrepreneur decides to appoint an 'external' manager, the lowest risk strategy is to approach informally an individual with whom the entrepreneur has previously worked. For growing businesses the particular configurations of managerial abilities is rarely optimal at any point in time. In most cases, while the managerial team may have been appropriate for a point in the past, it is unlikely to be relevant to current and future conditions.

Very little empirical evidence on the assembling of management teams in small firms is available. Even the authoritative study by Curran (1986) of research on UK small business only discussed owner-managers, and made no reference to non-owner-managers. To some extent this void has been filled by Wynarczyk et al. (1993) who look at the market for non-owning managers in small firms. They find that fast-growing firms are much more likely to seek to recruit managers externally than slow growth firms. The fast growth firms are also much more likely to employ an individual with a large firm employment history than a slow-growing firm. The fast growth firm is also more likely to employ a more qualified individual.

These results all suggest that a strong link exists between the motivations and aspirations of the firm and the type of (non-owning) managers which are appointed.

The problem with stage models of growth

The stage models discussed in the last chapter are helpful in highlighting that managerial style and role do vary widely, and are constantly evolving. However there are several key problems in utilising them. First there seems to be a presumption that, while not all firms follow the pattern of staged growth identified by the models, this is a fairly familiar developmental pattern. For example, Scott and Bruce

(1987) say, 'Not all businesses which survive grow to be large businesses', whilst Churchill and Lewis (1983) point out that previous researchers 'assume that a company must grow and pass through all stages of development or die in the attempt'. To face up to this problem, Churchill and Lewis have a third stage, which the firm can use either as a platform for further growth or as a basis for good life-styles for owners and managers. This they call the Success Disengagement Stage. In these senses there is a recognition by the authors that there is not an inevitable move from Stage I to Stage V through all intermediate stages. Nevertheless, despite this recognition, the vast majority of the discussion is devoted to factors influencing the movements between stages.

Our concern with the stage models, however, goes beyond a recognition that some firms may reach a given stage and then 'stick' or even disappear. Given our discussion of uncertainty and innovation, relatively few firms are likely to move from one stage to another, and the points of crisis are more likely to lead to the demise of the firm than to its movement to the next stage. Given that about 11 per cent of the stock of firms in the UK cease to trade each year (Daly, 1991) and that almost all of them are small, it is clearly impossible to discuss the small firm sector without discussing the question of failure. Essentially it is this fear, or at least recognition, of failure that leads to the types of responses by the small firm owner which we discussed in the section on uncertainty.

If firms rarely move from one stage to another this requires an explanation of how, at any one point in time, there are firms of different sizes and organisational complexities. Wynarczyk *et al.* (1993) suggest that firms which are currently at the 'growth' stage either never experienced the earlier stages or existed in that state for such a short period of time that it could not really be described as a stage, or reached their current size though acquisition rather than organic growth.

Furthermore the models imply that firms may be much more 'advanced' in some aspects than in others. For example, a firm may have a sophisticated organisational structure, yet have top management still attempting to involve itself in all aspects of the firm.

Fast growth firms

In essence the trajectory of development which the fast growth firm experiences is fundamentally different from that of the more typical small business. Furthermore virtually the only small firms which become medium or large size are those which were never very tiny firms, or were this size only for a very short period of time. By implication, their owners set out with the intention of becoming significant market players very quickly. Very few stumbled into becoming large firms.

The fast growth firm appears to begin with a managerial team of owners and professional managers. The top management role may then be classified as delegation and co-ordination. Even at start-up it would be difficult to imagine the organisation structure to be anything other than centralised, but strong elements of functionalism are quite likely. It is also likely that the management of a start-up small firm which is gearing up for rapid growth will have a highly entrepreneurial style, and yet be concerned to co-ordinate the activities of the existing team. In making these statements we define the growth to be organic, rather than through the acquisition of, or merger with, other businesses.

Almost no firms pass through each of the five stages of business growth. Indeed the vast majority have probably never moved from one phase to the next. The single most frequent response to the crises which are supposed to induce movement from one stage to another is the collapse of the business. The value of these stage models is to highlight that the managerial role in small firms varies widely and may be subject to considerable change over short periods of time. They should not be assumed to reflect a linear progression of the small firm through time.

Conclusions

This chapter has been concerned to place the development of management and management teams within the context of smaller firms. Instead of examining management theory developed for large firms and seeking applications within the small firm sector we have tried to ask the question: what is it that makes small firms different from large, other than the question of pure size? We have taken as our theme the point made by Penrose more than 30 years ago that, in the same way that the caterpillar is not a small butterfly, a small firm is not to be viewed as a scaled-down version of a large firm.

We have taken two key issues, those of uncertainty and innovation, and examined their meaning and relevance in the small firm context. In particular, we have clearly distinguished between the relevance of these terms for small and large firms. In each case we conclude that both concepts are central to an understanding of the role of management in a small firm and how that management develops and evolves. Probably the key concept is that of uncertainty, which is at the heart of the financial, marketing and motivational bases of smaller businesses, and is massively more significant than for large firms. The risk of failure, and the implications of this for the entrepreneur and his or her dependants, is the key factor influencing management decisions.

Yet innovation is the key factor which distinguishes the growing firm from 'the plodding man of business'. Innovation, in this context, is not the grand concept of a totally new product discussed by Schumpeter, but rather the ability to offer a product or service which can, in some way, be distinguished from that supplied by rivals. The ability to innovate can lead to growth, if that is an objective of the business owner. If growth takes place it both induces the crises which impose pressure on the existing management and facilitates further growth if these crises are satisfactorily negotiated. The key characteristic which distinguishes small from large firms in this context is that the decision to seek growth is likely to be influenced by different factors in the two types of firms. Put crudely, the owners of small firms make the decision taking account only of their own personal circumstances. In a larger firm the interests of external shareholders are assumed to be of major importance.

It is because small firms are fundamentally different from large firms that we reject the concept of stage models which see the transition of small to large firms as a set of hurdles or 'crises' which the organisation has to overcome. Instead theorists and practitioners have to identify those characteristics of a small firm, other than size per se, which distinguish small from large firms. Once these factors are identified, and we have begun that task in this chapter, it becomes much easier to obtain meaningful insights into decision making in smaller firms.

Exercises

1. Write an essay exploring the meaning of entrepreneurship.
2. Write an essay highlighting the importance of risk and uncertainty to the entrepreneur.
3. Write an essay that explores Schumpeter's meaning of innovation.
4. Write an essay that highlights the role of innovation in entrepreneurship.
5. List the main barriers to moving from an owner-managed to a team-managed firm.
6. Write a mini case on a small firm of your choice showing how it made (or did not make) the transition from owner-managed to team-managed business.
7. Write a critique of the stage models of growth.

References

Baumol, W.J. (1967), *Business Behaviour, Value and Growth*, Harcourt Brace.

Beesley, M. and R. Hamilton (1984), 'Small firms' seedbed role and the concept of turbulence', *Journal of Industrial Economics*, vol. 33, no. 4, December, pp.213–29.

Binks, M. and A. Jennings (1986), 'Small Firms as a Source of Economic Rejuvenation', in J. Curran and D. Watkins (eds), *The Survival of the Small Firm*, vol. 1, Gower, pp.19–37.

Birch, D.L. (1979), 'The Job Generation Process', MLT Program on Neighbourhood and Regional Change, Cambridge, Mass.

Boswell, J. (1973), *The Rise and Decline of Small Firms*, Allen & Unwin.

Bradburd, R.M. and D.R. Ross (1989) 'Can Small Firms Find and Defend Strategic Niches? A Test of the Porter Hypothesis', *Review of Economics and Statistics*, vol. LXXI, no. 2, May, pp.258–62.

Casson, M. (1982), *The Entrepreneur: An Economic Theory*, Martin Robertson.

Churchill, N.C. and V.L. Lewis (1983), 'The five stages of small business growth', *Harvard Business Review*, vol. 61, no. 3, May–June.

Cowling, M., J. Samuels and R. Sugden (1991), *Small Firms and the Clearing Banks: A Sterile, Uncommunicate and Unimaginative Relationship*, Association of British Chambers of Commerce.

Cressy, R.C. (1993) 'Loan Commitment and Business Starts: An Empirical Investigation on UK Data', SME Centre Working Paper No. 12, Warwick Business School.

Curran, J. (1986), *Bolton Fifteen Years on: A Review and Analysis of Small Business Research in Britain 1971–1986*, Small Business Research Trust.

Daly, M. (1987), 'Lifespan of Businesses Registered for VAT', *British Business*, 3 April, pp.28–9.

Daly, M. (1991) 'VAT Registrations and De-registrations in 1990', *Employment Gazette*, November, pp.579–88.

Davies, J.R. and M. Kelly (1972) *Small Firms in the Manufacturing Sector*, Research Report No. 3, Report of the Committee of Enquiry on Small Firms, Cmnd 4811, HMSO.

Ganguly, P. (1985), *UK Small Business Statistics and International Comparisons*, Harper & Row.

Knight, F.H. (1921), *Risk, Uncertainty and Profit*, Houghton Mifflin.

Marshall, J.N., N. Alderman, C. Wong and A. Thwaites (1993), 'The Impact of Government-assisted Management Training and Development on Small and Medium-Sized Enterprises in Britain', *Environment and Planning C: Government and Policy*, vol. 11, pp.331–48.

NEDC (1986), *Lending to Smaller Firms*.

North, D., D. Smallbone and R. Leigh (1994), 'Employment and Labour Process Changes in Manufacturing SMEs during the 1980s', in J. Atkinson and D.J. Storey (eds), *Employment, the Small Firm and the Labour Market*, Routledge.

O'Farrell, P.N. (1986), *Entrepreneurs and Industrial Change*, Irish Management Institute.

Penrose, E.T. (1959), *The Theory of the Growth of the Firm*, Basil Blackwell.

Phillips, B. and B.A. Kirchhoff (1988), *Survival and Quality of Jobs Generated by Entrepreneurial Firms*, US Small Business Administration.

Porter, M.E. (1980), *Competitive Strategy*, The Free Press.

Rothwell, R. (1986), 'The Role of Small Firms in Technological innovation', in

J. Curran, J. Stanworth and D. Watkins (eds), *The Survival of the Small Firm*, vol. 2, Gower, pp.114–42.

Schumpeter, J.A. (1934), *The Theory of Economic Development*, Harvard University Press.

Scott, M. and R. Bruce (1987), 'Five Stages of Growth in Small Businesses', *Long Range Planning*, vol. 20, no. 3, pp.45–52.

Shearman, C. and G. Burrell (1988), 'New technology-based firms and new industries: employment implications', *New Technology, Work and Employment*, vol. 3, no. 2, pp.87–99.

Storey, D.J. (1982), *Entrepreneurship and the New Firm*, Croom Helm.

Storey, D.J., R. Watson and P. Wynarcyzk (1989) 'Fast Growth Small Businesses: Case Studies of 40 Small Firms in North East England', Department of Employment Research Paper No. 67, London.

Storey, D.J., K. Keasey, R. Watson and P. Wynarczyk (1987), *The Performance of Small Firms*, Croom Helm.

Townroe, P. and K. Mallalieu (1994), 'Founding a New Business in the Countryside', in J. Curran and D.J. Storey (eds), *Small Firms in Urban and Regional Locations*, Routledge.

Utton, M.A. (1984), 'Concentration, competition and the small firm', in C. Levicki (ed.), *Small Business: Theory and Policy*, The Acton Society, Croom Helm.

Watson, R. (1990), 'Employment Change, Profitability and Directors' Remuneration in Small and Closely-held UK Companies', *Scottish Journal of Political Economy*, vol. 37, pp.259–74.

Watson, R. (1991), 'Modelling Directors' Remuneration in Small and Closely-held UK Companies', *Journal of Business Finance and Accounting*, vol. 18, pp.85–98.

Wynarczyk, P., R. Watson, D.J. Storey, H. Short and K. Keasey (1993), *The Managerial Labour Market in the Small Firm Sector*, Routledge.

CHAPTER 5

The entrepreneur

Jim Dewhurst

INTRODUCTION	94
SMALL BUSINESS IN THE UK AND EUROPE	94
ENTREPRENEURIAL MOTIVATION	96
PSYCHOLOGICAL TESTING FOR ENTREPRENEURS	97
THE POSITIVE SIDE OF ENTREPRENEURSHIP	100
THE DARK SIDE OF ENTREPRENEURSHIP	102
SOCIAL ATTITUDES	104
HARDSHIP, SELF RELIANCE AND DISCIPLINE	106
LESSONS FOR THE UK	107
EXERCISES	108
REFERENCES	108

Introduction

Because of the close relationship that exists between the entrepreneur and his business, the success or failure of the business is very much associated with two factors. These are the degree to which the aims of the business correspond with the real aims of the entrepreneur and, secondly to what extent the real aims of the entrepreneur can actually – given his or her psychological make up – be achieved in practice. This chapter will develop these themes and in the course of this will arrive at some general indications of small business success or failure, and in particular why small businesses in the UK are not widely seen – at any rate by the rest of the world – as being outstandingly successful.

Small business in the UK and Europe

It has long been held that small businesses in the UK have a vital part to play in its economy. The traditional wisdom is that small

businesses can achieve this because of their flexib
tive capacity and above all their high profitabilit
widely known (ever since the Bolton Report, 197
number of small businesses in the UK is smaller
other comparable country. Until recently it was h
reasons for this lack of input from the small busir
economy arose from the disadvantages that these businesses suffered
in terms of government support, fiscal measures and general funding
facilities. Ever since a report by the Economist Intelligence Unit (EIU)
in 1983, we know that this has not been true so far as the incidence
of taxation and tax incentives are concerned.

Burns and Dewhurst (1986) looked at small businesses in seven
European countries, and in particular compared the situation of
small business in France and West Germany with that in the UK.
They concluded that 'the UK small businessman faces neither the
burden of taxation nor the complexity of administration that many of
his European neighbours face'. They also noted that the UK 'stands
out as providing some of the best institutional facilities for equity
capital for small businesses', and concluded that 'compared to his
European neighbours the UK small businessman would seem to
have little to complain about'.

One other tenet of the traditional lore concerning small businesses
in Great Britain is also open to question: it has always been held that
despite the disadvantages small businesses suffer in this country,
their profitability record is high. Bolton, Wilson (1979) and a number
of other reports have shown that in terms of return of investment or
return on total assets, small businesses generally have performed
better than large.

Recent figures produced by the government in *Business Monitor*
seem to show that whatever the position may have been in the past,
the present tendency is for smaller businesses to do no better than
larger in terms of profitability. Indeed, small businesses' return on
invested capital has been only around 3 per cent (Burns, 1985).

In 1988 and 1989 it is true, small businesses were still performing
appreciably better than large businesses (CSO, MA3). However by
1990 the effects of the recession had hit small businesses badly, and
their profitability (except in manufacturing industry) dropped to
below that of large businesses. No comparable official figures exist
post-1990 as the central statistical office decided that extraction of
these data from published accounts was no longer cost-effective. The
CSO also commented that it had not been possible to use the data
directly in compiling UK national accounts.

There is not much evidence of a comparable recent poor performance by small businesses on the Continent. Why should this be?
The government tries to help small businesses in this country in a

...iety of ways, and yet small businesses do not respond. One clue ...s to a possible reason is provided when we recall that the close correspondence between the entrepreneur and his business is one of the characteristics of a small business. Can it be that the entrepreneur, or what he is trying to do with his business, is at fault? If this is the case we need at the very least to provide positive evidence that there are material differences between the UK entrepreneur and his counterpart on the continent and elsewhere overseas.

Entrepreneurial motivation

The Shorter Oxford English Dictionary defines an entrepreneur as 'a contractor acting as intermediary between capital and labour'. The French economist Cantillon was the first person to introduce the term; he said that the entrepreneur was 'the agent who purchased the means of production for combination into marketable products'.

Early English classical economists such as Adam Smith, saw the entrepreneur as having a rather minor role in overall economic activity; they thought that he provided real capital, but did not play a leading or directing part. For such economists, one person, or indeed a group of persons, did not count much in the scheme of things: it was the broad pattern of supply and demand which effected change and only macroeconomics mattered.

The first part of the nineteenth century saw, for the first time, the frequent use of the limited liability company as a means of business organisation. The second part was characterised by a growing separation of corporate ownership and management. This resulted in a re-examination of the position of the entrepreneur and greater emphasis on his role in the business. Much of the ensuing literature concentrates on the differences between the entrepreneur (the setter-up, the goal maker) and management which ran the business. Perhaps the main characteristic of truly small businesses is that this difference does not exist for them. Yet the role of the entrepreneur can hardly be discounted; no business ever started itself!

The goal to which the entrepreneur aspired was basically seen to be (or implied as being) profit maximisation. If we return again to the importance of the correspondence between the entrepreneur's own goals, and that of his or her business, we are faced with a problem. For nowhere in any of the psychological theories of the time, or indeed since, do we see profit maximisation as a *basic* motivation for individuals.

The social psychologists (mainly apostles of Sigmund Freud) saw drives 'as provided by the social environment in which man existed'. This, of course, differs from Freud's pan-sexualism with its implication that all other motivations and drives are derivatives of thwarted sexual desires. There are, of course, other groups – for example, self-theorists and the stimulus response theorists – but none of these considers profit maximisation, or indeed anything like it, as a good explanation of human, or business, behaviour.

In broad terms we have to conclude that if profit maximisation is indeed the goal of an entrepreneur then psychological theories, as such, are of little help to us. So how can we recognise, in practice, a good entrepreneur, how can we tell who is likely to be a successful one, or why he or she might fail, and – above all – why is the latter especially likely to occur in the UK?

Psychological testing for entrepreneurs

If psychological theory fails us in explaining the basic motives that drive an entrepreneur, will psychological practice help? Psychological tests come in two forms:

(i)   Projective tests
(ii) Pencil and paper tests, including psychometric tests.

Projective tests

Projective tests require that the individual writes – or, better still talks – candidly about something. For example, he or she may describe a picture or discuss a story. Which picture or story does not matter much; the assumption in this sort of work is that he projects his own inner feelings on to the description or discussion. The technique is entirely analogous to that used in the Rorschach ink blot test. Broadly, the psychologist will be looking for the real attitude of the subject to those matters accepted as being of importance to the small business entrepreneur. Risk-taking, innovative thought, and decision-making capacity are typical. But such projective tests are expensive in terms of time and the use of trained staff and, moreover, the interpretation and explanation of the results is very much a subjective matter so they are, inevitably, of somewhat limited use.

Pencil and paper tests

Pencil and paper tests really exist in two types, though only one type is much used. The first types seeks to determine whether an individual is likely to have the qualities necessary to succeed in setting up and running a small business. The second type seeks to determine what kind of small business activity is likely to be suitable for him.

The underlying question which the first type tries to resolve is simply whether the individual is likely to be happier as an employee or as an employer. This requires a degree of self-analysis and such analysis is always a task from which one tends to shrink. In any case we all think we know all about ourselves, so why bother? In fact, when the test is carried out, and the answers looked at objectively, it is usual to find that an additional level of self-knowledge has been achieved.

Small business literature abounds with such tests. Indeed, it is probably true to say that no comprehensive small business book is produced today which does not include at least a simple test on these lines. The format varies, but the subjects include, *inter alia*, talents, skills, abilities, experience, interests and values, and attitudes to work, people, products and leisure.

Psychometric testing is the most sophisticated and quantitative of these tests. Psychometric testing attempts to apply objective measurements to psychological variables. It then uses statistical methods to analyse the results. There are a number of psychometric tests. The Sixteen Personality Factor (16PF) test is one of the most widely used. In this test 16 basic personality factors, such as intelligencee, ego strength, dominance and guilt proneness, are directly measured by a written test. From the results of this test a number of second-order factors are constructed. These factors are of much more direct use in assessing aptitudes and attitudes which are of relevance to the business situation. Second-order factors include extroversion, aggression, independence and conformity to social norms.

Psychometric tests are generally long and exhaustive. Typically they involve some 200 or so questions. The normal time taken to answer is around three-quarters of an hour. The 16PF test must be administered by a registered psychometric tester. This test has been particularly popular in recruitment work in large organisations. Some of the second-order factors, such as independence and conformity to social norms, can be of substantial use in assessing the suitability of individuals for entrepreneurial work. However certain controversies surround the uses of psychometric testing. These psychometric assessments can be divided into ability tests, which measure numeracy and verbal skills, and personality tests, which measure people's perceptions of their own behaviour. It is widely accepted that ability tests can be highly effective provided they are well designed and relevant to the job concerned. Personality tests can be more controversial.

Anglian Water used personality tests when it decided to shed 900 staff as part of a big downsizing. All staff were given the tests to help management decide who would be given new jobs. Anglian announced that only 30 per cent of the decision would be based on the test results. But Unison (the union) argued strongly that the company gave too much weight to the tests.

The correct conclusion to draw would appear to be that these tests should only be used as part of a battery of selection techniques, such as interviews, group discussions and application forms. But they must be the right tests, properly tailor made for the situation.

Some years ago a psychologist tested 68 personnel managers and later gave them each *identical* reports describing their personality. In what is known as the Barnum Effect, half of them described what they believed was their individual assessment as 'amazingly accurate', 40 per cent said it was rather good, and the remaining 10 per cent saw it as 'half and half'.

Finally psychometric testing can give rise to legal claims. In the USA a court in California awarded $1.3m. against a supermarket chain which had used personality tests to recruit security guards. The complaint was that the questionnaires were intrusive and bore little relevance to the job.

The second type of paper and pencil test, though much less widely known, can be of much greater practical use. The aim of these tests is not only to assess the skills, aptitudes and experience necessary to set up and run a particular small business, but, more importantly, to determine whether that business satisfies the entrepreneur in terms of personal interests, social and economic conditions, job satisfaction, and so on. In other words, whether he will like it and whether the business is really 'him'.

For this test three columns are needed, one for the entrepreneur, one for the proposed business, and a third for the variance between the interests and desires of the entrepreneur and those offered by the prospective business. On the left of these columns are listed various interests and conditions: they will include such matters as place of work, hours worked, overtime work, and so on (see Appendix D, in the John Jederman case). Completing this sort of test and working out the variances is a long and complicated task, best done over several sessions. A high level of determination on the part of the entrepreneur is required, particularly when completing the column about his or her own interests, values and capacities in an entirely objective way. However, the benefits of such an analysis can be substantial. This simple format indicates to the budding entrepreneur, not what type of business he *fancies* he likes, but which type really suits his personal talents and abilities. In the John Jederman Case Study we include a practical example of how this type of test can be used in deciding which of two alternative business proposals is the more suitable for a potential businessman. In the example, the alternatives considered by the entrepreneur are those of setting up a retail business selling small gifts, or taking up tutorial and lecturing work in retail management with a Cambridge correspondence college.

The positive side of entrepreneurship

Many attempts have been made to find out what is the key characteristic of the successful entrepreneur. If there is one way of putting the characteristic succinctly it is probably contained in this statement by Joseph R Mancuso of the US Center for Entrepreneurial Management.

> It's not the critic, nor the observer who watches from a safe distance. Wealth is created only by doers in the arena who are marred with dirt, dust, blood, and sweat. These are producers who strike out on their own, who know high highs and low lows, great devotions, and who overextend themselves for worthwhile causes. Without exception, they fail more than they succeed and appreciate this reality even before venturing out on their own. But when these producers of wealth fail, they at least fail with style and grace, and their gut soon recognizes that failure is only a resting place, not a place in which to spend a lifetime. Their places will never be with those nameless souls who know neither victory nor defeat, who receive weekly paychecks regardless of their week's performance, who are hired hands in labor in someone else's garden. These doers are producers and no matter what their lot is at any given moment, they'll never take a place beside the takers, for theirs is a unique place, alone, under the sun.

This is a jubilant declaration of the high endeavours, delights and pains of entrepreneurship. It is effective because it immediately presents certain key words or phrases:

- doers,
- sweat,
- overextending themselves,
- venturing out on their own,
- style and grace.

Many studies of small business entrepreneurs just list a series of attitudes, skills, and physical and mental attributes. Frequently the most commonly cited characteristics apply equally to all executives, or indeed to all workers. But this positive statement concentrates on those which are special to successful small businesses.

Doers

All true entrepreneurs are believer driven. All have a strong desire to succeed. All wish to achieve new and challenging goals. All wish to get on with the job and hate delay. Though they accept that obstacles will be placed in their way, their belief in their capacity to overcome these problems seldom falters, their confidence in themselves hardly ever wavers. The tougher the going the more they 'get going'. Paradoxically, as we note in a later section, it is only when things are going well, and there is not much to fight against, that their drive may waver.

Sweat

Determination, commitment and, perhaps above all, perseverance are the hallmarks of the entrepreneur. Hard work and singleminded effort are in their blood. Most entrepreneurs work many more hours a week than their counterparts in larger organisations. The dividing line between work and home life and leisure hardly exists for them. Their hobby is their work.

Many entrepreneurs realise that the extraordinary workloads that their way of living imposes on them means that they have to be fit to be able to take the strain. Many entrepreneurs monitor what they eat and drink. Some establish exercise routines. Jogging, keep-fit classes, aerobics, swimming, walking and weight lifting are their favoured activities for what little 'leisure' time they allow themselves. In such circumstances leisure itself is little more than an extension of time dedicated to work.

Overextending themselves

Good entrepreneurs use personal or business failure as a learning experience. Most entrepreneurs are realistic enough to expect such setbacks. Temporarily they may become discouraged or even depressed, but in the long run they accept such difficult times and look for new opportunities. For them, great are the uses of adversity. Effective entrepreneurs are quick learners. They have a strong desire to know how well they are doing. Though they do overextend themselves they monitor their own performance. They use feedback intelligently.

Venturing out on their own

Successful entrepreneurs are no less gamblers than investors in equity shares on the stock exchange. When they take part in a venture they do so in a carefully though out, calculated manner. Good SME entrepreneurs try to maximise the odds in their favour.

They avoid taking risks as far as possible. Their strategies include making as sure as possible of their financial base by sensible long-term planning. They make arrangements well in advance with banks and other lending institutions, and they seek out financial partners to share the risks.

Good entrepreneurs are goal-oriented in their pursuit of opportunities. They focus on the market and how to satisfy it, rather than on what they like to produce, or what services they like to offer. They set the goal, then find the resources necessary to achieve it.

Style and grace

SME entrepreneurs know that a reputation for reliability and integrity is crucial to success. Their customers, creditors and their providers of funds will soon find out if they possess these attributes. Personal failure by a small business manager to come up to expectations in these matters will inevitably, in the long run, have a serious adverse effect on the business. SME entrepreneurs have to be flexible and creative. At one time creativity was believed to be exclusively an inherited trait. We are less certain now. Much recent work would seem to indicate that creativity can, to a large extent, be learned. Above all entrepreneurs have a vision. Not all visions remain constant over time: as the entrepreneur grows in experience – as the business develops – as circumstances change, so the vision will change too. But a vision – a distant, exciting goal – there always will be.

The dark side of entrepreneurship

It has been said by Derek du Toit (1980), an entrepreneur himself, that 'the entrepreneur who starts his own business generally does so because he is a difficult employee'. Since a small business is run by one man it seems certain that another characteristic of the man who wishes to run his own show is a need to be in control. The other side of this particular coin is that he probably finds it difficult to cope with alternating dominant and submissive roles. A manager in a large corporation, by contrast, has to play both these, when dealing with employees, and with colleagues more senior than himself. More specifically, he probably cannot play the submissive role very easily. So the picture we have of many hopeful entrepreneurs is of the man who is a failure in his managerial position in a large corporation because he hates being told what to do. He wants to be in a position where he tells other people – and no one tells him! But again, we have to ask if this background and these characteristics are likely to lead in the long run to success in a business controlled by one man.

Control

Kets de Vries (1985), a psychoanalyst at INSEAD, has argued that a desire for control often leads to over-control; that is a desire to let no one else have any authority. This does not matter too much – indeed, it may well be a good thing – in a very small business when total control by the man who 'lives' at his business may be both practical and useful. The danger is that he will continue these habits when the business has grown to a size when they are totally inappropriate. In one fruit-juice bottling plant with about 200 employees, and a substantial number of senior marketing and production staff, the owner-manager could not relinquish tight control over minor matters. Letters and communications of any sort sent by members of staff had to be made with a 'pink copy'. This was the owner-manager's copy and every day he read through his copies of all correspondence, feeling that in this way he had everything still where he wanted it. The problem, as de Vries points out, is that in such organisations subordinates become infantilised. They are expected to behave as incompetent idiots, and that is the way they do behave. They tend to do very little, take no decisions and circulate very little information. The better ones do not stay. A buyer of such a company will find that he is not purchasing a good management team. Incidentally, the owner-manager developed an ulcer as a result of trying to cope with everything himself.

Quirks

Entrepreneurs in such organisations typically, too, have quirks. Minor quirks hurt nobody so long as the business is small, but when the active co-operation and support of more people is required, they can be a great disadvantage. Frequently an entrepreneur in a growing organisation will become increasingly distrustful; he will begin to see all things as operating against him. Paradoxically, when the situation is bad, he may be at his best: he will feel that he has paid the price for success. Success, on the other hand, will reinforce distrust: he will go further along the road that he has already followed of only employing sycophants and business morale will inevitably deteriorate. One strange but not uncommon side effect of growing success in this type of entrepreneur needs mentioning. He may well have a desire for applause and recognition which needs to be institutionalised. He will wish to build a monument to himself. This may take the form of erecting a large office block with a large office for himself, or it may take less obvious forms. He may wish to support or endow local playing fields, swimming baths or parks. He may even wish to fund a chair (in his own name!) at a university.

One further problem may arise for the growing 'successful' business, which occurs when the entrepreneur wishes to cash in on his work, and decides to sell his business. Not infrequently, one of the terms of the deal is that he will stay on for a limited number of years 'at the helm'. This appears to be to everybody's benefit. The entrepreneur gets his money and retains his job satisfaction, since his work is unaltered; and the buyer gets the benefit of his expertise and connections. Customer loyalty will be unaffected. In fact, in such 'take-overs' all sorts of difficulties soon arise. The problems that we have mentioned: desire for control, personal quirks, distrust of subordinates and so on, all become magnified and this type of deal often does not work out well.

A parallel situation, one in which an entrepreneur takes over another small business, may show up other dark sides of entrepreneurship. Most small business vendors' stated aims will be in terms of cash and immediacy and they will wish to maximise total price. Their true aims may well be different. There are a wide variety of possibilities. Some are straightforward. They may be selling now in order to avoid future perceived problems. They may feel that the business for sale conflicts with their other activities. But many reasons are much more personal and emotional. They may be concerned with management succession, or much more subjective aims such as continuance of the existing name – typically that of the founder – or his or her physical, continuing connection with the business as a consultant. They may be concerned with avoiding staff dismissals. A proposed sale may even be a stalking-horse for one fraction of a family business trying to get at another. What is important is that, in all non-hostile bids both in the UK and elsewhere, the true aims of the vendor are established. This means personal contact and a great deal of listening and understanding. Only in that way will the hidden reasons for selling be laid bare. Only on that basis will a successful deal package be achieved by the entrepreneur.

Social attitudes

In the previous section we looked at the negative aspects of entrepreneurship. Throughout we have been trying to find reasons for the failure of small businesses in general and particularly those in the UK. Do entrepreneurs in the UK have too many failings? Are too many *cidevant* (but failed) corporate executives, now working out some of their failings in an alien arena? Are small businesses the last refuge of the low-rated individual? If this is at all true (and clearly we are stating the hypothesis in a very extreme form) then again we have to find reasons why this might be particularly common in the UK.

The attitudes within the UK to work in any industrial business by any other than the 'working' class, has been devastatingly attacked by many (but mainly non-UK!) writers. Martin Wiener (1981) in his review of English society in the nineteenth century 'the low status given to a career in trade and industry did serve a purpose – the Empire needed a large, confident and fairly conventional class of administrators, whereas the economy seemed to be taking care of itself'. A century later the situation had changed dramatically. By then the colonies and the Commonwealth needed comparatively little attention. The economy, by contrast, lagged. The need was for the best effort in industrial production, but attitudes were then, as now, unbelievably slow to change. James Callaghan, when he was Prime Minister in 1976, complained that 'many of our best trained students have no desire to join industry'. MBA students from UK business schools would have been happy at that time to have joined a respectable city institution (such as a stockbroker, a firm of chartered accountants or a merchant bank) or possibly a blue chip business such as Imperal Chemical Industries (ICI) or Rolls-Royce. But even if they did join the industrial *crème de la crème*, it was only in the functional areas of finance, personnel, marketing or administration. Production was, and still is, a dirty word. But the position is entirely different elsewhere; in both France and Germany a production manager or engineer is addressed by the courtesy title of 'Engineer'. This is a mark of respect and is seen as such. But in the UK, whilst doctors, rectors and professors are called by their titles and respected for their work, production people are neither called by a title nor respected for what they do.

In the UK this attitude of distaste for industry in general, and manufacturing industry in particular, spreads into all disciplines. In research we find a split between pure research (which is academically and socially acceptable) and applied research. One is seen as clean; the other dirty. The purest, cleanest research is probably 'pure' mathematics (again the same emotionally charged adjective) as compared with applied mathematics. Above the door of a well-known institution there is engraved the hope that pure mathematics 'never has been and never shall be of any use to anyone'. For supporters of this view, it must have been sad when the beautiful abstract conditional probability work of an eighteenth-century clergyman by the name of Bayes was two centuries later found to be of practical use in business decision-making. When George Boole created the complex mathematical structure since called Boolean algebra, he little thought that it would form the basis for work in switching circuits and logic gates for that most practical of all aids – the computer. What once was clean now is not!

In the UK, industry has only proved attractive to the well-to-do when the pull of money or family tradition has been very powerful. Most frequently it has been the profession of last resort, to fall back on when success in other, reputable, occupations has not been possible. The only other possible alternative in such situations was teaching. Many researchers in this area have confirmed this from their field work.

But if industry (and manufacturing industry especially) in the UK is one of the last resorts of the unsuccessful, what about small businesses? If we continue with our example of the employment of MBA students as providing a good indicator of job desirability at a reasonably high level, the conclusions are shattering. Until recently, small business was a total non-subject not only at any university but even in business schools. No courses were held and no students even considered working in this area. It is true that in the last few years the situation has changed dramatically; now we have well-attended small business option courses both at MBA and undergraduate levels. Courses for those wishing to set up their own small business are run at most universities.

The attitude to small businesses in the UK is indeed very different now from what it was only a few years ago, but in this country all we are doing is trying to correct our huge existing negative bias against such organisations. In the USA there has long been a tradition of a much more positive vision. The man who starts from scratch and becomes a millionaire (preferably before reaching the magic age of thirty) is held in the highest public esteem. He is a sort of latter-day folk hero. Again, we have to contrast this with the situation in the UK. A large number of potential business entrepreneurs are undoubtedly corporation 'cast offs', and in our present economic climate there are many of these. To the outside observer it has seemed for many years that most large corporations have had some staff posts which appeared to be for quite useless purposes. In fact they were for useless people; people who had fallen by the wayside, but which a benevolent company did not wish to cast aside. When corporations eventually did cut back, where did these people go? Many, it is clear, went into small businesses.

Hardship, self-reliance and discipline

One final example of the effects of this negative attitude to small businesses in our society will suffice. In the nineteenth century, making money in business was, as we have seen, always the work of the unfavoured few. So who were the people who filled the vacancies that the establishment declined? Some we already know about, but in many cases it was well-educated and well-informed people who were members of races and sects which were not highly regarded by society at large.

The Jews, for example, amongst others, helped to fill this vacuum, and we have a parallel today in the small business situation. Ethnic minority groups, such as Asians, prepared to work long hours in business such as retail shops and with a full family commitment, are amongst the most prolific and successful. But they are there because the opportunities are not available to them elsewhere. They are there because they are prepared to accept the tough conditions which, it is clear, often do occur in this socially unacceptable area of business management. There are parallels to this situation throughout the world. The 'Malaysian' Chinese in Malaya, Indonesia and other countries in South East Asia provide one example. In Malaya these 'many generation' Chinese expatriates are present in large numbers. They do not constitute a majority of the population, so that voting control and political power has always been with the indigenous Malays. Nevertheless, the control over business (still mainly small business) and over almost all professional work by this ethnic minority group is still – despite strenuous efforts by the ruling Malaysian government party – nearly absolute. The Chinese work long hours, they accept hard conditions and they thrive on it.

Malcolm Harper (1985) mentions many such examples: 'The Indians in East Africa, the Armenians in Egypt, the Lebanese in West Africa, the Kikuyu in Masailand, the Mahajans all over India except in their desert homeland of Rajasthan, the Tamils in Sri Lanka, the Palestinians in Arabia and the British almost everywhere except in Britain; all have shown that dislocation and hardship can lead to enterprise.' He argues that: 'The very experience of living in a difficult environment, and of planning, financing and executing a move and then surviving in a new and often hostile environment requires qualities of self-restraint, abstinence, hard work and voluntary postponement of gratification which are normally far more severe than those demanded by the lifestyle of those who remain at home, or of the indigenous people of the place in which these refugees relocate.'

Lessons for the UK

Perhaps in the UK, we should encourage small business training schemes which are themselves tough and which emphasise the characteristics of toughness and discipline required to succeed in this area. Perhaps we still tend to featherbed 'start-ups', to encourage new businesses with financial support in the early months which subtly deprives the entrepreneur of the need to fight hard for survival in a hostile business environment. If this, too, is true, we have some clear guidelines on how to encourage small business entrepreneurship in the UK: we need to make small business entrepreneurs realise that self-reliance, hard work and discipline are necessary factors for success. The other side of the coin is that, as we have argued, we need to change the attitude of our society to small business. We have to encourage the vision – so common on the Continent – of a hardworking small-business community which is respected and admired in its own right. We have to encourage the right people to move into this area and not until society sees success in small business as the sort of achievement which they would expect and admire from determined, hard-working, well-motivated, intelligent people, will these people become entrepreneurs.

Exercises

1. List the reasons you would want to start-up your own business.
2. Write an essay describing the entrepreneur.
3. Based upon an interview with a local owner-manager, write a mini case study outlining their motivations for setting up the business, attitudes towards the way the business is developing and views on their need for achievement, locus of control, risk taking, independence and innovative behaviour.
4. Based upon an interview with a local owner-manager from an ethnic minority group, write a mini case study outlining their motivations for setting up the business, attitudes towards the way the business is developing and views on their need for achievement, locus of control, risk taking, independence and innovative behaviour. Contrast this with the views expressed in exercise 3.
5. Write an essay describing how attitudes towards running your own business have changed in the UK in the last 20 years.
6. Assuming you are a bank official, write a report to your superior in the bank outlining how you would identify an entrepreneur from psychological tests.

References

Bolton Report (1971) *Report of the Committee of Enquiry on Small Firms*, Cmnd 4811, HMSO.
Burns, P. (1985), 'Financial Characteristics of Small Companies in the UK', paper presented to 8th National Small Firms Policy and Research Confer-

ence, 1985, and published as Strategy and Enterprise Working Paper 85.08, Cranfield School of Management.

Burns, P. and J. Dewhurst (1986), *Small Business in Europe*, Macmillan.

du Toit, D.E. (1980), 'Confessions of a Successful Entrepreneur', *Harvard Business Review*, November–December, p.44.

Economic Intelligence Unit (1983), *The European Climate for Small Businesses: A 10 Country Study*, EIU.

Harper, M. (1985), 'Hardship, Discipline, Entrepreneurship', Cranfield Working Paper 85.1, Cranfield School of Management, May.

Kets de Vries, M.F.R. (1985), 'The Dark Side of Entrepreneurship', *Harvard Business Review*, November–December, p.160.

Wiener, M. (1981), *English Culture and the Decline of the Industrial Spirit, 1850–1980*, Cambridge University Press.

Wilson Report (1979), *Report on Financing of Small Firms*, Cmnd 7503.

CHAPTER 6

Financing small firms

Martin Binks and Christine Ennew

INTRODUCTION 110
EQUITY FINANCE 111
DEBT FINANCE 115
BANKS AND SMALL BUSINESS 119
SERVICE GAPS 120
OTHER SOURCES OF FINANCE 126
SUMMARY 128
EXERCISES 128
REFERENCES 129

Introduction

As has been explained in the previous chapters, there is no typical or standard small firm. On the contrary, the small firms sector is highly diverse with respect to both structural characteristics (age, industry sector, growth rate and so on) and financing conditions and requirements. There are numerous sources of financial diversity in addition to those which may arise as a consequence of differing managerial abilities. For example, the extent of internal equity within businesses varies widely according to the process of accumulation, the age of the business and its profitability. Equally external equity may be significant for some small businesses, though many will resist any form of external involvement. The growth rate of the firm and the industrial sector in which it operates will have implications for financial requirements, as will the vintage and nature of plant and equipment. On the demand side, the nature of the customer base varies by sector and market, and variations in factors such as the extent of trade credit, payment terms, delayed payment, market power and many other influences will affect the revenue flowing into the business. Not only do these many characteristics of financing conditions vary between businesses, sectors and markets, but they also vary through time as a consequence of changes in both the internal and external environment of the business.

The most obvious manifestation of the varying financing conditions are the different gearing ratios which exist across companies. Although banks typically may look for gearing ratios of around 1:1, the problems associated with access to either internal or external equity may result in rather higher gearing (or constraints on the availability of debt). Equally, however, many firms may seek actively higher gearing ratios, given the implications for profitability. The nature of the operating environment will also have some bearing on gearing, with high-risk environments generally requiring a much lower gearing ratio than low-risk environments.

This chapter examines some of the diversity in the sources and provision of finance to small businesses in the UK, paying particular attention to some of the problems which may confront these businesses. The provision of finance to a small business can be regarded as a simple contract between the two parties in which the finance provider may be regarded as the principal and the small firm as the agent. In effect, the small business is undertaking a project and generating a return on behalf of the provider of finance. Broadly speaking, there are two generic and separable forms of external finance, equity and debt. Equity is risk capital whilst debt is generally fully secured. The provision of equity finance is examined first and it is argued that this source of funding is relatively unimportant for the majority of small businesses. Thereafter the provision of debt finance by the banking sector is discussed in some detail and particular attention is focused on the conditions under which small businesses may encounter problems with the availability of credit and the quality of the banking relationship. Finally alternative sources of finance are examined briefly. A case study at the end of the book highlight some of the difficulties which small businesses encounter in relation to the provision of finance. Where appropriate, similarities and differences between the UK and the rest of Europe are highlighted.

Equity finance

Sources of equity finance for small firms can be categorised broadly as either internal or external. Internal equity arises, as its name suggests, from within the business, while external finance constitutes the admission of external ownership into the business. Equity finance may largely be regarded as risk capital.

Internal equity

Internal equity may be provided by the owner-manager or directors of the company or come from retained profits generated through the company. For the purposes of this analysis we will assume that directors' loans are simply a form of internal equity, since their repayment is contingent upon the same success of the company which underpins straightforward equity involvement. A survey by Keasey and Watson (1992) noted that internal equity contributed around 31 per cent to firms' financing structure and in that sense was as important as bank debt as a source of funds to small businesses. As indicated in the opening section, the availability of internal equity will vary considerably between firms according to the wealth of the owner-managers or directors and the profitability of the business. Where internal equity finance is insufficient for the requirements of the firm then it must choose between attempting to attract external equity funding or debt finance.

External equity

Access to external equity has been identified as a problem area for small businesses for a considerable time. The first reference to a potential shortfall in external equity finance for smaller amounts of funding was provided by the Macmillan Committee in 1931. In their report they suggested that the raising of amounts of external equity of less that £200,000 would be difficult for most businesses owing to the costs of full floatation on the stock exchange. It should be stressed that the 'Macmillan Gap' referred to a much larger financial shortfall than is identified in the 1990s since the amounts involved were quoted at 1929 prices. Using the transformed values of the pound sterling for 1930 as suggested by *The Economist*, this amount would be approximately £4m. in 1993 prices. After the Second World War it was recognised that the problems of external equity funding still prevailed and in response the Industrial and Commercial Finance Corporation (ICFC) was established in 1945. ICFC was funded by the Bank of England and the main clearing banks and still operates as part of 3i. Although the Radcliffe Committee, reporting in 1959, indicated that the finance gap had effectively been closed through the operations of the ICFC, they indicated a different problem involving the funding of new technology. Technical Developments Capital (TDC) was set up as a result. Although the Bolton Committee, reporting in 1971, did not focus attention upon the efficiency of the financial market confronting small businesses, the Wilson Committee, in 1979, again drew attention to shortfalls in this area. Attention was focused upon the operation of the 'over-the-counter' (OTC) market for informal broking of small business shares and the need for alternative broking facilities which were cheaper than the full quotation option available. Subsequently the opening of the Unlisted Securities Market and the short lived Third Market extended the opportunities for smaller businesses to raise external equity, although typically the businesses that were able to benefit from these developments were probably medium-sized rather than genuinely small. Other initiatives to improve the supply of equity to small businesses included the Business Expansion Scheme (BES), introduced in 1983, which provided tax relief for private investments in smaller businesses provided the individual investors were unconnected with the business venture. The effectiveness of this scheme in closing the equity gap has been negligible (Boocock, 1989; Harrison and Mason, 1990) and the operation of the BES was finally terminated in 1993.

Venture capital

The venture capital industry which had developed so effectively in the USA began to develop rapidly in the UK during the early 1980s. Although seen by some at the time as a natural source of funds for entrepreneurial small businesses (as with the initial launch of ELECTRA), the venture capital industry was less than effective at delivering equity funding to small businesses. Hughs (1992) estimates that only 20 per cent of venture capital funds are used for projects with a value less than £250,000. Indeed this is widely recognised as the cut-off point for an equity gap. The existence of this gap can be attributed to both supply and demand problems. On the supply side, the evaluation and monitoring costs are typically such that it is rarely worthwhile for venture capitalists to consider proposals for small scale projects. On the demand side, there is evidence of significant levels of resistance to external equity funding by small business owners.

Information asymmetry

The supply-side problem essentially arises because of the existence of asymmetric information between the two parties involved. For the principal or potential provider of funds it is necessary to obtain a considerable amount of information about the agent or firm requesting finance. This information is necessary, first, in order to evaluate whether the proposition is sound and true in that it conforms to the facts presented in the proposal. Second, if funding is provided, the information is required on a regular basis in order to monitor the progress of the business and ensure that this is in line with the expectations provided in the proposal. These information costs do not rise or fall pro rata with size of the proposal. They are in effect fixed costs and thus tend to preclude the consideration of projects below a certain level.

Apart from information costs, there are other reasons for the effective operation of an equity gap threshold. Where propositions refer to new and unfamiliar technologies it is difficult to assess the risk involved without considerable research. As a result, a venture capital or development capital provider may avoid the funding of such technologies. Given a specific overall fund size to be invested in venture and development capital projects, it is also clear that smaller investments will make only a relatively small contribution to the performance of the overall funds; larger projects may make a greater contribution to the balance sheet.

Business angels

A trend which is also more prevalent in the USA and which is now emerging in the UK is the growing role of 'business angels' in the provision of external equity finance to small businesses. Business angels are specific individuals who wish to become involved in the financing of higher-risk projects in smaller, often entrepreneurial firms. They may wish to do so in order to attract the higher returns which may arise. They may also be motivated by a desire to become involved with these kinds of businesses. Either way it is possible for small businesses and 'angels' to be brought together in a mutually beneficial partnership which provides the firms with the requisite funding, and the business angel with a home for their investment. The main problem with an informal process such as this is that the network of business angels is poorly developed in the UK (Mason, 1992; Mason and Harrison, 1993). As a result, it is often extremely difficult to bring firms and individuals together. With a more effective network structure it is possible that these sources of external equity funding in much smaller amounts may become prevalent in the future.

Irrespective of whether small firms can gain access to external equity finance in practice, it should be emphasised that the large majority do not wish to do so. Evidence provided by the research from the Wilson Committee in 1979 suggested that as many as 75 per cent of small businesses would resist any external participation in the equity of the company. More recently Binks *et al.* (1990a) suggested that as many as 85 per cent of small business owners may resist external equity participation because of concern about a loss of control, while Cowling *et al.* (1991) quote a figure of 61 per cent.

Despite this general resistance to the notion of external equity participation, the significance of the equity gap should not be underestimated. Although the firms affected most significantly by the equity gap may constitute a very small proportion of the stock of businesses in the UK, they will often tend to be more dynamic businesses with rapid growth potential and entrepreneurial aspirations. Firms which are attempting to innovate and develop new technologies, or which are trying to grow rapidly from a relatively small base, will be particularly vulnerable to the shortfall of external equity finance which obtains in the UK at present.

Debt finance

As a result of the observations presented above, it is clear that, for the vast majority of small businesses in the UK, the main source of external finance is the debt provided by the banking sector. Furthermore it is also clear in the vast majority of cases that small firms rely upon banks in order to get debt funding. According to Keasey and Watson (1992) bank debt represents in the region of 31 per cent of business liabilities and may be as important as directors' equity and trade credit in terms of sources of business finance. The authors also provide evidence of an increasing reliance upon short-term bank finance in the late 1980s, while Hughes (1992) also notes that short-term debt has been much more important to small businesses in recent years than either long-term debt or equity. The high levels of provision made by the main clearing banks to cover defaults from loans undertaken in the late 1980s reflect some of the problems involved in ascertaining the liability of debt provisions to small businesses.

In providing debt finance a bank is in effect investing in a business and it needs to be confident that the opportunity provided will generate a sufficient income stream to enable repayment. The provision of finance acts as a constraint on growth only in those situations where a project that is commercially viable and profitable at prevailing and potentially higher interest rates is not undertaken because firms are not able to obtain funding.

The extent to which viable projects are unfunded is virtually impossible to measure. There is considerable debate as to the extent and, in some cases, even the existence of this form of credit rationing. Within the principal and agent framework outlined with respect to equity finance, it is possible to consider a simple model of this relationship in the context of debt provision. In effect the bank or principal requires the firm to undertake an investment project and generate a return on its behalf. The firm is the agent in this process. As with the case of equity provision, the bank, in order to enter this contract, would require certain information to ensure that the project is viable, that the firm is capable of understanding it and that, once the contract has been established, the firm will do what was agreed to the best of its abilities.

Information asymmetry

Under conditions of perfect and costlessly available information with no uncertainties regarding present or future trading conditions, such information requirements would not present a problem. In practice, of course, such conditions do not prevail and information is often expensive and difficult to obtain. The distribution of information between the parties is not symmetric and there are certain pieces of information which are pertinent to the contract between the two but which are only available to one of the parties. This information asymmetry poses two problems in the provision of debt funding. First the bank cannot gain access to certain information which is pertinent to the decision whether to enter into the contract. Typically this might refer to the actual abilities of the individuals applying for finance and the qualities of the project. This is often referred to as the 'problem of adverse selection'. Second it is quite possible that relevant small business management will fail to perform to the best of their abilities. As was the case with equity provision, this risk of moral hazard requires that the bank undertake certain monitoring exercises in order to observe this process if it begins to occur.

A number of studies have examined the implications of information asymmetries from a theoretical standpoint. When considering capital market failure, Stiglitz and Weiss (1981) identify debt gaps as a result of both adverse selection and moral hazard. Problems relating to adverse selection arise because borrowers have different degrees of risk attached to their projects. In this situation, as interest rates rise, banks anticipate that lower-risk borrowers with viable projects will tend to drop out of the market and, as a result, the price or interest rate attached to the provision of debt is higher than that commensurate with the risk involved in the project itself. This process may be augmented by the moral hazard problem associated with the bank's inability to monitor projects in an efficient and effective way without incurring very high costs. This approach argues that there will be equilibrium credit rationing and a shortfall in debt provisions (Bester, 1987; Bester and Hellwig, 1989). The opposite case is argued by de Meza and Webb (1987), who identify adverse selection in the presence of different entrepreneurial abilities as leading to an oversupply of credit rather than a debt gap. In practice these disagreements from a theoretical standpoint may not be mutually exclusive. Berger and Udell (1989) argue that, while the aggregate effects of credit rationing may be small, there is empirical evidence to suggest that, when credit is rationed to some firms, it is more readily available to others. The coexistence of oversupply and credit rationing may in part be due to the role of collateral in bonding debt finance. Where sufficient collateral can be made available, the bank may feel that less information is required because the debt can be recovered in the event of a default. In addition collateral may also reduce a bank's concern about potential moral hazard problems because it acts as an incentive to a borrower to ensure that every effort is made to ensure that the project succeeds. Consequently the availability of sufficient collateral may ensure that some, perhaps relatively weaker, projects are funded while the lack of sufficient collateral may result in other, commercially viable, projects failing to obtain finance.

Evaluating loan applications

The extent to which such a situation can arise will be contingent on the ways in which loan applications are evaluated. Typically banks will adopt an approach which is somewhere between the two extremes of income and capital gearing. In a purely income-geared approach the lending decision is driven by the anticipated profit stream of the project concerned. Where the projected profit stream is sufficient to cover the servicing of the debt with a margin for security, the finance is forthcoming. This approach lays full emphasis upon the prospects of the enterprise. In contrast the capital gearing approach emphasises the value of collateral and security available to the lender in the event of default. It refers, therefore, to the accumulated assets of individuals and businesses rather than to the prospects of the particular enterprise for which the loan is required.

In practice, attention will be given to the potential viability of the enterprise concerned and its prospects, while at the same time it will also be directed towards the assets which are provided as available collateral, the extent to which others may have a claim on such assets and their value in the event of default. Where available collateral is insufficient to justify the loan and a purely income gearing approach is prohibited owing to a lack of information, credit rationing will tend to occur in the absence of an efficient, fair and effective loan guarantee system.

Collateral

It is important to understand the process whereby banks place a value on collateral provided by businesses. Collateral provisions will refer either to the business assets of the company or the personal assets of its owner-manager and/or directors, or a mixture of the two. The valuation of business assets is difficult for banks since they must assume a process which would apply in the event of default and a realisation of the assets in the second-hand market. This 'carcass' approach to business asset valuation typically will place a far lower price upon the assets concerned than that which the firm has paid for them and which it can justify in a going concern environment. Banks may also experience problems in the valuation of personal assets and also business assets where they refer to land and buildings. The recent significant reductions in house and commercial property prices in the UK have led to a considerable dilution of the collateral underpinning and securing many debts.

Given the problems that banks confront when attempting an income gearing approach to loan evaluation along with those associated with collateral evaluation, it is clear that many firms will perceive the collateral requirements of banks as being far in excess of what should be required to secure debt funding. It is also clear that many firms will have insufficient business collateral to secure debt fully. This is also the case for growing firms where they are purchasing plant and equipment with term finance. In this case the problem of collateral is augmented because the acquisition of new plant and equipment adds far more to the expenditures of the firms in purchasing it than it does to the collateral base of the firm in securing that funding. The 'carcass' or 'gone' concern valuation described above leads unavoidably to this conclusion. Many small firms, and in particular growing firms, will therefore be subjected to debt gaps and also the requirement to yield expansion in order to protect the limited liability status of the company, rather than have this eroded through the provision of personal assets for collateral purposes.

Attempts to identify the existence or otherwise of a debt gap in practice are difficult since, in the absence of detailed (often confidential) micro data, there is no easy way of identifying whether failures to obtain funding or failures to obtain adequate funding are due to the quality of the project itself or to some form of credit rationing. However it has been argued (Hughes, 1992) that the most obvious manifestation of a debt problem arises not directly in relation to the amount of credit available but rather to the terms on which credit is available. In particular, a heavy reliance on collateral, particularly personal collateral, may effectively create a debt gap because of the resultant erosion of limited liability status (Binks *et al.*, 1990b).

Banks and small business

When considering the question of the provision of finance to small firms by UK banks, it is helpful to consider the changing competitive environment in which UK banks operate. Since the early 1970s there has been a gradual increase in pressure on the UK banks to improve the quality of their lending services to small businesses. This pressure has arisen as a result both of external competition from other institutions, potential and actual, and of direct criticism of existing bank practices.

External competition has increased through the changing role of the building societies and institutions such as Abbey National and the TSB. Although the anticipated level of effective competition may have been overstated, the potential for increased market penetration by institutions other than the clearers is fully recognised. Taken in conjunction with the variety of adverse comment directed at the quality of bank services, this potential for an alternative option serves to increase the significance of these criticisms. While few or no realistic alternatives to the main clearing banks had existed for much small business lending, the pressure to raise service quality has tended to be lower particularly if, as evidence suggests, the banks have been regarded as being very similar in their provisions (Binks *et al.*, 1989). Criticism of the clearers has arisen from a wide variety of sources, much of it being anecdotal and poorly addressed. The most significant criticisms refer to the approach to bank lending, the extent to which there is short-termism in UK bank practice and customer perceptions of service quality.

In 1979, the Wilson Committee provided evidence to suggest that bank managers may be overly cautious in their lending decision regarding small firms. In particular they drew attention to the security ratios which typically were applied to small business lending. The evidence which they provided of high security ratios has been reinforced by a variety of more recent studies, (Binks *et al.*, 1988, 1990, 1993). The criticism of the banks in terms of the short-term nature of most of the financial products used in practice has been cited as a major constraint on economic development by Edwards (1987). Clear evidence of the demand for longer-term, more flexible debt products was provided in a study by Binks (1987).

The corollary of these observations is that banks are under pressure to change as the result of a changing competitive environment and also of perceived weaknesses and imperfections in service quality. Although the pressures upon the banks may be similar, they themselves confront these from different positions. Banks vary according to their size, in terms of both assets and branch network, and also in the extent to which they are regionally based. Given the increasing level of effective competition between the clearing banks, they also vary according to the strategies which they adopt in their approach to the small firms market. Evidence from other countries such as Germany (Bannock and Doran, 1991; Binks *et al.*, 1991) suggests in particular that smaller more regionally based banks may be better placed to generate a closer relationship with their small business customers than larger universal banks. Their advantages tend to derive from a better knowledge and understanding of regional conditions and often greater continuity in terms of the loan officer–small business manager relationship.

The four main English clearing banks are still broadly similar, in the sense that they are all large with extensive branch networks, although Barclays and National Westminster bank have approximately double the market share of the small business community when compared to Lloyds and Midland. The Scottish banks, as a group, are also similar in many respects and are much more regionally specific than the English banks. They also tend to be rather smaller. Within the UK, therefore, it is possible to observe two separate groups of banks, the first being universal banks and the second being primarily regionally based banks. In the light of the observations made above, it is to be expected that the service quality associated with the two groups would be different. In order to test this expectation we can consider the perceptions of the small business customers of service quality for each group of banks.

Service gaps

The potential for a debt gap to exist arises as a consequence of asymmetric information. Although perfect information is an unobtainable goal, the quality and quantity of information flows between banks and small businesses will be influenced by the nature of the relationship between a business and its bank. A close relationship has the potential to provide the bank with a better picture of the operating environment facing a particular business, the qualities of the management team and a better overall picture of the prospects for the business. Equally a close relationship should provide the business with a better understanding of the constraints under which banks and bank managers operate and thus a more realistic picture of what the business can expect in terms of financing (Watson 1986). The failure to develop close working relationships has been identified as one of the weaknesses of Anglo-Saxon banking systems such as that of the UK (Yao-Su Hu, 1984; Edwards, 1987). Thus any consideration of finance provision to small businesses would be incomplete without some discussion of the nature of the banking relationship.

Table 6.1   Financing characteristics*

	1988	1990	1992	1994
% with overdraft	81.50	86.00	76.3	72.20
Overdraft limit (£000s)	50.28	58.61	64.22	48.63
Amount overdrawn (£000s)	27.89	40.97	45.89	22.86
Overdraft usage (%)	55	70	72	47
% Margin over base (overdraft)	2.82	2.80	3.08	3.28
Collateral ratio on overdraft		4.78	3.48	2.35
% with loan	41.5	44.9	42.3	39.7
Size of loan (£000s)	–	62.46	80.17	59.20
Collateral ratio on loan	–	3.85	2.09	1.92
Term of loan (years)	8.8	9.2	10.0	9.8
Margin over base (loan)	2.96	2.63	2.79	3.12

Source: Binks and Ennew (1994a).
*These results are based on re-analysing the original data in order to ensure consistency in methods of calculation. As such, some of the figures may differ slightly from those presented in earlier reports.

One of the largest information sets concerning the bank–small business relationship is provided by regular surveys of the membership of the Forum of Private Business (FPB). This membership was surveyed in 1988, 1990, 1992, and 1994.[1] The response rates concerned were respectively 35, 30, 38 and 30 per cent. This corresponded to absolute numbers of 3,500 in 1988, 4,200 in 1990, 6,100 in 1992 and 5589 in 1994. From a sampling perspective, the FPB sample is not wholly representative of the population of small businesses. In particular, the FPB sample has a bias towards the larger businesses and towards those making more active use of their bank. However, in order to gain some understanding of the relationship between banks and small businesses, these sample characteristics may be particularly desirable.

The evidence collected relates to a wide variety of questions, including financing terms and conditions, service quality and constraints and the banking relationship. Prior to examining aspects of the banking relationship it is appropriate to consider some more general features of the financing of small businesses as described by the FPB sample. The proportion of firms with bank finance has declined over the period reflecting what is generally though to be a move by the banks towards term loans. It is also interesting to note that there is evidence of a decline in usage of bank finance; the average overdraft and loan size and the degree to which overdrafts

---

[1]Full details of each of these surveys are contained in Binks *et al.* (1988, 1990a, 1993) and in Binks and Ennew (1994a, 1994b).

are used reaches a peak in 1992 in the depth of the recession and has declined thereafter. Interest rate margins (points above base) have increased significantly over the period. In part this reflects declining collateral ratios. However, even allowing for the effects of change in collateral and changes in the characteristics of firms, there is still evidence of a significant increase in interest rates over the period. There are a number of variations in interest rates between banks; in part these may be attributable to differences in the size of facility and differences in collateral. Nevertheless, some differences remain with the Scottish banks typically appearing to offer lower rates than the English banks.

It is apparent that between 1988 and 1990 there was a significant increase in the proportion of firms which had considered changing bank. Thereafter, the proportion is relatively constant with a slight drop in 1994. Assessments of the degree to which charges represent 'value for money' have also changed significantly over the period 1990 to 1994. Banks are now perceived as offering much poorer value for money than in either 1992 or 1990.

Moving on to consider the broader aspects of the banking relationship, Table 6.2 examines the impact of different aspects of bank policy on businesses. The figures highlight the extent to which owner-managers believe their business to be constrained by bank actions. There is a high degree of consistency in perceived constraints with charges and interest rates regularly cited as the aspects of bank policy which most constrain respondents businesses. In general the customers of Scottish banks perceive that their businesses are less constrained than is the case with the customers of English banks.

Firms in the sample were divided into two groups according to their responses on a series of questions relating to their willingness to participate in the banking relationship.[2] As indicated earlier, a customers willingness to participate in the banking relationship is likely to be an important determinant of the effectiveness of that relationship. Evidence with regard to the constraint variables (presented in Table 6.3) suggest that the more participative firms generally perceive their business to be less constrained than the less participative firms.

Two further aspects of the relationship between banks and small business require consideration: the overall quality of service provided and the relationship between business owner and bank manager. A consideration of quality of service provided gives an indication of the ability of the banks to meet and satisfy the needs of

---

[2]The allocation of firms to groups was carried out using cluster analysis. Further detail on this procedure is contained in Ennew and Binks (1995).

Table 6.2 Ranking of main constraints in 1988, 1990, 1992 and 1994

	1988		1990		1992		1994	
	% Citing	Rank	% Citing	Rank	Mean score	Rank	Mean score	Rank
Collateral	14.20	3	13.60	3	2.72	3	2.99	4
Interest rate	19.70	2	37.20	1	3.18	2	3.22	2
Credit availability	12.90	4	3.70	4	2.65	4	2.88	5
Charges	30.70	1	26.60	2	3.23	1	3.53	1
Competence of manager	6.90	5	2.70	5	2.24	6	2.56	6
Speed of service	1.50	6	1.10	6	2.12	7	2.52	7
Term of loan	0.70	7	0.10	7	2.60	5	–	–
Termination of overdraft	–	–	–	–	–	–	3.00	3

Source: Binks and Ennew (1994a).

Table 6.3   Constraints for participative and non-participative firms

	Non-participative	Participative
Collateral	3.14	2.91*
Availability of credit	3.36	3.14*
Bank charges	3.71	3.45*
Competence of manager	2.98	2.34*
Speed of Service	2.78	2.39*
Threat of termination of overdraft	3.20	2.91*

*Difference is statistically significant.
Source: Binks and Ennew (1994b).

their customers. Equally, the relationship with the bank manager provides some understanding of the potential for information sharing and co-operation which can serve to reduce the extent to which debt gaps may occur.

Survey respondents were asked to score their perceptions of the quality of provision (on a five-point scale) for a number of different service characteristics. These included factors such as knowledge of business, industry and market, competitive charges, access to loan officer, efficiency and reliability. These characteristics were aggregated to represent five general aspects of service provision. These groupings provide a means of comparing the relative quality of service provision across customer groups. As Table 6.4 shows, there is a degree of variability between the different dimensions of service quality and there are also significant differences between the participative and non-participative firms. Specifically, the banks appear strongest in relation to knowledge, operations and accessibility but disappointingly weak in relation to core product areas and the pricing of services. Equally it is clear that participative firms generally perceive the quality of service to be higher than is the case with non-participative firms.

However, the concept of a good banking relationship extends beyond the quality of service provided. It is perhaps important, if not more so, to consider the relationship between the business and the bank manager. Indeed there is evidence to suggest that it may be the bank manager who is of most significance rather than the bank itself (Binks, Ennew and Reed, 1990a). While the quality of the service provided by the bank manager will vary according to the personalities of the individuals who are party to the relationship, there are reasons for believing that systematic variations may exist because of different training processes and different internal procedures policies and culture. Furthermore, there are also grounds for expecting that a better relationship would prevail when business

Table 6.4 Service quality for participative and non-participative firms

	Non-participative	Participative
Basic Product	2.87	3.26*
Price	2.67	2.94*
Knowledge and understanding	2.39	2.93*
Operations	3.32	3.67*
Accessibility	3.28	3.51*

*Difference is statistically significant.
Source: Binks and Ennew (1994b).

Table 6.5 Banking relationship for participative and non-participative firms (1)

	Non-participative	Participative
Trust and confidence	2.56	3.02*
Information flows	3.25	4.21*
Approachability	2.88	3.94*

*Difference is statistically significant.
Source: Binks and Ennew (1994b).

owners display a greater willingness to participate in the relationship. Information on a number of aspects of the relationship between bank manager and small business owner was collected as part of the survey and the responses were grouped into summary variables. A comparison of the responses of participative and non-participative customers is presented in Table 6.5, with higher scores indicative of a higher perceived quality of relationship. The maintenance and development of trust and confidence appears to be one of the weaker aspects of banking relationships and it is also apparent that participative customers have the more favourable perceptions of their banking relationship.

Finally, it is useful to examine the degree of loyalty of small businesses to their banks and the degree to which this varies across customer groups. In practice only a very small proportion (possibly less than 5 per cent) of a banks customers actually change bank during any one year. This may be partly explicable by satisfaction with the services provided, partly by the high degree of switching costs associated with a change of bank and partly by a perceived lack of differentiation. To gain some indication of the relative importance of these factors, the survey distinguishes between those who had considered changing bank and those who had not, and the reasons for not considering a change of bank. Table 6.6 provides a comparison of data for responses to these questions.

Table 6.6   Banking relationship for participative and non-participative firms (2)

	Non-participative	Participative
Not considered changing bank (%)	46.9	61.7
Reason: No difference (%)	47.8	33.4
Satisfied (%)	44.6	60.3
Effort and difficulty (%)	25.7	19.9

Source: Binks and Ennew (1994b).

The figures in Table 6.6 suggest a much higher degree of loyalty among the participative customers and also a much higher level of satisfaction with bank services. A much smaller proportion of non-participative customers had not considered changing bank and, when asked why, this group was much more likely to cite negative factors such as the lack of perceived differentiation and the effort and difficulty involved in changing bank.

A key feature of this analysis of the relationship between banks and small businesses is the importance of the customer in influencing its quality. A good banking relationship can help to ameliorate some of the problems of asymmetric information, but only if customers are willing to participate and share information. The potential benefits of such participation are apparent from the results presented in the previous paragraphs. More participative customers are generally more satisfied, they perceive fewer constraints on their business, a better quality of service and a better banking relationship.

Other sources of finance

Although small businesses rely heavily on the banking sector for the provision of debt finance, there are a number of alternative non-bank sources of funding, such as factoring and leasing.

Factoring

Factoring is essentially a means of improving short-term cash flow and reducing the problems associated with delayed payment. The factor receives duplicate copies of all invoices and assumes responsibility for collecting payment from trade debtors; in return, the business can draw immediately on the funds represented by the value of the invoices up to a specified maximum (typically around

80 per cent). The remaining funds are made available once the factor has received full payment from the firm's customers. Full service factoring includes the factor assuming responsibility for chasing up debts, while invoice discounting simply provides finance against the value of the invoices but leaves the responsibility for chasing debtors with the business. Full service factoring will attract a fee in the region of 0.5–4 per cent of the value of the invoices, while invoice discounting is much cheaper, with fees generally less than 1 per cent of the value of the invoices. In addition a fixed fee is usually payable.

There are many advantages to factoring. The use of a factor improves cash flow and helps to avoid overtrading, as well as reducing overheads by allowing someone else to take responsibility for debt collection. However many firms are resistant to factoring because it is often argued that recourse to a factor is a sign that a firm is experiencing trading problems. If this were the case then that firm's supplier might lose their own trade credit arrangement and be required to pay invoices in advance of receipt of the goods or services involved. Furthermore, where firms experience delays in payment of more than a specified number of days, the factor will reclaim the funding already issued. Finally firms may find that, once they rely upon the services of a factor, they may be 'locked in' to the relationship even when conditions improve, because of the cash flow implications of any disengagement.

Leasing

In contrast to factoring, leasing provides a means of financing capital investment. Equipment such as photocopiers, computers and cars provide the simplest example of leasing whereby, rather than a purchase being made, the equipment is leased from a supplier who assumes responsibility for servicing and maintenance. This has the clear advantage of making the costs of this equipment known in advance and payable on a regular and predictable basis. Other forms of leasing are available for more specialist types of equipment, although often this form of leasing is only available for very large-scale purchases which are outside the range of most small businesses.

Hire-purchase is a variant of leasing, although there is a clear difference in that, when making a hire purchase agreement, the business has the option to become the owner of the equipment once the purchase price has been paid. This purchase price includes an element for the cost of finance and is typically more expensive than a bank loan, but may be a viable alternative in instances in which bank finance is not available.

Summary

In this chapter we have explained why some small firms will experience difficulties in raising external finance. Underpinning much of this problem is the cost of obtaining regular reliable and accurate information which can drive and sustain the lending decision. In the case of external equity, these information costs create a threshold size for project submissions below which few formal institutional providers will consider applications. For debt finance the same costs create a need for collateral which, if unavailable to the firms concerned, may constrain access to loans because they are unable to provide sufficient security. We have established the importance of a well informed and trusting relationship between banks and their small business customers, and provided evidence on the state of this relationship as perceived by firms. There is clearly scope for improvements in this relationship which would aid communication between the parties.

We believe that significant reductions in information costs are crucial to more effective financial provision by providers of equity and debt. In the future there will be far wider and more imaginative use made of expert- or knowledge-based decision support systems by most financial institutions. These will have the effect of reducing information costs while raising quality and consistency. This in turn will greatly increase the effectiveness of the decision-making process and also provide a system of continuous updating to management information systems. Finance gaps will never disappear completely, but they will become much less of a constraint for the vast majority of firms.

Exercises

1. As an owner-manager, list the pros and cons of obtaining equity finance. What is the major reason for your not wanting it likely to be?
2. Write an essay exploring whether the 'Macmillan Gap' still exists. If it does, what are the likely consequences?
3. Write a report to the government outlining the problem of information asymmetry, its consequences and any potential solutions.
4. Write a report to your superiors in the bank outlining how you think the provision of services to small firms might be improved.
5. What sources of finance are available to small firms, other than debt or equity? List the pros and cons of using each one.
6. Write an essay exploring the likely consequences of the structure of financing available to small firms in the UK.

7. Write an essay that compares the provision of finance for small firms in the UK with that available in Germany. Why is the German system so different from that in the UK? Should or could the UK system be changed?

References

Bannock, G. and A. Doran (1991), *Business Banking in the 1990s: A New Era of Competition*, Lafferty Group.

Berger, A.N. and G.F. Udell (1989), 'Some Evidence on the Empirical Significance of Credit Rationing', Working Paper, Salomon Brothers Centre for the Study of Financial Institutions, New York University.

Bester, H. (1987), 'The Role of Collateral in Credit Markets with Imperfect Information', *European Economic Review*, vol. 31, no. 4, pp.887–9.

Bester, H. and M. Hellwig (1989), 'Moral Hazard and Equilibrium Credit Rationing: an Overview of the Issues', in G. Bamber and K. Spremann (eds), *Agency Theory, Information and Incentives*, Springer-Verlag.

Binks, M.R. (1987), *Long Term Debt and the Financing of Investment in the UK*, Employment Department.

Binks, M.R., C.T. Ennew and G.V. Reed (1988), 'The Survey by the Forum of Private Business on Banks and Small Firms', in G. Bannock and E.V. Morgan (eds), *Banks and Small Businesses: A Two Nation Perspective*, Forum of Private Business/National Federation of Small Business.

Binks, M.R., C.T. Ennew and G.V. Reed (1989), 'The Differentiation of Bank Services to Small Firms', *International Journal of Banking and Marketing*, vol. 7, no. 4, pp.29–32.

Binks, M.R., C.T. Ennew and G.V. Reed (1990a), *Small Businesses and their Banks 1990*, Forum of Private Business, Knutsford.

Binks, M.R., C.T. Ennew, and G.V. Reed (1990b), 'Finance Gaps and Small Firms', paper presented to the Royal Economics Society Annual Conference, Nottingham.

Binks, M.R., C.T. Ennew and G.V. Reed (1991), *Small Businesses and their Banks: An International Perspective*, National Westminster Bank.

Binks, M.R., C.T. Ennew and G.V. Reed (1993), *Small Businesses and their Banks 1992*, Forum of Private Business, Knutsford.

Binks M.R. and C.T. Ennew (1994a), *Small Businesses and their Banks 1994: Report 1*, Forum of Private Business, Knutsford.

Binks M.R. and C.T. Ennew (1994b), *Small Businesses and their Banks 1994: Report 2*, Forum of Private Business, Knutsford.

Bolton, J. (1971), *Small Firms*, Report of the Committee of Inquiry on Small Firms, Cmnd 4811, HMSO.

Boocock J.G. (1989), 'The Role of Specialist Financial Intermediaries in the Financing of Small and Medium Sized Businesses in the United Kingdom: A Review of Recent Developments', Research Papers in Banking and Finance no 89/9, University College of North Wales.

Cowling, M., J. Samuels and R. Sugden (1991), *Small Firms and Clearing Banks*, Association of British Chambers of Commerce Report.

de Meza, D. and D.C. Webb (1987), 'Too Much Investment: A Problem of Asymmetric Information', *Quarterly Journal of Economics*, vol. 102, pp.281–92.

Edwards, G.T. (1987), *The Role of Banks in Economic Development*, Macmillan.

Ennew, C.T. and M.R. Binks (1995), 'The Provision of Finance to Small Firms: Does the Banking Relationship Constrain Performance?' *Journal of Small Business Finance*, vol. 4(1), pp.69–85.

Ennew, C.T., G.V. Reed and M.R. Binks (1993), 'Importance–Performance Analysis and the Measurement of Service Quality', *European Journal of Marketing*, vol. 27, no. 2, pp.59–70.

Harrison, R.T. and C.M. Mason (1990), 'The Role of the Business Expansion Scheme in the UK', *Omega*, vol. 17, no. 2, pp.147–57.

Hughes, A. (1992), 'The "Problems" of Finance for Small Firms', Working Paper No. 15, Small Business Research Centre, University of Cambridge.

Keasey, K. and R. Watson (1992a), 'Banks and Small Firms: Is Conflict Inevitable?', *National Westminster Bank Quarterly Review*, May, pp.30–40.

Keasey, K. and R. Watson (1992b), *Investment and Financing Decisions and the Performance of Small Firms*, National Westminster Bank.

Keasey K. and R. Watson (1993), *Small Firms Management*, Basil Blackwell.

Macmillan, H. (1931), *Report of the Committee on Finance and Industry*, Cmd 3897, HMSO.

Mason, C.M. and R.T. Harrison (1993), 'Promoting Informal Venture Capital: An Evaluation of a British Initiative', paper presented to Babson Entrepreneurship Research Conference, Houston, March.

Mason, C.M., R.T. Harrison and J. Chaloner (1992), 'Informal Risk Capital in the UK: A Study of Investor Characteristics, Preferences and Decision Making', in M. Robertson, E. Chell and C. Mason (eds), *Towards the Twenty-First Century: The Challenge for Small Business*, National Books.

Stiglitz, J. and A. Weiss (1981) 'Credit Rationing in Markets with Imperfect Information', *American Economic Review*, vol. 71, pp.393–410.

Watson, I. (1986), 'Managing the Relationship with Corporate Clients', *International Journal of Bank Marketing*, vol. 4(1), pp.19–34.

Wilson, H. (1979), *The Financing of Small Firms*, Report of the Committee to Review the Functioning of Financial Institutions, Cmnd 7503, HMSO.

Yao-Su Hu (1984), *Industrial Banking and Special Credit Institutions: A Comparative Study*, Policy Studies Institute.

CHAPTER 7

Venture capital

Gordon Murray[1]

INTRODUCTION	131
VENTURE CAPITAL AND THE EQUITY GAP	132
GENESIS AND GROWTH OF THE INDUSTRY	134
CONTINENTAL EUROPE	136
STRUCTURE OF THE UK INDUSTRY	138
MANAGEMENT BUY-OUTS AND BUY-INS	150
THE INVESTMENT PROCESS	152
CORPORATE VENTURING	155
THE FUTURE: ISSUES AND PROGNOSES	157
EXERCISES	162
REFERENCES AND SELECTED BIBLIOGRAPHY	163

Introduction

The severity of the recession in the UK over the period 1989–92 and its consequent marked increase in the number of liquidations and insolvencies among small and medium-sized firms (SMEs) has added further impetus to the long-running debate on the appropriate financial structure for small firms. For over 60 years, since Macmillan's 1931 governmental review of the state of finances of SMEs, a stream of academic and public enquires have cited the deleterious effects of a chronic shortage of long-term, risk capital to support the growth of the small firm sector. This shortage of risk capital or long-term equity within the balance sheet of small businesses, and the alternative reliance on security based lending, primarily bank overdrafts, have, it is argued, placed firms in a position of excessive vulnerabil-

---

[1]The author is grateful for the helpful and insightful observations made on this chapter by Chris Beresford, partner, KPMG, Corporate Finance.

ity in the event of a downturn in sales or other threats to the firm's profitability or, more critically, cash flow.

Clearing banks operating more rigorous credit controls in the recent UK recession came under a spate of public criticism as their reduction or curtailment of commercial credit facilities exacerbated a marked rise in small firm failures after 1989. The Confederation of British Industry's Smaller Firms Council noted the adverse consequences of excessive debt and gearing for smaller businesses (CBI, 1993). It also reiterated the commonly held view that there continued to be a dearth in the provision of smaller amounts of equity (<£250,000), the so-called 'equity gap', through the capital markets available to SMEs. However, despite the intuitive popularity of the equity gap proposition, there is not uniform consensus as to its existence and effect. Storey (1994), preferring the term 'market failure', has argued that the withholding of equity to firms of questionable potential cannot in itself be considered a failure if the commercial risks are considered unacceptable by the equity providers. Bannock (1991) suggested that the supply of third-party equity and its take-up are roughly in balance if the number of potential fast growth, new companies in the UK is estimated and compared to the supply of equity financings on an annual basis.

Venture capital and the equity gap

It is within this context of the appropriate financial structure of SMEs that the potential and actual role of venture capital is most commonly debated. It is suggested that there is often a widespread misunderstanding regarding the exact nature and purpose of venture capital finance among the small firm population. Importantly this confusion, or lack of awareness, also appears to extend to embrace a significant number of the advisors, including accountants and bank managers, who counsel owner-managers of SMEs (Hovgaard, 1991).

Two definitions by leading participants in the UK venture capital industry illustrate the nature of this form of specialised investment activity: 'Venture capital in its widest sense is the investment in equity capital in unquoted companies to support their future development and profitable growth' Hugh de Quervain, Managing Director Midland Montagu Ventures, 1990 (now Midland Private Equity); 'Venture capital is the investment in long term, risk equity finance where the primary reward for the providers is an eventual capital gain, rather than interest income or dividend yield' (Tony Lorenz, Managing Director ECI Ventures, 1989). Thus the venture capital industry is characterised by a focus primarily on *unquoted* companies with the potential to *grow rapidly* and to yield a level of *return on capital* comensurate with the additional risk and illiquidity of an investment which cannot be traded during the lifetime of the investor's commitment to the enterprise. Particularly for start-up and other early stage investments, annual dividends or yield on the investment are either absent or play a minor role in the total returns to the venture capital investor. The venture capital firm's reward is primarily made on the capital gain at realisation or exit of its equity stake through the eventual sale or, more rarely, the flotation of the business on either the main or secondary stock markets. However there are a number of later stage investors, including 3i and several captive venture capitalists, who can structure their financial returns on the basis of annual yield. Such arrangements reduce the need for an early or inappropriately timed exit but require the investee company to be sufficiently cash-generative to pay annual dividend and interest payments.

Depending on the degree of risk of a proposal, which may loosely be correlated with the maturity and track record of the investee company, the venture capitalist will usually demand annualised rates of return between 30 per cent and 60 per cent (Murray and Lott, 1995). The ability of the majority of small firms to meet financing costs of this order is negligible. Thus venture capital is a financing instrument which is only relevant to those fast-growth firms able to demonstrate the probability of achieving *exceptional*, commercial returns. Storey *et al.* (1989) showed in their North of England study that these 'fast track' firms only represented 4 per cent of the total sample of new firms investigated. That venture capitalists reject in excess of 95 per cent of the approximately 50,000 applications made to them each year (Bannock, 1991; Dixon, 1991) is a reflection of their own views of the scarcity of such fast-growth firms.

The general proposition that venture capital is only suitable for firms able to demonstrate super-normal growth and profitability needs one important qualification. In the case of later stage development capital deals, and particularly management buy-outs (MBOs) and buy-ins (MBIs), the deal negotiated between equity and debt holders can be structured to give an attractive rate of return on equity. This is accomplished by increasing the project risk through the use of substantial debt within the financing structure. The ability to engineer the returns to equity are not conditional on the buy-out vehicle having to show substantial growth prospects. Rather it is adequate for the new company to demonstrate a solid record of profitable operation. However the losses incurred by debt providers (including several foreign banks) in what can be viewed with hindsight as excessively overpriced and 'overgeared' MBO/MBI deals in the late 1980s has made lenders extremely wary of financing structures which resulted in their taking equity-type risks for debt-type rewards. In consequence, the levels of both senior and unsecured (mezzanine) debt within MBO/MBI deals have fallen significantly since 1989 (CMBOR, 1993). This concern about the excessive use of debt in the deal structure, primarily articulated by bank lenders but also conceded by equity providers, has acted as a substantial brake on larger MBO and MBI opportunities in recent years (Financial Times MBO Survey, 8 December, 1993).

This situation has lead Bannock to argue that the limitation on venture capitalists investing more of their resources into SMEs and particularly early stage investments is not fundamentally a supply or 'equity gap' issue concerning the availability of venture capital funds but rather a problem occasioned by the lack of attractive investee companies for venture capitalists. This view is supported by Dixon's (1991) findings. He notes that 63 per cent of the respondents in his UK venture capitalist survey argued that they had more funds than attractive applicants in which to invest.

Thus, when authors have criticised the limited contribution of formal, venture capital organisations to overcoming the barriers to growth of small firms (see ACOST, 1990; Pratt, 1990), the debate has on occasions reflected more the perspectives and interests of the writers than the logic of capital markets. With the exception of publicly financed venture capital firms with a local or regional economic development focus, the majority of the hundred-plus members of the British Venture Capital Association (BVCA) have an exclusively commercial remit as investors of institutional clients' moneys. These firms have a fiduciary responsibility to their investors, not to the small business community per se. While the industry is embarrassed at the paucity of investment that has been allocated to particularly start-ups and new technology-based firms (NTBFs) within the UK (Murray 1994a&b, and Lott 1995), there is a pervasive belief among venture capital practitioners, based on investment experience, that the risks associated with start-ups and young companies are unacceptably high in relation to the costs and potential rewards of such investment.

Nonetheless the UK venture capital industry which has shown meteoric growth in the 1980s and has attracted funds for primarily unquoted, equity investment of over £9b. since 1980 will, perforce, remain the subject of considerable interest and debate.

Genesis and growth of the industry

Venture capital is not a contemporary phenomenon. Throughout antiquity, rich individuals and money managers invested speculatively in commercial and trading opportunities, taking a calculated decision on the risks and rewards of backing potentially attractive enterprises. Individual investors and financial institutions helped create and fund new manufacturing and transport enterprises during Britain's Industrial Revolution via common stock ownership. Similarly, in the 1930s, rich individuals and family trusts contributed to the rapid growth of US economic enterprise. Hannah (1992) has noted the innovative role of a number of insurance companies before the Second World War in taking unsecured equity positions in business with high growth potential, including the fledgling British car manufacturing industry.

However the development of specialist, equity investing organisations in new and growing businesses did not emerge until after the Second World War. In 1945 the Bank of England and the major clearing banks created ICFC, the forerunner of Investors in Industry, which is now renamed 3i plc (and was listed on the UK main market in 1994). In America, General Doriot, a professor at Harvard Business School, founded in 1946 American Research & Development (ARD), the first independent venture capital company (Bygrave and Timmons, 1992). ARD's structure of a general partnership, creating in turn a management company which raised specialist funds from financial institutions, that is, the limited partners, was to set the general blueprint for independent venture capital firms on both sides of the Atlantic.

Unlike the US industry, which grew rapidly during the postwar period, the UK venture capital did not show rapid development for nearly a quarter of a century after the formation of ICFC. By the mid-1970s there were less than 20 venture capital operations in existence, the majority of which were 'captive' offshoots of the major clearing banks and a small number of institutional investors, including pension funds and insurance companies. In 1981 some 40 UK venture capitalists committed £66m. to 163 investee companies (Lorenz 1989). However, in the succeeding ten years, investments made by the formal UK venture capital industry (defined as full members of the industry's representative body, the BVCA) grew at a real rate of over 20 per cent per annum. By 1991 BVCA statistics showed that in that year the industry invested £1,153 million in 1,386 enterprises. At its zenith, in 1989, the UK industry, comprising 124 firms, invested over £1.65b. in 1,569 companies. The vast majority of these funds (86 per cent) was directed domestically to unquoted UK companies (Figure 7.1).

This dramatic increase in activity was a result of Britain experiencing in the early to mid-1980s one of the longest periods of sustained growth in economic activity since the war. Real economic growth, falling interest rates and liberal credit policies, sustained growth in stock market prices prior to October 1987, a burgeoning mergers and

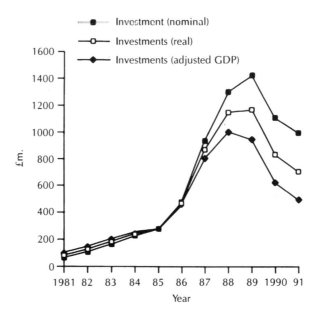

Source: Murray (1992).

Figure 7.1   Annual value of venture capital investment, 1981–91

acquisitions market coupled with a trend for major restructuring and rationalisation of large and mid-sized companies, and the active involvement of government in incentives for new firm formation each helped fuel what was to become known as the 'decade of the entrepreneur' (Bannock, 1987). The venture capital industry was successful in exploiting this conducive and bullish investment environment. New products, particularly the management buy-out, attracted both suppliers and potential recipients of investment funds. Between 1985 and 1992 the UK venture capital industry invested over £8.8b. in approximately 10,000 client companies (BVCA press release, June 1993).

Continental Europe

Just as there had been a lag between the growth of US and British venture capital activity, a similar but far shorter delay was experienced in the widespread uptake of venture capital finance in continental Europe. Venture capital as a financial product/service appears to demonstrate the concept of the 'international product life cycle' (Murray, 1991b and 1995). However, by the mid-1980s, the major

Table 7.1   Total European venture capital annual investment by stage of finance, 1992

	Amount of investment (ECU 1000)	%	Number of investment	%
Seed	27,001	0.6	133	2.2
Start-up	251,014	5.3	797	12.9
Expansion	2,150,937	45.8	3,527	56.4
Replacement	402,650	8.6	631	10.2
Buy-out	1,869,641	39.8	1,109	17.9
Total	4,701,243	100	6,197	100

Source: EVCA (1993).

countries of Western Europe and Scandinavia were experiencing comparable growth rates to those of the UK in the provision of venture capital. Between 1985 and 1986 funds available for investment grew by 62 per cent to ECU 2,285m. in 12 European countries including the UK. While the UK's venture capital industry has dominated European figures, by 1986 it represented less than half of all funds raised or invested annually for the first time (EVCA, 1987). The Netherlands, France, Germany, Belgium and Denmark were each starting to develop rapidly. Unlike Britain, where the greatest increase in activity was coming from independent firms, the domestic banks with captive venture capital subsidiaries were a major engine of growth in most continental European countries (Table 7.1).

By 1992, the 17 national members of the European Venture Capital Association had cumulatively raised ECU 38.5 billion of investment funds. Annual investments made by its members, in a year in which Europe was experiencing the deepest recession in a generation, totalled ECU 4.7 billion in 6,197 companies. This represented a year on year increase in the value of investments of 1.5 per cent, although a decrease of 10.3 per cent in the number of investments made. The UK still represented some 40 per cent by value of all European investment in 1992, a figure approximately twice as large as for France and three times as large as for Germany, the two largest venture capital industries in continental Europe. By 1991, the European industry, as measured by annual investment levels, had become substantially larger than the US industry with respective figures of ECU 4,632m. and ECU 1,050 million. While Europeans trends were still marginally upwards, even in recession, 'disbursements' to investee companies in the USA by 1991 had hit a ten year low (Venture Economics Inc., 1992).

Structure of the UK industry

Venture capital firms are intermediaries in the investment chain. They act essentially as agents on behalf of their investors with a responsibility to identify and execute attractive investments which will make economic returns commensurate with the risks and illiquidity of investing in young and growing unquoted enterprises. Thus the three key elements of the industry may be categorised as the providers of investment finance, the venture capital firm intermediaries and the entrepreneurial users of venture capital finance.

The providers

In describing the formal venture capital industry it is sensible to ignore informal, individual providers of venture capital, a group often termed 'business angels' (see Harrison and Mason, 1992; Wetzel, 1986). Research in the USA has shown that the informal sector invests in aggregate substantially greater sums than the formal sector, particularly in early stage enterprises. The potential of business angels to help address the problem of the limited availability of small tranches of risk capital for young businesses has created considerable interest in both the UK and continental Europe. These informal investors generally operate independently of the professional venture capital firms. However a number of venture capital funds are at present exploring with informal investors means by which common experience, finances and investment opportunities could be pooled.

The financiers of formal venture capital activity are primarily large institutional investors managing a portfolio of investment choices or 'asset classes'. Although the BVCA cites eight sources of funding for independent venture capitalist funds in its 1992 Report on Investment Activity, pension funds and insurance companies represented two-thirds of the total of £347 million raised in that year. However these figures ignore the role of captive organisations which invest their own finances via, usually wholly owned, subsidiary venture capital operations. Purely captive funds, which may have either bank or other institutional parents, in 1992 invested £361m. (29 per cent) of the total value of UK annual investments of £1,251m. This understates the role of captives, as 'semi-captive organisations', which manage both parents and externally generated funds, represented a further £269m. (21 per cent) in that year. (It should be noted that 1992 BVCA figures include, for the first time, debt as well as equity investments by UK venture capitalists. Thus 1992 figures are not directly comparable with earlier years.) (Table 7.2).

Table 7.2 Institutional sources of capital for UK independent funds, nominal and real (1985) values

	1983	1984	1985	1986	
Nominal £m.	112	195	278	239	
Real £m.	125	207	278	233	
	1987	1988	1989	1990	1991
Nominal £m.	684	612	1684	830	368
Real £m.	634	532	1360	621	260

Source: Venture Economics Ltd. (1991) and BVCA (1992).

It remains debatable whether or not venture capital should be termed an 'asset class'. The level of information, particularly on risks and returns, is particularly poor when compared to established assets classes such as UK stocks or gilts. Even at the height of the popularity of venture capital among institutional investors, the moneys placed in venture capital never reached 1 per cent of total annual institutional investment in the UK. Compared to investment in stocks, bonds and gilts, venture capital is essentially a peripheral activity in value terms. This plausibly explains why most institutional investors are prepared to allow independent venture capital firms to manage their limited exposure to this specialist activity rather than bringing the investment responsibility 'in house'.

The attraction for the institutional investor is the potential superior return to venture capital. Small firm stocks, in periods other than recession, regularly outperform the main market. Research on the Hoare Govett Smaller Companies Index (HGSCI) by Dimson and Marsh (cited by Brakell, 1988) showed that in the period 1955–87, the annual rate of return on the HGSCI was 20.6 per cent against 15 per cent for the overall market. There is also the ill-defined, social or ideological benefit of investing in young companies which may become the international corporations of tomorrow. However the advent of recession and the failure of a number of well-publicised venture-backed companies have caused institutional investors to reduce both their expectations from, and their investment in, venture capital. In 1989, UK independent funds raised £1.68 billion, a sum similar in scale to the total funds raised for the four preceding years. In the two years after 1989, the funds raised were halved each year to a plateau of under £400m. Senior UK venture capitalists have acknowledged that the industry 'oversold' the attractiveness of venture capital investment returns in the mid-1980s (Murray 1991a).

It is likely that this situation will result in a 'funds famine' for all but the most successful venture capital firms as disillusioned investors redirect future funds to more attractive opportunities (Murray, 1991a; Financial Times MBO Survey, 8 December 1993). However the consequences of investors' caution will not be uniform. A number of both captive and independent UK venture capital firms have raised substantial new funds recently. Thus the UK industry will show aspects of both 'feast and famine'. The more successful venture capital firms will continue to attract an increasing share of institutional investors' allocations, while those firms with a poorer investment history will be obliged to downsize their operations and/or exit from the industry.

While the role of third-party equity is pivotal to the venture capital process, it is important to appreciate that it is only one element of the financing of the venture capital transaction. The final structure negotiated between the owner-manager(s) of an investee company and their venture capital backers will also require the commitment of a range of other critical investors in the agreed deal. On occasions, the nature of the financing package can be extremely complex. It therefore becomes critical that the entrepreneur seeking funds is well advised by a professional financial intermediary throughout the often lengthy negotiation process. In addition to one or more venture capitalists' provision of equity, the following additional sources of finance may also be contributed by other interested parties to the deal structure.

1. Owner's equity: the investees' contribution to the total equity package.
2. Senior debt: a package of primarily secured lending, which can include working capital facilities, provided by banks or other corporate lenders.
3. Mezzanine: unsecured debt with the opportunity to convert in part to equity-provided specialist finance houses, banks or, more rarely, the venture capital firm.
4. Loan notes: additional debt from any party to the deal.
5. Vendor finance: financial support from the seller including equity and/or debt.

In broad terms, the smaller the transaction value, the greater the dominance of senior debt and equity within the total finance structure. Other forms of finance rarely amount to more than 25 per cent of the total deal value. The likelihood of the owner-managers retaining a majority of ordinary, voting shares is in inverse proportion to the size of funds sought. The question of equity dilution and particularly the retention of majority ownership is an area of considerable potential contention between the investee owner-managers and the external equity providers (University of Cambridge, 1992). Furthermore the more perilous the economic environment for venture-backed businesses, the more likely that investors will demand a greater contribution of risk capital and/or guarantees from the investees themselves. For example, the Centre for Management Buy-Outs Research at Nottingham University's six monthly, average figures for all UK MBOs for the period from January 1989 to June 1992 show a marked change in the total contribution of equity and senior debt during a period of increasing economic downturn. The average equity contribution over the three-year period rose from 19 per cent to 41 per cent, while senior debt declined from 61 per cent to 39 per cent (CMBOR, 1992).

Venture capital intermediaries

The '1992 Report on Investment Activity' (BVCA, 1993) notes that the BVCA had 115 full (that is investing) members. Although BVCA members represent over 95 per cent of all available venture capital resources in the UK, there are a number of other sources of venture capital not represented by BVCA membership. The Levy Gee database of UK venture capital suggests a population of approximately 140 sources. A KPMG Peat Marwick/HMSO 1992 publication looking at UK sources of venture capital under £25,000 lists 197 firms providing equity, including BVCA members. The majority of non-BVCA providers cited are smaller sources with a specific economic development remit, although a number of corporate and private investors are also listed.

Venture capital firms may be generically classified by three criteria:

- ownership of the venture capital operation,
- investment focus of the fund(s),
- venture capital management behaviour/investee relationships.

These criteria are not exhaustive. Depending on the purpose of analysis, venture capital firms may also be categorised, for example, by the size of the funds at their disposal or their geographic location and dispersion.

Ownership

As already noted, venture capital firms may be described as captive, semi-captive and independent. Captive and semi-captive firms commonly represent the presence of diversified financial institutions in the area of venture capital. The ability of captives to raise additional funds from outside the parent organisation increases flexibility and also allows the resultant 'semi-captive' to offer performance-linked remuneration in line with the benefits of becoming a partner or employee within the management organisation of an independent fund (Murray, 1991a). Clearing bank-owned operations represent the single biggest source of captive activity. The four largest clearing banks in the UK each have an associated venture capital operation, as do a number of smaller retail banks and merchant banks. The strength of the clearing banks' names and the ability to use their countrywide networks of retail banking operations give their operations a national reach. In 1991 all captives took a 25 per cent share by value (£240m.) of total UK deals financed, of which bank captives represented 53 per cent.

An analysis of the market share of UK venture capital must necessarily reflect the significant presence of one organisation: 3i plc. Since its inception in 1945 as ICFC, 3i has invested approximately £6b. in 11,800 independent companies (3i plc, 1993). While generally regarded as a type of captive, given its size and organisational structure, the 1991 BVCA Report of Investment Activity categorises 3i as 'an independent via unquoted vehicle'. Certainly, in its national (and international) scope, with some 20 regional offices throughout Britain, 3i is comparable to the bank-type, venture capital operations. The absence of a reliance on fixed-term, institutional fund raising and 3i's common practice of providing investee firms with debt as well as equity finance also increase the similarity of 3i to its major clearing bank competitors. In 1992, 3i made 559 investments totalling £259m. to take a market share by number of total UK companies financed by venture capital to 48 per cent. These investments, including both debt and equity, represented 20 per cent of the value of total 1992 UK financings (BVCA, 1993), indicating 3i's continued publicised involvement in all stages of investment, particularly the early stage and smaller deal, where it is UK market leader.

As already noted, recent changes to the manner in which the BVCA categorises investments have increased the difficulty of making direct comparisons between captives, independents and 3i. However, in round terms, independents represented in 1992 some 60 per cent of all BVCA full members and were responsible for 50 per cent by value of all UK investment. It was the independent sector which grew most dramatically in the period 1980–89 and was responsible for the greatest increase of funds into the UK venture capital industry.

Independents are essentially agents acting on behalf of their predominantly institutional investors. Potential investors are invited to contribute to a fund which is constructed as a separate legal entity owned by the limited partners which provide the finance. The venture capitalist, which is more commonly organised as a partnership although several quoted investment trusts exist, is contracted to manage the fund. The management partnership or company gains income from its management services to the fund in undertaking the investment process from potential client selection to the final harvesting or realisation of the mature investment. The management organisation will also participate in the success of its activities through the negotiation with the investors of a 'carry'. This is a share of the capital gains realised by the fund subject to reaching minimum performance targets which are usually referenced to traded stock performance or the cost of capital over a comparable period.

Independent venture capital firms typically attempt to create a fund of a specific target size, defined period of commitment and target sector or investee scope. For example, in the UK, several venture capital firms in the mid-1980s were actively raising new, 'closed end' funds (for example, with a ten-year life) specialising in UK management buy-outs with a focus on manufacturing and consumer-based market sectors. Such funds, which were marketed internationally to potential investors, were typically between £50–200m. in size and would expect to attract between ten and 30 investors. The industry has seen a pronounced concentration in the allocation of investors' finances. The largest 30 full members of the BVCA, each with funds in excess of £100m., now represent approximately 90 per cent of the total funds under management of the UK industry (Murray 1992). The independents among these larger venture capital firms typically manage three to five separate funds and operate on a fund-raising cycle of approximately five years.

Investment focus

Venture capital firms invest at all stages in the life cycle of an enterprise, from inception to final sale. However it is rare for individual firms, other than the largest organisations, to cover the full spectrum of investment stages. The BVCA (1993) categorises eight investment stages of interest to individual venture capital firms (although the last two categories are strictly not stages).

1. *Start-up:* financing provided to companies for use in product development and initial marketing. Companies may be in the process of being set up or may have been in business for a short time, but have not sold their products commercially.
2. *Other early stage:* financing provided to companies that have completed the product development stage and require further funds

to initiate commercial manufacturing and sales. They may not yet be generating profit.

3. *Expansion financing:* capital provided for the growth and expansion of an established company. Funds may be used to finance increased production capacity, market or product development and/or provide additional working capital. Capital provided for turnaround situations is also included in this category, as is the refinancing of bank debt.

4. *Secondary purchase:* purchase of existing shares in a company from another venture capital firm, or from another shareholder or shareholders.

5. *Management buy-out:* funds provided to enable current operating management and investors to acquire an existing product line or business.

6. *Management buy-in:* funds provided to enable a manager or group of managers from outside the company to buy into the company.

7. *New investment:* first occasion of investment in a company by a venture capitalist.

8. *Follow-on investment:* further investment by the same venture capital organisation.

As Figure 7.2 indicates, MBOs (including MBIs) continue to be the single largest stage of investment activity, taking nearly two-thirds of all investment value provided by venture capital firms in the UK in 1992. The UK is different in this respect from the rest of the European venture capital community, where 'expansion capital' is

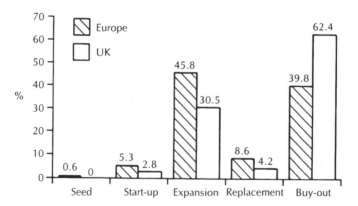

Source: EVCA (1993).

Figure 7.2 Percentage distribution of annual investment by stage of finance, Europe and UK, 1992

Table 7.3   UK venture capital activity in start-up and other early stage investments as a percentage of aggregate annual investment less MBO values

	1986	1987	1988	1989	1990	1991
% Total UK investment in start-ups and other early stage	40.9	28.5	23.0	38.9	24.4	13.0

Source: Murray and Lott (1995).

the largest single activity at 46 per cent of total value and 57 per cent of all investments in 1992.

It is noteworthy that the BVCA does not include 'seed capital' activity within its categorisation of venture capital. Seed capital may be defined as 'equity investment in the earliest conceptual or ideas stage of a new product, process or service in order to test the fundamental feasibility of a proposal'. This omission is perhaps understandable, given the wholesale unattractiveness of this investment category to commercial investors (Murray, 1994b). The EVCA 1993 *Yearbook* indicates that in 1992 £0.53m. was allocated in the UK to this activity. This sum represents 0.04 per cent of annual investments by value and, with ten recorded deals, 0.5 per cent of the total number of completed investments. The BVCA considers these figures too small to record and no information is provided on seed capital activity in their Annual Reports of Investment Activity, yet Murray and Francis' study (1992a) of ten European countries indicates the importance of this highly speculative, risk finance, particularly to new technology-based firms (NTBFs), a conclusion shared with American researchers (e.g. Bygrave and Timmons, 1992). The European Community's pilot initiative, the European Seed Capital Fund Scheme (ESCF), created in 1988, was formed to address directly this important funding gap.

An analysis of UK investment allocation over the period 1986 to 1991 (Table 7.3) indicates the decreasing share of total funds accorded to early stage (start-up and other early stage) financings when MBO/MBI figures are removed from the analysis. Murray (1994a) could only identify 16 specialist, early stage venture capital firms in the UK. Similarly there are less than ten specialist seed capital operations despite the underlying demand for small tranches of speculative equity. (One Cambridge based, British venture capital firm specialising in technology-based, seed capital investments received 350 applications for equity finance over the period 1990/91. It decided to make three investments during this period.) This trend away from early stage deals in the UK has also been corroborated by other authors (Sweeting, 1991; Dixon, 1991).

This relative decline in the support of new and young enterprises by *venture* capitalists is a source of embarrassment to the industry (Murray 1991a). Practitioners cite the unacceptably high levels of firm failure associated with early stage deals and their resultant unattractiveness when compared to later stage investments, particularly development capital and MBOs. Venture capital managers also noted the impracticability of the industry, as it is presently structured, to evaluate and support, post-investment, literally thousands of young, and frequently inexperienced, entrepreneurs seeking funding in the equity gap range of less than £250,000. The time and monetary costs of the process of project evaluation and the associated 'due diligence' are broadly insensitive to project size. Conversely project income and potential capital gain are directly related to the size of the investment. Accordingly the majority of UK venture capital firms decline an involvement in start-up and, particularly, seed capital investments while actively competing for the more scarce supply of MBOs, and other later stage deals in the greater than £10 million category.

Some observers have argued that the term 'venture capital' is misleading and unhelpful. They argue that early stage, *venturing activity*, which Murray (1991a, 1994a) has termed 'new capital' and Bygrave and Timmons (1992) label 'classic venture capital', encompasses the financing of new and early stage enterprises. Thus the great majority of the industry's activity and finances are now focused on later stage, *development capital* or, in Murray's terms, 'replacement capital'. A development capital deal can frequently include an injection of additional capital from the institutional investors. However, development capital is essentially concerned with changing the ownership structure of the shareholding of the business.

It is no coincidence that a number of venture capital firms have, over the last three years, publicly changed their names. Most notably, 3i now calls itself 'an investment capitalist' and the Midland Bank's venture capital subsidiary, Midland Montagu Ventures, is now renamed as Midland Private Equity.

Management behaviour and investee relations

A successful venture capital firm has to demonstrate two cardinal skills: it has to be able to attract and identify firms that will realise exceptional profit performances, and it has to be able to direct its commercial, financial and industry experience in a manner which will directly add value to the activities of the client investee firm. Venture capital firms may be divided into two broad camps defined by the degree of active involvement which they take in their investee companies. 'Hands on' venture capital firms actively engage in the management processes of their portfolio of investee firms. They are involved in strategic decision making and, on occasions, may also become involved directly in day-to-day operations during periods of particular problems or critical activities. There is an explicit belief held by these investment executives that their industry knowledge and skills, along with their experience of a wide range of client operations, can have a direct influence on the successful outcome of the enterprise. 'Hands off' venture capitalists take a diametrically opposed view, arguing that it is not their role to become involved in the direct managerial operation of the investee company. They argue that this responsibility must remain exclusively that of the entrepreneur or owner-management team. Hands off investors will only directly intervene in the management of the investee firm when exceptional, and usually difficult, circumstances dictate that they must take greater control in order to protect their investment.

A number of American academics have looked at alternative typologies for describing the nature of the relationship between the venture capitalist and the management of the investee company. Sapienza and Timmons (1989) defined three role types: strategic, supportive and networking. They noted that these functions are broadly consistent with MacMillan *et al.* (1989) four categories of 'sounding board, financier, contact and management recruiter'. While these categorisations may add further useful insights, they do not conflict with the more fundamental hands on and hands off dichotomy.

The freedom to operate a hands on or hands off regime is strongly influenced by the investment policy of the venture capital firm. A 'portfolio approach' to investment is commonly adopted by the larger venture capital firms, particularly 3i and the bank captives. The diversification of risk by a portfolio operator dictates that client companies come from several stages of investment and/or from a wide range of industry sectors. With portfolios frequently including between 50 and 200 investees, it is unrealistic to assume that the investor managers can allocate significant time to each company outside crisis situations. Gorman and Sahlman (1989) showed that the average US 'hands off' investor spends on average 80 hours per year on each investee firm in onsite contact, plus a further 30 hours of telephone contact. This can be contrasted to the average contact time of 200 hours per firm allocated by hands on investors in Murray and Francis' study of seed capital providers. 3i, particularly, has made a virtue of the reality of its scarce managerial resources (given that it had investments in over 3,700 companies in 1992) by advertising to potential investees that it does not wish to interfere in their businesses. Investor control in hands off operation relies on rigorous ex ante evaluation of the investment proposal and a strong reliance on timely management accounting and financial reporting from the client firm, supported by monthly or quarterly visits by the responsible investment executive.

Hands on venture capital operations are smaller and more specialist in industry and/or technology focus. They are usually confined to a limited geographic focus in order to enable close involvement and supervision. They are frequently associated with early stage operations where the entrepreneur is likely to need substantial support and advice in areas outside his or her particular competence. Seed capital operations in the UK, continental Europe and the USA are universally hands on relationships. The seed capital investment executive is likely to be responsible for a maximum of five client companies as opposed to an industry average of ten clients per investment executives (Venture Economics Ltd, 1990). Hands on venture capital firms will select proposals where their own industry knowledge, experience and contacts can become a direct resource to the client. Sapienza (1992) argues that venture capital firms are more likely to add value for 'innovator' entrepreneurs who are seeking a longer-term partner, rather than exclusively a new source of finance. In the event of having limited direct industry experience, it is common for hands on investors to ensure that their interests are represented by placing on the board of directors a non-executive representative with material industry-specific knowledge. However it is common practice for both hands on and hands off investors to require non-executive representation on the investee company's board of directors.

As the recent UK recession threatened the viability of many young or small companies, it has become more common for venture capital firms, perforce, to become more hands on in operation. Their ability to accomplish this has been helped by an industry trend to recruit more investment executives from senior positions in sectors and industries of relevance to the market focus of the venture capital firms (Murray, 1991(a)). However the majority of executive personnel in venture capital firms, with the exception of technology investors (Murray and Lot, 1992), continue to be recruited largely from financial disciplines (Venture Economics Ltd, 1990; Davie, 1991)/

The logic of the hands on mode of operation is that the involvement of the venture capital adviser can directly add value to the operation of the client firm, yet there has been very little testing of this critical assumption. MacMillan *et al.* (1989) in the US and Fredrikson *et al.* (1990) in Sweden have attempted to test this assertion. In each case, these researchers did not find a robust correlation between the provision of hands on advice and the subsequent economic success of the investee companies receiving this form of support. Murray and Francis found that surveyed owner-managers of seed capital investee companies in eight European countries rated the advice of their venture capital sponsors less useful than alternatives sources of advice in all areas other than finance. Similar concerns with the competencies of advisers available to new NTBFs in the former East Germany were found by Lange and Crossfield (1993).

While the ability to share the broader experience of investment executives with their investee clients remains intuitively attractive, there is as yet negligible empirical support of the effectiveness of this mode of venture capital operation. This reality is of particular relevance to seed capital operations and regional development funds supporting early stage venture capital investments where a hands on style of management is viewed as a necessity rather than a choice.

The users

The users of venture capital finance can also be defined by the various stages of finance, ranging from the tentative idea of a technology entrepreneur seeking seed capital finance to the established company seeking additional finance for a specific product or market opportunity. Venture capital is rarely the first choice of funding of any entrepreneur or management team. It is usually sought after own funds and bank borrowing facilities have been exhausted. For this reason, venture capital is sometimes viewed as 'the funding of last resort'. The reason for such a tentative approach is understandable. The majority of SME entrepreneurs do not easily give up exclusive ownership of a firm which they may have nurtured and supported over the first critical years (Small Business Research Trust 1990). However rapidly growing firms often find that working and investment capital constraints are a severe brake on their ambitions. Storey *et al.* (1989) noted that it was common for the 'fast track' firms in their sample to have clashed with their bank managers regarding their very high growth ambitions and thus need for increasing increments of working capital financed by further bank debt.

It is just these fast growth firms with management of exceptional commitment and ambition that the venture capitalists would see as their natural customer base. Fast track entrepreneurs want growth, and venture capital investors need growth. Investee companies approaching venture capital firms have commonly used up their borrowing capacity with tangible assets already assigned to secure existing borrowings. Thus an external injection of equity remains one of the few options left to the management. The firm which is considering venture capital is unlikely to be large or profitable enough to consider a listing on the secondary market. (In the UK, the Unlisted

Securities Market is being terminated in 1996. Firms seeking a stock market listing may use its replacement, the Alternative Investment Market, if they are not of sufficient size to consider a main market listing.) It is also largely excluded from the diversity of instruments available to larger firms (Buckland and Davies 1987). For the MBO/ MBI management teams, their objective is partial ownership and operating control of the target business. When the market value of the business exceeds the unencumbered asset base from which new loans can be raised, institutional equity often becomes the most feasible source of new finance.

The established but financial constrained firm may ultimately choose to accept a lower rate of growth, rather than agree to the equity dilution consequent on venture capital involvement. For the start-up project requiring substantial capital expenditure or the MBO opportunity presented to incumbent management, the freedom to proceed without external equity is severely proscribed. Murray and Wright (1996) found that approximately three-quarters of MBOs of £2–10m. were initiated by the parent company's decision to sell the MBO team's division or business. The MBO teams were, in consequence, commonly put under severe time pressure to raise the necessary purchase finance. This urgency gave the venture capital partners a considerable negotiating advantage and Murray and Wrights' respondents held ambivalent attitudes regarding the high costs associated with using venture capital finance. Conversely, Murray and Francis (op.cit) found that the majority of recipients of seed capital within the ESCF scheme believed that the deal arrangement with their equity providers was fair and reasonable. Their positive attitudes might be a consequence of their clear understanding of the projects' critical reliance on an outside investor, coupled with a recognition of the very limited supply of such funding.

Management buy-outs and buy-ins

The single biggest product for the UK venture capital industry throughout the 1980s has been the management buy-out (MBOs). Over the years 1979–91, the Centre for Management Buy-Out Research (CMBOR) at Nottingham University recorded 3,506 MBOs with an aggregate deal value of £19.1b. There were also 994 Management Buy-Ins (MBIs) worth £7.2b. over the same period. While management buy-out/buy-in volumes reached a record high in 1990 at 594 deals, the value of annual transactions dropped from £7,501 million in the previous year to £3,110 million. This 58 per cent drop was, in large part, due to the decline in frequency of the largest deals (greater than £250m.). In 1989, 12 listed company buy-outs,

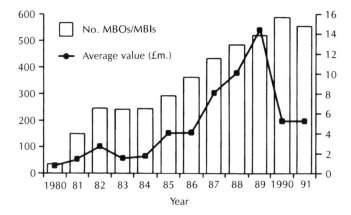

Source: CMBOR (1992).

Figure 7.3   Growth of management buy-outs and buy-ins, 1980–91

valued in total at £3,780m. occurred. In 1990 there were only four listed buy-outs totalling £170m. MBO/MBI figures for 1991 show a continued decline in the total value of transactions since 1989. At £2,829m. the aggregate value of MBO/MBI deals was the lowest since 1986 (CMBOR, 1992) (Table 7.3) The importance of MBOs/ MBIs to the UK venture capital industry can be evidenced if their value is removed from UK annual investment statistics. When excluded, annual venture capital investment has declined in nominal value terms over the last four years from £565m. in 1988 to £445m. in 1991.

Twenty of the leading UK venture capitalists in the Autumn of 1990 (Murray, 1991a) estimated that MBOs would continue to be the single most important product in the UK venture capital industry, still representing 51 per cent of the value of annual transactions in 1995. They cited the necessary restructuring to the UK economy during the recessionary period, coming after a period of historically high merger and acquisition activity from 1986–89, as an opportunity for continued MBO deal flow. The record number of MBOs in 1990, and the sustained level of 444 deals in 1991, supports this assertion. This restructuring would also give opportunities for management buy-ins but, with two exceptions, of the venture capitalists specialising in MBIs, the majority (77 per cent) of respondents believed the additional risks of MBIs would continue to constrain interest among venture capital investors. MBIs were estimated to take 26 per cent of annual funds invested in MBOs/MBIs in 1995. In 1991, the percentage split in value terms between MBO and MBI venture capital investments was 76 and 24, respectively.

Murray's respondents also believed that, while MBOs would continue to be the single largest product in value terms by 1995, a greater proportion of annual investment (estimated at 36 per cent; 1991 actual 34 per cent) would be applied to later stage financing including development capital, secondary finance and, reflecting the problems of recession, rescue-type refinancing deals. The ability to provide capital for firms that remain basically sound but are financially constrained as traditional sources of borrowing and new equity become less available was seen as the single biggest contemporary opportunity, being mentioned by 59 per cent of respondents.

The continued resilience of MBOs/MBIs as a venture capital mainstay, even in times of recession, is illustrated by the '1992 Report on Investment Activity' published by the BVCA (May 1993). At a total venture capital investment value of £807m. in 1992, this one investment category was responsible for 64 per cent of annual investment by BVCA members and represented just over a quarter of all financings in the year. Given that an increasing number of MBOs and MBIs were the result of rescue and receivership situations, the aggregate demand for this product has the additional attraction of appearing to be relatively less sensitive to recessionary factors.

The investment process

Tyebjee and Bruno's (1984) five stage, decision process model of venture capital investment activity (Figure 7.4) accurately illustrates the role played by the venture capitalist, namely identifying, appraising, investing in and subsequently advising the management of client investee firms. Interestingly the model does not include the deal realisation or exit from the venture capitalist's portfolio, a critical factor in the success of an individual investment. However the authors do note the importance of 'cash out potential' in their appraisal of venture capitalists' evaluation criteria.

The initial contact may be via an entrepreneur approaching the venture capital firm directly. A number of major UK venture capitalists, particularly the largest UK firm, 3i plc, undertake substantial advertising activity directly to the business community. The venture capitalists also have a network of 'intermediary' organisations such as accountants, clearing and merchants banks, commercial law firms and so on who also direct potential investees to the equity providers. However the efficacy of the financial adviser as a conduit of proposals to venture capital financiers cannot be assumed. In a 1993 study of MBOs in the £2–10m. deal size, 40 per cent of the management teams argued that their financial advisor was not influential in iden-

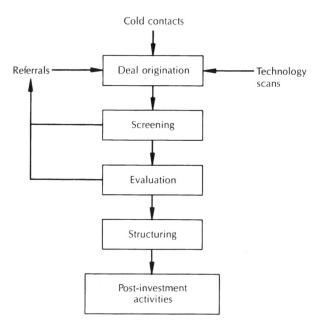

Figure 7.4 Tyebjee and Bruno's decision process model of venture capital activity

tifying or helping select the venture capital company that eventually financed the MBO (Murray and Wright 1996). In addition, venture capitalists may syndicate the financing of deals with other venture capitalists, in part to offset risk but also for reasons of reciprocity in deal flow. According to the respondents from Murray's 1990 survey, this practice is declining. The two primary reasons given for reduced syndication were the increasing scarcity of attractive project proposals in a competitive market-place and the added complexity of investor control in a syndicated deal.

As Bannock (1991) and Dixon (1991) both note, venture capitalists receive vastly more applications that they could, or would wish to, finance. Initial screening, usually based on a brief appraisal of the business plan submitted with the original proposal, will invariably result in the rejection of approximately 80 per cent of all applications. The rejection may be for tangible reasons that the venture capitalist believes the deal is too small (or too large), is in a sector or activity which is unattractive to the fund or is one where a sufficient exposure to similar investments is already achieved. The rejection may be for the more subjective reasons of the appraiser's initial personal reaction to the investment proposed. However many investors are overwhelmed by applications, with entrepreneurs commonly making multiple applications to several venture capital firms. Thus this first 'cut' at the deal flow is invariably cursory.

It is for the remaining 20 per cent of applicants that the serious evaluative experience of the venture capitalist is largely employed. The business plan becomes the foundation document on which further product/market and financial investigations are conducted. These internal analyses are supported by external appraisals including accountants' reports and specialist evaluations by consultants experienced in the proposed area of activity. During this process the entrepreneur and management team are invited to participate in repeated appraisals and reformulations of the proposed plan. Investigations will also encompass the personal and career histories and ambitions of the entrepreneur and management team.

It is only after the venture capitalist has convinced him/herself of the merit, attractiveness and commercial feasibility of the project, including the capabilities of the management team, that the negotiations on the nature of the deal structure are seriously pursued. The allocation of potential rewards on the successful outcome of the investment is seen by the investee managers as a 'zero sum game' and negotiations can be protracted and occasionally heated. For most management teams such negotiations are a 'once in a lifetime' exercise, while for the venture capitalists they are their professional milieu. Managers who have gone through this experience repeatedly comment on the complexity and stress of what can be an extremely protracted exercise, often lasting over six months. The emotional tension during this process is raised on the occasions where an attractive proposal is being bid for by a number of competing venture capital firms in a so-called 'beauty parade' – a free market situation that venture capitalists and other corporate financiers generally find unattractive.

Determining the decision criteria on which venture capitalists appraise investment proposals is one of the most popularly researched areas by academics (see Wells, 1974; Pointdexter, 1976; Tyebjee and Bruno 1984; MacMillan *et al.*, 1985; Goslin and Barge, 1986; Dubini, 1989; Dixon 1991; Murray and Francis, 1992). The conformity of findings is high and can well be summarised by MacMillan *et al.*'s pithy conclusion: 'There is no question that, irrespective of the horse (product), horse race (market), or odds (financial criteria), it is the jockey (entrepreneur) who fundamentally determines whether the venture capitalist will place the bet at all.' More numerically put, Gormann and Salhman (1989) noted that, in their survey of 49 venture capitalists, 91 of 96 cases of failure were in part ascribed to the 'shortcomings of senior management' and that this was the overriding factor in 62 of the cited cases.

Thus, despite the wealth of market and financial data frequently available to the evaluators of project proposals, the final decision pivots on the venture capitalist' objective and subjective assessment of the quality of the entrepreneur and project management. While objective managerial track records may be available for later stage deals and, particularly, MBOs/MBIs, in the case of seed capital and start-up projects, the entrepreneur may well be a completely unknown quantity. As one venture capitalist ruefully noted to the author, 'You only know that you have invested in a maniac when he has cashed the cheque!'

The quality of the business plan and the rigour of the financial data included may well indicate the competence of the entrepreneur (or, possibly, the professional skills of his/her accountant or consultant advisor). However, Dixon (op. cit) has noted the limited use by venture capitalists of modern financial theory in choosing investments and constructing their portfolios to optimise risk/returns. Sampling 30 specialist UK venture capital organisations, Dixon evinced surprise that none of his respondents explicitly classified projects into risk categories: 83 per cent of his sample evaluated risk on an individual project basis without reference to overall portfolio risk. In a related question, only 27 per cent of the sample attempted to mitigate risk through an actively diversified portfolio. Dixon attenuates his implicit criticism by noting the difficulties of information asymmetries between the investor and the prospective applicant for venture capital finance.

In preference to more sophisticated models, the venture capital industry uses almost universally the annualised Internal Rate of Return (IRR) threshold for individual project financial assessment. The predominant use of IRRs is despite the well known shortcomings of this statistic (Brieley and Myers, 1984). The projected target IRR is primarily determined by the stage of investment. The IRR value becomes, in effect, the surrogate for risk (Murray and Lott 1995). The high IRR threshold against which a project is appraised is the result of the reality that less than one project in five will likely achieve the outstanding level of returns necessary to ensure the performance of the overall fund (Table 7.4).

Corporate venturing

A discussion on the purpose and nature of corporate venturing arguably sits somewhat awkwardly within a chapter on venture capital. Corporate venturers are not banks or other types of financial professionals but are international trading and manufacturing com-

Table 7.4   Venture capital firms' minimum IRR requirement by investment stage for technology and non-technology investment

Investment stage	Non-technology mean IRR %	Stnd dev. %	N	Technology mean IRR%	Stnd. dev. %	N
Seed	55.0	20.31	9	57.1	16.95	14
Start-up	49.5	11.64	22	52.4	11.07	23
Expansion	36.3	6.91	28	39.1	8.14	31
MBO/MBI	32.7	4.55	22	35.5	4.80	22

Source: Murray and Lott (1995).

panies. Their logic for investing in new or young companies is not primarily for shorter-term, financial returns but is related to issues of innovation and strategic foresight. However corporate investors do represent a specialised source of equity to new businesses, albeit one which is restricted largely to new technology sectors. Accordingly corporate venturing can properly be viewed as a variant of venture capital.

Corporate venturing may be defined as the involvement of industrial corporations in the creation of new business enterprise using the organisation's resources of finance, management and technical expertise to support new opportunities outside the formal business structure of the corporation. The created or supported venture is frequently operated autonomously from the parent body, although close links are maintained. Ultimately the enterprise may be incorporated into the parent or 'spun off' as a separate entity, depending on the relevance of the enterprise and technology to the current and future core competencies and products/markets of the parent. In financing and resourcing the new enterprise, the corporate parent is acting in an analogous manner to a venture capitalist.

With few exceptions, corporate venturing is noteworthy by its absence rather than its popularity. As Lorenz notes (*Financial Times*, 2 July, 1993, p.13) corporate venturing is a concept that regularly falls in and out of fashion in the UK. It is more established in the USA where there are indications of a renaissance in popularity. In the USA, 180 corporate/small venture company relationships, with a total of $950m. equity purchases, were recorded in the first three quarters of 1990 (Mast, 1991). Exemplars, which span industry sectors but concentrate on high technology areas, include General Electric, Monsanto, Xerox, Elf, Apple, 3M, IBM and Kyocera.

The current interest in corporate venturing, in Mast's opinion, is a consequence of the need of the corporation to keep in close contact with strategically important technological innovations occurring externally to the firm, particularly in areas peripheral to the firm's present R&D effort. Increasingly scrutiny of the cost effectiveness of huge corporate research budgets has also engendered interest in alternative means of gaining access to new technologies by utilising the creativity of NTBFs. The benefits of 'first mover advantage' in a critical new technology can be immense. The cost of corporate venturing is the time and effort necessary to create, manage and nurture the delicate relationship between the founder managers of a relatively tiny enterprise and the corporation.

Corporate venturing has moved from an earlier logic of attempting to find major diversification opportunities to a means of supporting existing business units. The activity may be used as one channel for capturing new and potentially attractive technologies. It is for this 'technology search' reason that Hurry *et al.* (1992) suggests that Japanese venture capital firms retain an interest in technology investments in the USA. The initial investment becomes a 'shadow option' on the new technology. Alternatively, corporate venturing may also be used to gain a return on accumulated research investment by spinning out non-core, but still valuable, technologies to trade buyers. Monsanto, Apple, 3M and Xerox have all used independent venture capital conduits for this purpose.

Corporates may invest via the vehicle of their own, internally managed fund or through the agency of a third-part venture capital fund. Mast notes a trend towards investment in specialist rather than generalist funds. Alternatively the corporate may allocate equity finance for ad hoc investments and dispense with a fund structure. The recent creation of venture funds in the UK, including British Telecom and a number of other privatised utilities, is a recognition of the imperative of exploring all avenues of technological innovation, and the importance of NTBFs in this process. If a fashion, corporate venturing may well become in vogue.

The future: issues and prognoses

Industry cyclicality and maturity

The UK venture capital industry is entering its 'teenage years'. The majority of firms, particularly independents, currently operating in the UK are less than ten years old. Since 1979, the more established firms in the industry have seen a period of recession, followed by several years of increased economic growth, only to be replaced by a second recession at the start of the 1990s. As Figure 7.1 shows, the industry has grown more rapidly than the underlying economy, only to contract at a faster rate when the latest recession undermined the prosperity of smaller companies. In essence, the industry has gone through one economic cycle in a sector which American experience has shown is highly cyclical (Sahlman 1989; Bygrave and Timmons, 1992). One outcome of cyclical activity is that the time at which a fund is raised and starts investing has a major effect on the subsequent profitability of the fund (Pointdexter, 1976; Bygrave *et al.* 1989).

Irrespective of the influence of the wider economic environment, Murray (1992) argues that the UK venture capital industry is entering a period of 'industry maturity'. Using a framework by Porter (1980), the UK venture capital industry fits closely the criteria for maturity that Porter isolates. Again in this context, a dynamic use of Porter's well-known 'competitive forces model' (Porter, 1979) clearly illustrates the changing nature of competition facing the UK industry (Murray, 1991b). The competitive forces model has been used by Sahlman (1989) in the USA and Lloyd (1989) in the UK to describe the two countries venture capital industries. Murray's model differs from these two authors in describing the institutional investors as the primary 'customers' of the venture capital firms rather than, as Sahlman and Lloyd suggest, the institutions being suppliers' to the venture capital firms. Similarly Murray descries the investee firms seeking funds as suppliers, to which the venture capitalists attempt to add value, rather than as customers in the two authors' alternative translation of Porter's model. Murray's view is supported by recent observations from senior management from major institutional investors including Postel Investment Management in the UK (Brakell, 1988) and the CEO at Hambros International Venture Fund in the USA.

In summary, Murray argues that the bargaining power of the external forces having an impact on the venture capital industry and its component firms can be seen to have altered significantly if viewed in two time spans: 1980–87 and 1988–93. In the later and more contemporary period (Figure 7.5), the industry is characterised by (1) powerful and sceptical institutional providers of capital assisted by specialist investment consultants (commonly termed 'gatekeepers'), and (2) a shortage of attractive investee clients who are, in turn, more informed about the nature of venture capital and the competitive offerings available. Both of these groups can exert increased bargaining power over the price of the venture capitalist's product/service, thereby eroding the returns to the venture capitalist. In the venture capitalist's favour, the threat from new entrants to the industry has diminished and the total number of BVCA full members has declined by 7 per cent since its peak of 124 members in 1989. During the recent period of the clearing banks' concern over their high exposure to SME lending, the availability of bank debt as a 'substitute product' for investee firms has similarly diminished. However institutional funders continue to have a full range of alter-

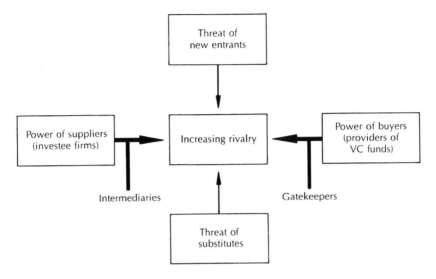

Source: Murray (1991b).

Figure 7.5 *A 'competitive forces' analysis of the UK venture capital industry in 1993*

native asset classes as substitute products for venture capital. The threat of a funds famine remains in a period of uncertainty as to the long-term profitability of venture capital investment.

Fund profitability

Arguably the most serious issue facing the UK venture capital industry centres on the question of the profitability of venture capital investment. It is an extraordinary fact that the industry has attracted several billion pounds of investment over the 1980s with little substantive evidence as to the profitability of such investment. Given that the majority of independent venture capital firms have raised the bulk of their funds on ten-year fixed terms since 1985, there are few organisations which have fully terminated individual funds and distributed the net proceeds of their investment activity. Thus new funds have had to be marketed to potential investors on the basis of interim figures and expected terminal returns. In a contemporary environment of investors' concerns as to the likely outcome of historic investments, there are substantial pressures on venture capital companies to demonstrate unequivocally the success of their investment performance to date. A number of venture capitalists investing late in the cycle of the early to mid-1980s boom and paying high prices for companies which were subsequently to suffer in the recession after 1989, will be hard put to demonstrate adequate track records to new investors. These potential casualties will further drive the present process of industry concentration as investors discriminate in favour of those venture capital firms with demonstrably successful track records.

Industry 'shake-out' or 'fade-out'

The term 'shake-out' is frequently used to describe the likely removal of unsuccessful venture capital firms from the industry. However this graphic description ignores the substantial short-run barriers to exit for investors holding a portfolio of unquoted, small companies. For those venture capital firms with attractive portfolio companies but a shortage of uncommitted capital, the opportunity of a fund refinancing or a change in fund management is feasible. Conversely, for those distressed funds with limited finances and portfolio companies of dubious potential, the outcome may be a gradual running down of the portfolio with exits negotiated at discounted prices. In these cases the description of market exit may be more accurately termed a 'fade-out'.

The threat of a funds famine and the consequent prospect of a long-run decline in the number of UK venture capital firms may be to the direct advantage of the captives and 3i plc. Provided that the captives can convince their parent organisations of the strength of their present and future performance, their preferential access to secured finances becomes a significant strategic advantage in a market characterised by capital scarcity. Similarly the size of 3i, the diversity of its investee portfolio and the security of its owners, give it a unique capability to exploit its access to international capital markets as a source of additional funds. Thus, if the supply of finance into the UK industry continues to remain a problem, it is expected that one consequence could be an increase in the market share of captives and 3i.

Future venture capital firm strategies

McNulty *et al.* (1993) have noted the difficulties of professional firms moving to a marketing-focused culture. Their observations also have currency within the venture capital industry. A 1991 study by Cranfield Management School MBA students of a sample of UK venture capital firms indicated the apparently modest attention given by the management teams to issues of marketing and strategy (see also Murray and Wright 1996). In a contemporary environment characterised by a shortage of funds, an oversupply of venture capital firms relative to the declining demand for their services, and increasingly discriminating and informed investee companies (including their advisers), venture capital firms have little choice but to embrace a strategic perspective.

It is argued that venture capital firms will be obliged to make coherent decisions about product/market choices. They will also have to define the nature of their 'sustainable competitive advantage' (Porter, 1980). In the absence of strategic differentiation, there is a pronounced danger that venture capital will become a commodity with customer/client choice made purely on price between firms offering, in reality, near identical services. Nixon's (1993) survey of MBO management teams indicated that a majority of respondents harboured some misgivings about the professionalism of both their advisers and their venture capital firms. Venture capital firms are also going to have to take issues of customer service and quality more seriously.

For the larger and more financially secure venture capital firms, a portfolio approach to investment will remain an attainable investment strategy. For smaller funds, there are likely to be greater pressures for specialisation, whether by, for example, stage of investment, industry sector knowledge or geography. Chronic funding problems will also encourage novel prescriptions in the manner in which venture capital firms relate to both investors and investee clients. Venture capital firms will also increasingly come to recognise the strategic information contained within their historic portfolios. Better information used strategically is a classic form of competitive advantage.

Just being a 'me too' provider of equity finance with negligible distinguishing benefits will not be a sustainable position in the harsher competitive environment of the later 1990s. The 'Klondike Years' of the early to mid-1980s are over. Successful venture capitalists are going to have to work harder and more cleverly.

The future for investee applicants

Overall about one proposal in 20 is accepted by the venture capital industry. This statistic has all the shortcomings of aggregated figures. It is suggested that, given the increasing profit performance demands which will be placed on venture capital funds, it is unlikely that project evaluators will relax their existing selection criteria. Saying 'no' will remain a cheaper and less risky decision than taking on an investee firm of dubious viability. There remains little indication that the industry will devote more of its resources and interest to early stage deals. European or domestic government policies may attenuate this situation at the margin, but do not address the fundamental issue of the high risks and low profitability of investing equity in seed capital, start-up and other early stage deals. Unless governments accept arguments for the wider social good of encouraging early stage venture capital investment (for example, the BJTU scheme in Germany, which underwrites part of the costs and risks of investing in NTBFs via direct support of the venture capital investors), the prognosis for an increase in the availability of equity specifically addressed at the equity gap level of less than £250,000 remains poor.

However the outlook for later stage deals (replacement capital) is more positive. Both in the UK and in continental Europe, investing equity in established businesses with assessable management track records and defined markets already takes the lion's share of venture capital investment. In the UK, MBOs will continue to attract competition from equity providers, particularly medium and larger MBOs of more than £10 million. Post-recession restructuring of mid-sized to large firms and the present trend away from diversified organisations will continue to ensure a regular supply of such opportunities. However post-recession management teams are likely to face increased competition from trade buyers for attractive enterprises. It is also probable that MBO opportunities will continue to grow in the major economies of continental Europe from their current modest levels.

Nonetheless, it is worth reiterating that venture capital will only be made available to a minority of companies deemed to have exceptional profit and growth potential, and managed by entrepreneurs who are viewed by the investor as having the skills and experience to realise these projections. Prospective applicants for venture capital would be well advised to use their management skills in the identification, selection and marketing of their proposals to their target equity providers. At the first cut, project proposals receive less than 20 minutes of a venture capital assessor's time in making the decision to investigate further. An unprofessional and amateur approach to a venture capitalist by an applicant company makes a rejection that much more probable.

Exercises

1. Write an essay exploring whether the 'equity gap' really exists. If it does, can anything be done to fill it?
2. Write a report outlining the criteria that should be used to assess whether a potential investment is suitable for venture capital funding.

3. Write a report highlighting why MBOs and MBIs are attractive investments for venture capitalists.
4. List the pros and cons of investing in start-up, other early stage and expansion stage as a venture capitalist. Write a report evaluating their attractiveness.
5. Write an essay evaluating the importance of 3i to the UK economy. Has their investment portfolio changed since they were floated on the stock market?
6. Write a report to your superior in British Telecom outlining why the company should become involved in corporate venturing and how such an initiative should be administered.
7. Write an essay exploring whether the venture capital industry really is entering a period of maturity.
8. Write an essay comparing the provision of equity finance in the UK with the provision in Germany.

References and selected bibliography

Advisory Council on Science and Technology (ACOST) (1990), *The Enterprise Challenge: Overcoming Barriers To Growth In Small Firms*, HMSO.
Bannock, G. (1987), *Britain in the 1980s: Enterprise Reborn*, 3i plc.
Bannock, G. (1991), *Venture Capital and the Equity Gap*, National Westminster Bank.
Brakell, J.R. (1988), 'Institutional Investor Expectations from Investment in Venture Capital', *1988 Guide to European Venture Capital Sources*, Venture Economics Ltd.
Brieley, R. and S. Myers (1984) *Principles of Corporate Finance*, 2nd edn, McGraw-Hill.
British Venture Capital Association (1984–92), *Annual Reports on Investment Activity*, BVCA.
British Venture Capital Association (1995), *Directory*, BVCA.
Buckland, R. and E.W. Davis (1987) 'Barriers to Entry in the Unlisted Securities Market: the Significance of Administrative Expenses', *Accounting and Business Research*, 17/68, pp.301–10.
Bygrave, W.D. and J.A. Timmons (1992), *Venture Capital at the Crossroads*, Harvard Business School Press.
Centre for Management Buy-Out Research (1992), *UK Management Buy-Outs 1992*, CMBOR.
Bygrave, W.D., N. Fast, R. Kholyian, L. Vincent and W. Yue (1989), 'Early Rates of Return of 131 Venture Capital Funds Started 1978–1984', *Journal of Business Venturing*, vol. 4, pp.93–105.
Confederation of British Industry (1993), *Finance for Growth*, CBI.
Davie, J. (1991), 'Finding and Keeping Good Venture Capital Managers', *Venture Capital Journal*, July, pp.21–6.
Dixon, R. (1991), 'Venture Capital and the Appraisal of Investments', *Omega*, vol. 19, no. 5, pp.333–44.
Dubini, P. (1989), 'Which Venture Capital-Backed Entrepreneurs Have the Best Chances of Succeeding?', *Journal of Business Venturing*, vol. 4, pp.123–32.

European Venture Capital Association (1992), *1992 EVCA Yearbook. Venture Capital in Europe*, KPMG.

Financial Times Survey (1993), *Management Buy-Outs*, 8 December, pp.1–XII.

Fredriksen, O., C. Olofsson and C. Wahlbin (1990), *The Role of Venture Capital in the Development of Portfolio Companies*, Paper for the SMS Conference Strategic Bridging Stockholm, September.

Gorman, M. and W.A. Sahlman (1989), 'What Do Venture Capitalists Do?', *Journal of Business Venturing*, vol. 4, no. 4, pp231–48.

Goslin, N.L. and B. Barge (1986), 'Entrepreneurial Qualities Considered in Venture Capital Support', *Frontiers of Entrepreneurial Research*, Babson College.

Hannah, L. (1992), *The Finance of Innovation 1880–1980*, Economic and Social Sciences Research Council funded project, ESRC.

Harrison, R.T. and C.M. Mason (1992), 'International Perspectives on the Supply of Informal Venture Capital', *Journal of Business Venturing*, vol. 7, pp.459–75.

Hovgaard, S. (1991), *London Business School/British Venture Capital Association Survey on Venture Capital in the UK*, BVCA.

Hurry, D., A.T. Miller and E.H. Bowman (1992), 'Calls on High-Technology: Japanese Exploration of Venture Capital Investments in the United States', *Strategic Management Journal*, vol. 13, pp.85–101.

Lange, A. and N. Crossfield (1993), 'Marketing Perspectives of State-Supported NTBFs in Former East Germany', unpublished MBA dissertation, University of Warwick, England.

Lloyd, S. (1989), 'Special Report: an Industry on the Brink of the 1990s', *UK Venture Capital Journal*, November, p.10.

Lorenz, T. (1989), *Venture Capital Today*, 2nd edn, Woodhead Faulkner.

MacMillan, H. (1931), *Report of the Committee on Finance and Industry*, Cmd 3897, HMSO.

MacMillan, I.C., D.M. Kulow and R. Koylian (1989), 'Venture Capitalists' Involvement in Their Investments: Extent and Performance', *Journal of Business Venturing*, vol. v, no.1, pp.27–47.

MacMillan, I.C., R. Siegal and P.N. Subba Narishima (1985), 'Criteria Used by Venture Capitalists to Evaluate New Venture Proposals', *Journal of Business Venturing*, vol. 1, no. 1, pp.126–41.

Mast, R. (1991), 'The Changing Nature of Corporate Venture Capital Programs', *Venture Capital Journal*, March/April, pp.26–33.

McNulty, T., R. Whittington and R. Whipp (1993), 'Market-Driven Change in Public and Private Sectors', paper presented at Warwick Business School seminar on ESRC-financed research project.

Murray, G.C. (1991a), *Change and Maturity in the UK Venture Capital Industry 1991–95*, British Venture Capital Association, 1991.

Murray, G.C. (1991b), 'The Changing Nature of Competition in the UK Venture Capital Industry: a Competitive Force Analysis', *National Westminster Bank Quarterly Review*, November, pp.65–80.

Murray, G.C. (1992), 'A Challenging Market Place for Venture Capital', *Long Range Planning*, vol. 25, no. 6, pp.79–86.

Murray G.C. (1994a), 'The Second "Equity Gap": Exist Problems for Seed and Early Stage Venture Capitalists and their Investee Companies', *International Small Business Journal*, vol. 12, no. 4, pp.59–76.

Murray, G.C. (1994b), 'An Assessment of the First Three Years of the European Seed Capital Fund Scheme', *European Planning Studies*, vol. 2, no. 4, pp.435–461.

Murray, G.C. (1995), 'Evolution and Change: an Analysis of the First Decade of the UK Venture Capital Industry', *Journal of Business Finance and*

Accounting, vol. 22, no. 8, pp.1077–1107.

Murray G.C. and D. Francis (1992), *The European Seed Capital Fund Scheme: A Review of the First Three Years*. DGXXIII, Commission of the European Union, Brussels.

Murray, G.C. and J. Lott (1995), 'Have UK Venture Capital Firms a Bias Against Investment in New Technology Based Firms?', *Research Policy* vol. 24, pp.283–299.

Murray, G.C. and M. Wright (1996 forthcoming), 'Management's Search for Venture Capital in Smaller Buy-Outs: the Role of Intermediaries and Marketing Implications', *International Journal of Bank Marketing*, pp.12.

National Venture Capital Association (1992), *Annual Report 1991*, Venture Economics Inc.

Nixon, B. (1993), 'The Role of Intermediaries in UK Venture Capital Deal Flow', unpublished MBA dissertation, University of Warwick, England.

Poindexter, J.B. (1976), 'The Efficiency of Financial Markets: The venture capital case', unpublished doctoral dissertation, New York University.

Porter, M.E. (1979), 'How Competitive Forces Shape Strategy', *Harvard Business Review*, March/April, pp.137–45.

Porter, M.E. (1980), *The Competitive Strategy: Techniques for Analysing Industries and Competitors*, The Free Press, Macmillan Inc.

Pratt, G. (1990), 'Venture Capital in the United Kingdom', *Bank of England Quarterly Bulletin*, vol. 30, no. 1, February, pp.78–83.

Roberts, E.B. (1991), *Entrepreneurs in High Technology*, Oxford University Press, New York.

Sahlman, W.A. (1989), *The Changing Structure of the American Venture Capital Industry*, National Venture Capital Association Conference, May.

Sapienza, H.J. (1992), 'When Do Venture Capitalists Add Value?', *Journal of Business Venturing*, vol. 7, pp.9–27.

Sapienza, H. and J.A. Timmons (1989), 'The Role of Venture Capitalists in New Ventures. What Determines Their Importance?', *Academy of Management Best Papers Proceedings*, pp.74–8.

Small Business Research Trust (1990), *Quarterly Survey of Small Firms in Britain*, vol. 6, no. 2.

Storey, D.J. (1994), *Understanding the Small Business Sector*, Routledge.

Storey, D.J., R. Watson and P. Wynarczyk (1989), *Fast Growth Small Business: Case Studies of 40 Small Firms in North East England*, Research Paper No 67, Department of Employment.

Sweeting, R.J. (1991), 'UK Venture Capital Funds and the Funding of new Technology-Based Businesses: Process and Relationships', *Journal of Management Studies*, vol. 28, no. 6, pp.601–22.

Tyebjee, T.T. and A.V. Bruno (1984), 'A Model of Venture Capital Investment Activity', *Management Science*, vol. 30, pp.1051–66.

University of Cambridge (1992), *The State of British Enterprise: Growth, innovation and competitive advantage in small and medium sized firms*, Small Business Research Centre, Cambridge.

Venture Economics Inc. (1992), 'Disbursements Hit 10 Year Low', *Venture Capital Journal*, June, pp.27–31.

Venture Economics Ltd. (1990), 'Special Report: Resources of the UK Venture Capital Industry', *UK Venture Capital Journal*, July, pp.8–14.

Wells, W.A. (1974), 'Venture Capital Decision Making', unpublished doctoral dissertation, Carnegie-Mellon University.

Wetzel, W.E. (1986), 'Entrepreneurs, Angels and Economic Renaissance', in R.D. Hisrich (ed.), *Entrepreneurship, Intrapreneurship and Venture Capital*, Lexington Books, pp.119–39.

CHAPTER 8

Franchising

Colin Barrow

INTRODUCTION	166
FORMS OF FRANCHING	166
THE GROWTH OF FRANCHISING	168
THE BUSINESS SECTORS COVERED BY FRANCHISING	170
ADVANTAGES AND DISADVANTAGES OF FRANCHISING	172
A MUTUAL DEPENDENCE	175
MATERIAL WORLD	178
EXERCISES	178

Introduction

Franchising is something of a half-way house, lying somewhere between entrepreneurship and employment. It holds many of the attractions of running a small business while at the same time eliminating some of the more unappealing risks. For example, the failure rate for both franchisors and franchisees (see Table 8.1) is much lower than for the small business sector as a whole, which can range upwards of 30 per cent.

Forms of franchising

Let us look at the various types of relationship between licensee and licensor which are described under the general heading 'franchises'.

A distributorship

This could be for a particular product, such as a make of car. It is also sometimes referred to as an *agency*, but there is a fundamental

Table 8.1   Percentage of franchise chains and franchisees that ceased trading

	Business failures		Voluntary withdrawals	
Franchise chain	0.2	1.1	1.0	0.8
Individual franchises	3.6	4.6	4.4	3.9
Total	3.8	5.7	5.4	4.7

difference between these two concepts. An agent acts on behalf of a principal. Even though he or she is not employed by the principal, and even though he or she may have an agency for the products and services of more than one principal, what the agent does, says or represents to third parties is binding on the principal in question, as if they were employer and employee. A distribution, however, is an arrangement where both parties are legally independent, as vendor and purchaser, except that the purchaser, in exchange for certain exclusive territorial rights, backed up by the vendor's advertising, promotion and, possibly, training of his or her staff, will be expected to hold adequate stock and maintain his or her premises in a way that reflects well on the vendor's product or service

A licence to manufacture

This applies to a certain product within a certain territory and over a given period of time. The licensee may have access to any secret process this involves and can use the product's brand name in exchange for a royalty on sales. Licensor and licensee are independent of each other, except that the licensor will no doubt insist that the licensee complies with certain specifications as regards content and quality in order to preserve the good name of his or her product. The arrangement is often found in industry and two well-known examples have been the Rank Organisation's licence to produce the photocopying devices pioneered by the Xerox Corporation and the licences granted by Pilkington's for their revolutionary plate glass manufacturing process.

The use of a celebrity name

The name of a well-known person can be used to enhance the sales appeal of a product and guarantee, at least by implication, its quality. The most common example is the endorsement, by a sports personality, of equipment associated with his or her activity and bearing his or her name, in return for a royalty payment by the manufacturer.

The realisation that a 'personality' can sell things bearing his or her name came about principally through the exposure of sports in the media. In the 1930s there were some attempts to capitalise on movie stars' names in a similar way – an early poster associating Ronald Reagan with a brand of cigarettes has been much reprinted since he became prominent in another sphere – but sports men and women have been more ready, and perhaps better organised, to cash in on the advertising spin-off from the media coverage they get. A name can be franchised, at least for a while, to validate a product, particularly if there appears to be a direct connection between them: Arnold Palmer golf clubs, for instance.

The use of a trade mark

Here a widely recognised product is exploited commercially for a fee – subject to certain licensing conditions – rather than the name of an individual. An instance with which many readers will be familiar was Rubik's cube, always shown with the symbol TM beside it.

Business format franchising

Borrowed from the French, the term 'franchise' originally meant being free from slavery. Today, business format franchising is the name given to a relationship in which the owner of a product, a process, or a service allows a local operator to set up a business under that name, for a specified period of time. The local operator (the franchisee) pays the parent organisation (the franchisor) an initial fee and, usually, continuing royalties for the privilege.

The franchisor lays down a blueprint of how the business should be operated: the content and nature of the goods and services being offered, the price and quality of these goods, and even the location, size and layout of any premises to be used. The franchisor also provides the franchisee with training and other back-up support, such as accounting systems, advertising programmes and personnel recruitment and selection advice.

The growth of franchising

Sales from franchising now account for 32 per cent of all US retail sales, and operate out of some 350,000 business format franchise outlets. In the UK the number of franchised outlets grew from 2,000 outlets to nearly 20,000 in the decade up to 1991. Sales now exceed £6b. and nearly 200,000 people are employed in the industry. Strong franchise sectors also exist in Japan, Canada, Australia, France and throughout most of Europe.

Although all the above forms of franchising continue to flourish, it could be said that business format franchising has emerged as the dominant and certainly the most rapidly expanding mode. This is because it meets the commercial needs of the present time in the same way as some other forms of operation in response to conditions at that time. Looking back into the history of franchising for a moment, it is interesting to note that distributorship franchises were first applied to Singer sewing machines after the American Civil War when the United States emerged as a vast market, but when communications were too poor across great distances to make centralised distribution effective.

Contrary to popular opinion, the business format style of franchising did not begin with the boom of fast-food franchises such as McDonald's in the 1950s. In fact, franchising can date its beginnings back to the early 1800s. However it was in 1898 that modern franchising really got under way when General Motors began franchising dealerships. Still alive and well today, their franchise system boasts 12,000 dealers scattered throughout the USA and as many again throughout the world.

Franchise systems were also created by Rexall in 1902 and Howard Johnson in 1926 – as were many oil, grocery, motel and fast-food franchises during those years. So great has been its growth that most industries have already been touched by franchising. According to the American National Federation of Independent Business, about 10 per cent of the nation's 18 million businesses now run under some kind of franchise agreement.

In essence, franchising thrives because it merges the incentive of owning a business with the management skills of big business. And personal ownership is one of the best incentives yet created to spur hard work.

Franchising may benefit not only the franchisee but also the franchisor. For example, it may enable the franchisor to grow rapidly by using other people's (that is, the franchisee's) money. That is largely how giant franchisors like McDonald's and Baskin-Robbins mushroomed into billion dollar businesses in so short a time.

The idea that franchisees are independent business people is something of a myth. Franchisees generally are not free to run their business as they see fit. They are often hamstrung by the franchisors' policies, standards and procedures. Nor do franchisors encourage their franchisees to improve the way they do business. To quote the

Bank of America: 'The best franchisee, as far as many franchisors are concerned, is someone who is smart enough to understand and operate the system, but not smart enough to try to improve on it.'

One franchisor describes the ideal franchisee as the sergeant type – midway between the general who gives the orders and the private who merely follows them. People who want their own business to escape taking orders from others frequently see franchising as the answer. They are subsequently frustrated by lack of autonomy.

The business sectors covered by franchising

In the 1990s, in the UK the largest fields of activity in terms of systems units are business services (23 per cent), home improvements (13 per cent), property maintenance (9 per cent), health and beauty (8 per cent) and leisure (7 per cent).

Food, divided up between fast food and 'other food, accounts for a total of 15 per cent, but when you look at turnover percentages a significantly different picture emerges. The percentage of turnover accounted for by fast foods is in line with the percentage of units (7 per cent), but 'other' foods, which has 8 per cent of the total number of systems, accounts for no less than 22 per cent of industry turnover, only just behind business services with 24 per cent of industry turnover. By contrast, home improvement, the second biggest in the number of units, only accounts for 5 per cent of turnover. This suggests that one of the factors to look out for in choosing a franchise is not so much the number of units in operation, but the turnover (and, of course, the profitability) per unit.

It is also worth noting that the pattern of franchises seems to change from year to year. In 1989/90 business services grew to over 40 per cent of the total, whilst in 1990/91 they contracted to 23 per cent. By contrast, vehicle and property maintenance and property improvements were sharply low, against the tide of recession, though this may be more a reflection of people using redundancy money to set up a business in these areas than of the size of the market. The fact that print franchises were sharply down from 15 per cent – the second biggest proportion in 1989 – to 3 per cent in 1990, was a clearer indication of recession.

The simplest form and usually the cheapest to acquire is a job franchise service which is run from home, a cleaning service, for instance, or a vehicle maintenance franchise such as Hometune. Much the largest group of franchises, though, are those which entail acquiring premises and often a substantial investment in equipment in addition to the initial fee payable to the franchisor: fast food restaurants and print shops are two of the most visible and widespread franchises of this type.

At the top end of the market are investment franchises like Holiday Inn, where the start-up costs can run well into six figures. A prime Wimpy bar franchise will now also run to over £500,000, as will some computer franchises. Overall, the range of activities which can be franchised is very wide and some 65 have been identified in the USA, ranging from hotel ownership at the top end to the soft drink bottling franchise with the unlikely name of Cock 'n Bull Ltd at the other. The latter is an indication that not all American enterprises can be readily transplanted into the international market. There are at the moment at least 40 types of franchise in Britain, covering a wide variety of fields from fast food to dry cleaning.

In the USA large franchisors – those with 1,000 or more units each – dominate business format franchising, with 57 companies accounting for 5 per cent of sales and 55 per cent of establishments. These figures should be viewed against a backdrop of over 4,000 franchisors operating in 50 business sectors in this market, employing some 7 million people between them.

Only 70 per cent of outlets in franchise chains in North America are franchisee-operated. The remainder are company-owned stores using hired managers. These 'company stores' are acknowledged to be less profitable than franchised outlets.

In general franchising is viewed as being a relatively 'safe' way into business with only a small fraction of a per cent of the country's 350,000-plus franchises failing in any one year. There is also evidence that franchisees are generally satisfied with their lot. Some 90 per cent sign up again when the term of their agreement expires.

The main growth in US business format franchising is in the service sector, encouraged in part by the low cost of entry compared with established car repair and fast-food franchises. This high-growth sector includes such areas as:

- financial counselling services,
- home repair,
- insurance,
- legal services centres,
- accounting services centres,
- medical services,
- dental clinics,
- business brokers,
- weight reduction centres,
- figure control centres,
- smoking control centres,
- exercise studios,
- safe deposit box locations.

Many of these activities are still either in their infancy or even non-existent in the UK franchise market. Restrictive practices permitting, it seems inevitable that these types of franchise will make their presence more strongly felt in the UK in the coming decade.

Advantages and disadvantages of franchising

The advantages and disadvantages of taking up a franchise depend to some extent on the content of the agreement, but there is a core of balancing factors which are largely common because they relate to the nature of the kind of activity which franchising involves.

The franchisor

ADVANTAGES

From the franchisor's point of view, the advantages are that he or she does not have any direct investment in an outlet bearing his or her name. The inventory and equipment are owned by the franchisee. Because of the shortage of prime sites, there is a growing trend for franchisors to acquire leases on behalf of franchisees, or at any rate to stand as guarantors. Nevertheless the effect on the liquidity of the franchisor, in contrast to expansion by opening branches, is enormous – though if he or she does their job properly there are heavy start-up costs in piloting the franchise and in setting up and maintaining training. Thereafter there are further costs in providing a continuing service to franchisees in such matters as research and development, promotion, administrative back-up and feedback and communication within the network. The expectation is that these costs will be offset by the fact that the franchisee, as the owner of the business, is more likely to be highly motivated than an employee and more responsive to local market needs and conditions; that the franchisor receives an income from the franchise; that he or she saves on personnel and administrative costs; and that, without direct financial involvement, he or she may in this way derive some of the benefits of expansion, inasmuch as franchising provides economies of scale from centralised purchasing and, if he or she wished it and it is feasible, some degree of centralised administrative facilities.

DISADVANTAGES

The disadvantages are that, although the failure of an individual franchise may reflect badly on the franchise operation as a whole, all the franchisor can control is the format itself and he or she can only influence the running of individual operations by pulling the reins on this or that clause in the agreement – the broad terms of which we shall discuss shortly. In extreme cases the franchisor may terminate the agreement or at any rate not renew it, but he or she cannot throw the franchisee out as if he or she were the employee. The franchisor is therefore dependent on the willingness of the franchisee to observe the rules and play the game, while at the same time any failure to do so is equally, and perhaps more, damaging to the franchisor (and to other franchisees) than to the franchisee concerned because of its adverse effects on the franchise as a whole.

Another disadvantage sometimes turns out to lie in the curious mixture of dependence and independence that franchising produces. The franchisee is encouraged to think of him or herself as an independent business entity, and to a large extent this is indeed the situation. Nevertheless he or she is operating the franchisor's business concept under a licence for which a fee is payable. There are cases where a franchisee identifies so closely with the particular business he or she is running that they ultimately resent the payment of the fee. The success is felt to be due to the franchisee's own effort, not to the franchise concept or to the franchisor. This is apt to be particularly so if the franchisor adopts a lower profile than he or she should, either in terms of direct help or in matters such as national advertising. Clearly, of course, the franchisee would be obliged to pay under the terms of the agreement, but a sour relationship is not good for either party, so it is up to the franchisor to maintain his or her part of the bargain both in letter and in spirit. Franchises are a matter of mutual interest and obligations.

The franchisee

From the point of view of the franchisee, also, there are advantages and disadvantages which might, perhaps, be most clearly expressed in the form of a list.

ADVANTAGES

- A business format or product which has already been market tested and, presumably, been found to work. As a consequence, major problems can be avoided in the start-up period.
- A recognised name of which the public is already aware and which has credibility with the suppliers.
- Publicity, both direct, in that the franchisor advertises his or her product or services, and indirect promotion through signage and other corporate image promotion in all the franchisor's outlets.

- Although taking up a franchise is not cheaper than starting on your own, it is considered that the percentage of expensive errors made by individuals starting on their own is substantially reduced by the adoption of a tested format.
- Direct and close assistance during the start-up period.
- A period of training on production and management aspects.
- A set of standard management, accounting, sales and stock control procedures incorporated in an operating manual.
- Better terms for centralised bulk purchase negotiated through the franchisor, though he or she may be looking for mark-ups in this area as a source of revenue from the franchise.
- The benefit of the franchisor's research and development in improving the product.
- Feedback throughout the network on operating procedures and the facility to compare notes with other franchisees, both formally and informally.
- Design of the premises to an established scheme saves on interior design fees and may eliminate these altogether where the franchisor has a set of specifications.
- The benefit of the franchisor's advice on equipment selection and initial inventory levels, though this may be partial where the franchisor is also the supplier.
- Help with site selection, negotiating with planning officers and developers.
- Possibly, though not universally, access to the franchisor's legal and financial advisers.
- The protected or privileged rights to the franchise within a given area.
- Improved prospects of obtaining loan facilities from the bank.
- The backing of a known trading name when negotiating for good sites with letting agents or building owners.

DISADVANTAGES

- Business format franchising is, of necessity, something of a cloning exercise. There is virtually no scope for individual initiative in matters of product, service or design. However the franchisor will demand uniformly high standards of maintenance, appearance and packaging in whatever the franchise entails. These are usually monitored by regular inspection.
- The royalty (sometimes called a management fee) paid to the franchisor. This is usually based on gross turnover or on profit. The problem here is that if the franchisor is not pulling his or her weight, or if the franchisee does not feel this to be the case, the royalty can be subject to bitter dispute. The franchisee may then feel justified in

withholding all or part of it on the grounds of non-performance by the franchisor, but this is always a difficult matter to prove in the courts. Furthermore the franchisor's resources to conduct a long-drawn-out case will usually be greater than the franchisee's.

- A further problem is that a high turnover does not necessarily imply a highly profitable operation. If the franchisor's income is wholly or partially based on turnover, he or she may try to push for this at the expense of profitability.
- The franchisee is not absolutely at liberty to sell the franchise even though he or she is in many respects operating the business independently. The sale has to be approved by the franchisor, who is also entitled to vet the vendor and charge the cost of any investigations made to the existing franchise. Furthermore, although the business would be valued as a going concern in trading terms, the goodwill remains the property of the franchisor. Again the franchisee may feel that, at least to some extent, the goodwill has been built up by his or her own efforts. The resale of a franchise, in other words, is a process rich in those grey areas which can lead to expensive litigation.
- Territory agreements may be difficult to enforce in practice. For instance, the hypothetical firm of Calorie Countdown may have the exclusive rights in the suburb in which it is located, but there is nothing to prevent the citizens of that suburb from buying their slimmers' meals in some other neighbouring Calorie Countdown outlet.
- The franchisee, as well as paying a royalty to the franchisor, may be obliged to buy goods and services from him or her as well – possibly at disadvantageous rates.
- Though the franchisor places all sorts of controls and obligations on the franchisee to maintain the quality of his or her image, the scope for doing the reverse is more limited. If the franchisor's products or service get bad publicity, this is bound to affect the franchisee adversely, and there is very little he or she could do about it. Equally the franchisor may engage in promotional activities (and involve the franchisee in them as well) which, though perfectly harmless, may, from the point of view of a particular outlet, be an irrelevant waste of time.
- The failure of a franchisor may leave the franchisee with a business which is not viable in isolation.

A mutual dependence

From the above list of advantages and disadvantages to both parties a more detailed picture emerges of the business format franchise as a relationship of mutual dependence which allows each party to realise his or her own strength to their mutual and, at best, equal advantage.

The franchisor is able to expand without further investment and, though the return is obviously lower than from expansion by ownership, he or she does receive an income from the franchisee as well as getting both an outlet for his or her product and more muscle in negotiating the purchase of materials and equipment. The franchisee, on the other hand, is able to concentrate his or her entrepreneurial skills at the sharp end of sales and customer service, while the administrative headaches of setting up the business are mitigated by the uniform nature of the format. By the same token he or she is saved, through feedback to the franchisor of the accumulated experience of the franchises, from making the errors to which businesses are prone in their earlier and most vulnerable stages. This relationship is expressed as agreements – the purchase agreement and the franchise agreement. But before considering these, it is necessary to evaluate the franchise as a whole.

A study by Professor Russell M. Knight of the University of Western Ontario (see Table 8.2) illustrates the close agreement between franchisees and franchisors on the advantages of franchising, though in general, franchisees were slightly less enthusiastic. But much of the advantage of franchising lies in getting franchises with appropriate characteristics.

A study of the personal franchisee characteristics required for success (see Table 8.3), also carried out by Professor Knight, concluded that franchisees and franchisors have a large measure of

Table 8.2   The advantages of franchising

	Franchisees in agreement %	Franchisors in agreement %
You can make more money in a franchise than in an idependent business	51	47
A franchise is less risky than going it alone	78	88
A franchise offers greater job satisfaction than salaried employment	95	82
A franchise offers more independence than salaried employment	92	83
A franchise offers a proven business formula	83	99
A franchise offers the benefit of a known trade name	96	99
You can develop a franchise more quickly than an independent business	92	86

Table 8.3 Personal franchise characteristics required for success

	Franchisee %			Franchisor %		
	Very important	Important	Not important	Very important	important	Not important
Previous management experience in same industry	0	20	80	2	14	84
Previous own business experience	12	46	42	16	47	37
Management ability	84	15	1	66	31	3
Desire to suceed	90	10	0	93	7	0
Willingness to work hard	92	8	0	93	6	1
Creativity	26	56	18	12	44	44
Strong people skills	63	32	5	64	34	2
Financial backing	71	27	2	67	27	6
Support from family	52	28	20	46	32	22

Note: Study size: 148 franchisors and 105 franchisees replied to questionnaire, with follow-up interviews with 25 members of each group.

agreement on what makes for success. They disagreed only in rating management ability and creativity – a point that may provide some clues as to what franchisors are really looking for in a franchise.

Material world

Miles O'Donavan's franchise, Material World (named after the Madonna hit record, 'Living in a Material World'), is a good example of how to turn a successful conventional business into a franchise. He is an up-market version of a market trader, buying up manufacturers' ends-of-lines and seconds, and selling them to an apparently appreciative public. 'It is a very simple business,' he says. And he never doubted that it would succeeded because, the way he looks at it, it's providing a service at both ends of the equation. Not only is he helping out those people who would love to make their home 'very Sanderson' but currently find themselves strapped for cash; he is also helping out the manufacturers who have to rid themselves of their surplus stock somehow.

This mutually beneficial system is already well established in the clothing business, where disposing of chain store cast-offs is the basis of several retail chains. O'Donavan, however, operates with goods from rather up-market. Much of what he stocks would normally sell at £15 to £20 a metre but he has a blanket price of £7.95 a yard. The fact that he sticks to yards is not just a hankering for days gone by: it gives him a 10 per cent price advantage.

O'Donavan woke up one morning about 18 months ago and decided that with nine of his own shops he was about as exposed as he would like to be. Watching Coloroll and Lowndes Queensway sink without trace, he decided the time had come to share the risk with others. After a brief flirtation with the idea of venture capital, he plumped for franchising and has never looked back. His new franchisees helped lift turnover from £1.8m. to £3m. in 1991, and his business is now expanding fast in the UK and Europe. Best of all, he can sleep easy at night with the comfort of knowing his franchisees are as exposed as he is to the consequence of failure, something no Queensway store manager ever was.

Exercises

1. List as many franchise chains as you can.
2. Develop a service, manufacturing and retailing idea that would be suitable for franchising. List the reasons why they are suitable for franchising.

3. For a local retail franchise (for example, Body Shop, Tie Rack), write an essay outlining what the franchisor provides.
4. Based upon an interview with a local franchisee, write a mini case study outlining why they purchased the franchise and how successfully they think it operates.
5. Select a national franchise chain and write a report evaluating the franchisor's performance.
6. Write an essay outlining how franchising might develop in the 21st century.

CHAPTER 9

The business plan

Paul Burns

THE IMPORTANCE OF THE BUSINESS PLAN	180
KNOWING WHERE YOU ARE: THE POSITION AUDIT	181
KNOWING WHERE YOU ARE GOING: SETTING OBJECTIVES	183
STRATEGIES, OPERATING NEEDS AND BUDGETS	185
THE INVESTOR'S VIEW	186
THE FORMAT OF THE BUSINESS PLAN	189
PRESENTING A CASE FOR FINANCE	195
EXERCISES	197

The importance of the business plan

One of the most important steps in establishing any new business is the construction of a business plan. It can help the owner-manager to crystallise and focus his ideas. It can help him set objectives and give him a yardstick against which to monitor performance. Perhaps of more immediate importance, it can also act as a vehicle to attract any external finance needed by the business. It can convince investors that the owner-manager has identified high growth opportunities, and that he has the entrepreneurial flair and managerial talent to exploit that opportunity effectively, and that he has a rational, coherent and believable programme for doing so.

The business plan entails taking a long-term view of the business and its environment. A good plan should emphasise the strengths and recognise the weaknesses of the proposed venture. Above all, it should convey a sincerity of purpose and analysis which lends credibility both to the plan and to the entrepreneur putting it forward.

Knowing where you are: the position audit

The whole planning process is shown diagrammatically in Figure 9.1. For an existing business this process first involves coming to terms with the personal objectives of the owner-manager.

- Do we want income, or capital growth?
- Do we want to sell the business as a going concern when it gets to maturity, or do we want to pass it on to our children?
- Do we want to take risks in the business or do we value security more?

Second, it involves coming to terms with the strengths and weaknesses of the existing business, and the opportunity and threats that it faces. This is often called a 'position audit' or 'SWOT' (Strengths, Weaknesses, Opportunities, Threats) analysis. We are seeking to answer the following sorts of questions:

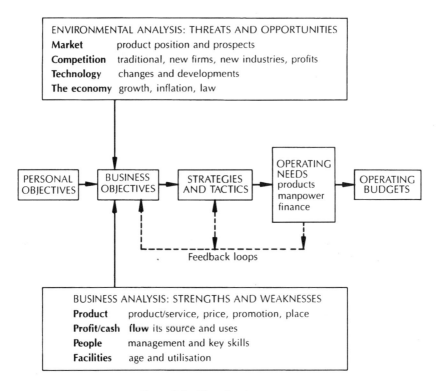

Figure 9.1   The planning process

- Where are we and how did we get there?
- What condition are we in?
- What lessons can we learn for the future?
- What threats need to be countered?
- What opportunities are open to us, and how can we exploit them or create new ones?

In other words we need to determine where we *can* go and where we *want* to go.

The in-depth analysis of the business will cover our products or services, finances, personnel and facilities. The sorts of questions we would as would be the following.

Products or services

- Are they quality products or services?
- How do our prices compare with our competitors'?
- How much do we spend on promotion?
- Where do we sell the product or service?
- Should be change the product or service in any way?

Finances

- What is our current level of profit and cash flow?
- Which products or services does it come from?
- How strong is our balance sheet?
- What potential sources of capital are available?

Personnel

- Are there gaps in our management?
- Are there gaps in the skills of our workers?
- What do they do best?
- What do they do worst?
- How well do we pay them?

Facilities

- How old are our building, machines and vehicles?
- What is their life expectancy?
- How efficient are they?

These questions are by no means exhaustive. They simply illustrate the sort of searching questions that need to be asked and answered truthfully.

As far as the environment is concerned, we also need to ask about four key areas: the customer (the most important person so far as any business is concerned), the competition, the technology, and finally the economy as a whole. The sorts of questions we would ask would be:

Customer

- Who is the customer?
- What does he want from the product or service?
- How important to him are quality and price?
- Where does he buy the product or service?
- How important is promotion?
- Why do customers buy our product or service, in particular?
- What developments in the product are taking place?
- Can we estimate the size of the market and its future growth?

Competition

- Who are our competitors?
- What size of business are they and where are they located?
- How profitable are they?

Technology

- Is technology changing?
- What are the changes?

Economy

- What are the growth prospects in the UK?
- Can we sell overseas?
- Will we be affected by any changes in legislation?
- What will happen to the price of our raw materials?

Knowing where you are going: setting objectives

The planning process really gets under way with the development of a mission statement. This is a statement of what business we are in.

It defines the boundaries of the business. It must be narrow enough to give direction and focus, but open up a large enough market to allow the business to grow and realise its potential. It should not be too restrictive to prevent development, nor so broad as to be meaningless. For example, a coalman might say he is in the business of 'marketing and distributing home fuel requirements'.

Ultimately your mission statement should contain something that is uniquely different from your competitors'. Therefore it should be based upon the benefits your product or service confers on an identified target market. The mission statement should also contain elements of what you want the business to become. These elements might include growth, profitability or other values. They should convey some image or vision that your employees can aim for. This vision should be quantifiable, otherwise nobody will know when it is achieved. It should also be realistic, otherwise nobody will care whether it is to be achieved.

An ever-increasing number of organisations regularly produce business plans. At the core of the plan is always the mission statement. A medical general practice developed the following mission statement; see how it gives a clear direction for the practice and defines a mission that will it will have to strive to achieve: 'To provide the best possible health care for patients at all times by responding to the needs, providing accessible medical and anticipatory care of the highest quality and doing all that is possible to improve the social environment of the community.' Mission statements for small firms often contain elements about the quality of work and the working environment. On the other hand, larger companies must have a clear vision that all staff can identify with. Probably the most widely quoted mission statement is that of Avis, the car rental people. It contains a simple vision expressed purely in financial terms: 'To become the fastest growing company with the highest profit margin in the business of renting and leasing vehicles without drivers.'

The next stage is to set quantified primary objectives that will reflect not only what you want the business to achieve but also what you think it realistically can achieve, given the market it faces. For many companies this will probably involve factors such as profitability, asset levels and growth. For example, an objective of an annual real growth in profit of after tax of 10 per cent with a minimum return on capital of 15 per cent achieves growth objectives while maintaining an asset base for the business. Of course, whilst objectives normally include financial elements, they also include other elements such as quality levels, customer service levels, new clients or customers, working environment and diversification targets. In fact the objectives can include any elements that take the firm along the path the owner-manager decides for it. They are 'what' statements. They tell you what you want the business to achieve. To be effective, objectives must be:

• Quantifiable,
• Bounded in time,
• Realistic and achievable.

They can then serve as useful goals and yardsticks against which to judge the performance of the firm. Objectives tell you where you are going and allow you to judge when you have arrived.

Strategies, operating needs and budgets

Strategies are 'how to' statements. They specify the tasks needed to be undertaken to achieve the objectives of the firm. These need not be complicated. They should, however, be comprehensive and consistent. The strategy is just the series of linked tasks. Their development involves co-ordination of the different management functions – marketing, accounting, operations and personnel. You might evaluate a number of different strategies that could help you achieve your objectives. They might include various pricing, distribution, staffing or financing options.

The next stage is to quantify these strategies into the operating needs of the firm:

• Should we be developing new products or services?
• Do we need to recruit new staff to undertake these tasks?
• Do we need new equipment or other forms of investment?
• How do we finance all of these things?

Often the objectives and strategies have to be changed at this stage simply because it becomes clear that you do not have, and cannot obtain, the resources to carry out the plan. These are shown as feedback loops in Figure 9.1.

The final stage in the planning process is the drawing-up of the detailed budgets for the business. This involves quantifying the costs and revenues associated with all aspects of the plan. It also involves drawing up detailed forecasts for:

• Cash flow,
• Profit and loss,
• Balance sheets.

The great advantage of the business plan is that it forces you to think in detail about the direction of the firm. It forces you to think through the options that are open to you and justify your decisions about which course of action to follow. That is not to say that you will anticipate all the problems that the firm will face, but it will mean that you are better prepared to meet those challenges because you have a thorough understanding of the business and its market-place. In many ways it is the process of planning that is important, rather than the business plan itself.

The investor's view

Banks

Over 60 per cent of external finance for small firms now comes from the banks. To obtain loan and often overdraft finance these days you frequently need to provide the bank with a business plan. The important thing to remember with them, however, is that, unlike the equity investor, they are not in the risk business. They are looking to obtain a set rate of interest on a loan and to have their capital repaid. They do not share in the extra profits if a firm is particularly successful, so they do not expect to lose money if they are not.

A business plan prepared for a bank could show how the interest on the loan will be paid, even in the worst possible set of circumstances, and that the capital can be repaid on the due date. It should seek to reassure the bank about the risks the business faces. The bank manager gains little from the success of the business but stands to lose a lot if it fails.

Equity investors

The institutions investing risk capital in unquoted companies today are becoming highly sophisticated. Most businessmen submit invest-ment proposals to more than one institution for consideration. However, on the other side of the coin, most investment institutions are inundated with investment proposals. It has been estimated that only one in 20 of these proposals ever reach the negotiation stage. To a very great extent, the decision whether to proceed beyond an initial reading of the plan will depend on the quality of the business plan used in supporting the investment proposals. The business plan is the first, and often the best, chance of an entrepreneur to impress prospective investors with the quality of his investment proposal.

An investor needs to be convinced of two things:

1. That a business opportunity exists which has the potential to earn the investor the high return he demands;
2. That the company proposing to exploit this opportunity can do so effectively.

Any business plan must therefore address both issues. This requires a careful balance between making the proposal sufficiently attractive, on the one hand, while on the other realistically addressing the many risks inherent in any business venture and showing how they can be acceptably minimised. To do this the business plan should emphasise the strengths of the company, particularly in comparison with its competitors. Behind all the plans and strategies the business plan must demonstrate convincingly the determination and credibility of the owner-manager and other key personnel involved in the business venture. It has been said that the most important factor in the decision whether or not to invest is the credibility and quality of the firm's management.

The most difficult aspect of any deal is deciding upon the split in equity between the various partners involved in a deal. The simple answer is that there are no simple rules and the final result will depend on the attractiveness of the investment proposal and the negotiating ability of the individuals involved. However *Venture Capital Report*, a monthly publication of investment opportunities, suggests the following starting-point:

For the idea: 33 per cent.
For the management: 33 per cent.
For the money: 33 per cent.

But it must be stressed that this is only a very rough guide. If an entrepreneur can provide no capital, he may receive less equity. If the idea is a breakthrough, he may receive more, and so on.

It is also advisable to consider the objectives of the investing institution. It will be interested in generating income from its investment by way of dividends or interest and, over the long run, through capital gains. But will the institution take dividends or interest, and when will these be paid? A venture capitalist may require dividends, but it could be in the entrepreneurs's interest not to take them because of tax problems. Indeed it may not be in the interests of the company to pay dividends or interest in its early years. A further issue is how much of the control of the business the owner-manager is actually willing to surrender. Most entrepreneurs wish to part with as little as possible of their business. Indeed venture capitalists now rarely demand even a 50 per cent stake in the business. At the end of the day, a sensible financing package involving equity and deferred interest terms or convertible loans might be the answer.

The second question is: how will the institution realise its capital gain, and over what period? This issue is frequently called the problem of 'exit routes'. It is a major problem for many investing institutions, since it can often take quite a number of years before it can realise its investment. Related to this is the issue of further funding needs and their availability from the investing institution. Exit routes and their time scale need to be seriously considered and openly discussed. Is the business looking to go on the stock market? If not, the investing institution might be tempted to promote a merger with a larger company, once the business has taken off. Another possibility is for the owner-manager to 'buy-out' the investing institution at a later date.

Also investing institutions have very different ways of operating. Some prefer a 'hands off' approach whereby, once they have invested, they have little to do with the business, perhaps meeting the owner-manager once a year to review the progress of the business. In contrast, some institutions prefer a 'hands on' approach, insisting on placing a non-executive director on the board and perhaps being in contact with the owner-manager up to eight times a month, with at least one visit. They may require consultation on budgets and plans and even changes in senior management.

Finally it must be realised that funds have different risk/reward profiles. Some specialise, either by size of business or industry sector. Frequently they have minimum investment levels. Certainly obtaining equity funding below £100,000 is still a problem in the UK. Many sound proposals are turned down by particular institutions simply because they do no fit the institution's investment profile. In which case other institutions should be approached. Undoubtedly deciding upon the appropriate financial structure and choosing the right investors will be a major task for most entrepreneurs.

Sphinx Ltd

Pamela Gray set up Sphinx Ltd, a UNIX software house in 1983 with £20,000 of her own and her partner's money and £400,000 from the venture capital organisations Alan Patricof Associates and Abingworth. She surrendered 60 per cent of the equity to these organisations in a series of negotiations that lasted over six months. They asked her to rework the business plan many times over, saying they needed to have it to present to their own boards for approval. Sphinx became highly successful and, with a turnover in excess of £6m., Pamela decided to sell it as a going concern for many millions of pounds. She views the process of obtaining funds as an obstacle course which proves a business person's dedication, commitment and tenacity. She sees the business plan as the necessary vehicle for communicating with any investors.

The format of the business plan

Any format for a proposed business plan should be viewed as providing general guidance only. Every business is different, and consequently a standard plan is totally inappropriate in every circumstance. Having said that, in Table 9.1 we attempt to outline the skeleton of a business plan. When looking at this it should be noted that it is unlikely that in every circumstance all the items mentioned here will be of sufficient importance or relevance to warrant inclusion in every plan. In particular there is one overriding principle with all business plans:

KEEP IT SHORT!

Any business plan should be sufficiently long to cover the subject adequately but short enough to maintain interest. Some business plans requiring a large amount of venture capital could be well over 50 pages long, but more normal projects should be restricted to 10 to 20 pages.

Clearly Table 9.1 is no more than an outline, and an outline that will have to be judiciously precised. Nevertheless it is an outline that is worth following. Plans for internal use can be even shorter. A few comments on the main headings in this plan may be of help.

Overview/summary

The executive summary must be brief – no longer than one or two pages. This should be treated as a stand-alone selling document. It is essential that the highlights of the entire business plan are contained in this summary. For many investors it will be the only part of the plan that they read. Indeed some advisors recommend that investing institutions are only sent this summary initially. Only if they are sufficiently interested should the full business plan be sent.

The company and its industry

This section attempts to establish the credibility of the owner-manager and his business in the eyes of potential investors. It is

Table 9.1   Outline contents of business plan

1. Overview/summary
   Purpose of plan
   How much finance is required, and what it is for
   Highlights of financial projections

2. The company and its industry
   Purpose of company
   History of company
   Past successes of company
   Discussion of industry

3. The products/services
   Description of products/services and applications
   Distinctive competences or uniqueness of product/service
   Technologies and skills required in the business
   Licence/patent rights
   Future potential

4. Markets
   Customers
   Competitors (strengths and weaknesses)
   Market segments
   Market size and growth
   Estimated market share
   Customer buying patterns
   Critical product/service characteristics or uniqueness
   Special market characteristics
   Competitor response

5. Marketing
   Market positioning – critical product/service characteristics or uniqueness in relation to competitors
   Pricing policy
   Selling/distribution policy
   Advertising and promotion
   Product/service support policy
   Interest shown by prospective customers

6. Design and development (if appropriate)
   Stage of development
   Difficulties and risks
   Product/service improvements
   Product/service developments in future

7. Manufacturing and operations
   Premises location
   Other facilities
   Production/service capacity
   Sources of supply of key materials or workforce
   Use of subcontractors
   Nature of productive process – machinery and critical points

Table 9.1   Continued

8. Management
    Owners/directors and other key management
    Expertise and track record (detail CVs as an appendix)
    Key management compensation
    Summary of planned staff numbers and recruitment plans
    Training policies
    Consultants and advisors

9. Financing requirements
    Funds required and timing
    Deal on offer
    Anticipated gearing
    Exit routes for investors

10. Financial highlights, risks and assumptions
    Highlights of financial plan (sales, profit, return on capital, net worth, etc)
    Commentary on financial plan
    Risks and how they will be tackled

11. Detailed financial plan (for 3 years)
    Profit and loss
    Contribution and break-even analysis
    Cash flow analysis (monthly in first year)
    Sensitivity analysis
    Balance sheets (annual only)

12. Items frequently included in appendices
    Technical data on products
    Details on patents, etc
    Consultants' reports on products or markets
    Order and enquiry status
    CVs of key managers
    Organisation charts
    Audited accounts
    Names of accountants, solicitors and bankers

important, as a common way of evaluating future potential is to look first at past performance. If, however, past performance is not a reliable indicator of future potential, it may be best to leave out this section entirely. Nevertheless the owner-manager must display a thorough understanding of his own company and the industry in which it is seeking to compete.

The products/services

This section should define precisely the products and services to be marketed. Clearly it will vary according to the number and complexity of the products or services to be marketed. While it is important to display a grasp of the technology involved, it is important that this section is written in clear, concise, layman's language. Detailed information can be relegated to appendices. It is important that in this section, and in others, the distinctive competences or uniquenesses of the product/service are emphasised. These can take many forms: new technology, product quality, low production cost or the fit with customer needs. It is also important that the owner-manager demonstrates his ability to develop the product or service beyond its present form. Investors rarely participate in a one-product company without indications of future developments.

Markets

Markets and marketing are critical to all companies. Brilliant new technologies are useless without customers. Most institutional investors see this as an area where major mistakes are made by new businesses. It is important to define precisely the market segments that the business hopes to attack. Estimates of market size, growth, share and competitive reaction should be based on the market segment, not on some wider market definition. Having identified the market segment to be attacked, customer-buying patterns need to be understood and, once more, the investor convinced that the product/service characteristics or uniquenesses that the business is offering will meet a ready market. Investors are always interested in the reaction of competition. Any business, particularly one with a good product/service idea, will meet competition sooner or later. It is important to identify current competitors and their strengths of weaknesses. This is especially important in the case of small or new businesses entering markets dominated by larger and more powerful competitors. Every business must develop a strategy for dealing with its competitors.

Marketing

Marketing strategy can only be developed on the basis of a thorough understanding of the market. Often the exact details of the marketing strategy can be complex, covering such areas as market positioning, pricing policy, selling and distribution policy, advertising and promotion, and product service support policy. Nevertheless, any business must analyse all of these factors in detail when formulating sales projections. These projections should be built up in as much detail as possible to act as a cross-check against the sales targets developed from the market analysis process outlined previously. Sales estimates based simply on targets without the detailed nuts and bolts of how these targets are to be achieved will inevitably prove unconvincing to a potential investor. Frequently this section can prove to be very lengthy. If this is the case it could, once more, be included as an appendix with only a summary in the main body of the plan.

Design and development

Many new businesses that are developing products which have not yet been marketed need to give a potential investor considerable information, not only on the stage of development the project is currently at, but also on the difficulties and risks that it faces, as well as the time scale involved in getting the product into the market. Even existing products and services must look to improvements as well as new developments in the future.

Manufacturing and operations

In this section the manufacturing or operations process should be briefly described. The section should highlight any potential problem areas such as new or untried technology or production facilities. It should highlight the intended use of subcontractors. Investors are very interested in how the business will control the quality of its product and in the case of a service operation it may be necessary to explain how the business is organised and controlled. Premises location and other facility needs should also be discussed. Finally lead times in crucial supplies, how many sources there are, and how quickly output can be increased or decreased, should also be addressed.

Management

The importance of management cannot be overemphasised. In many ways, the development of a coherent business plan simply proves the ability of management. Investors invest in people, not in a business plan. This section is therefore vitally important, particularly for start-up companies. It is worth remembering that for a substantial business to emerge it will be necessary to talk, not about individuals, but about teams of people with complementary skills. Ideally these skills will cover all the functional areas of business. However it is unlikely that a start-up would be able to bring together a balanced team at such an early stage. It is therefore reasonable to mention areas both of strength and weakness for a start-up business. Weaknesses can often be addressed by using consultants. Key managers should be described in terms of their experience and abilities, together with a statement of their specific responsibilities. Detailed CVs may be included in the appendices. Investors are naturally interested in track record since this gives them some indication about the management's ability to meet the targets set in the business plan. The summary contained in this section should therefore concentrate on the major achievements and experience of each key manager. Investors will also be interested in the mechanisms for retaining key managers and motivating them to achieve the target set in the business plan.

Financing requirements

The next three sections of the business plan focus on the translation of these plans and strategies into financial statements and financing requirements. The purpose of this section is to outline the funds that the owner-manager requires and the terms and conditions he is willing to offer to obtain those funds. Invariably the precise nature of any financial deal will have to be negotiated with the investor. Indeed investing institutions are frequently expert at constructing financial deals in such a way as to meet both their own objectives and those of the owner-manager. It is therefore appropriate simply to set down the skeleton of any deal (total funding required, timing, equity/debt structure) and leave the details for further negotiations. The key is to provide sufficient guidelines to indicate the main features of the financial structure of the business and indicate a fair price for the share of the business on offer, while allowing sufficient flexibility, particularly on minor points, to accommodate the wishes of investors. Remember that this is a negotiating situation.

Financial highlights, risks and assumptions

The purpose of this section is to pull out from the mass of financial data contained in the next section the highlights for potential investors. For example, the possible worth of the company if forecast results are achieved should be highlighted, as indeed may sales, profit and return on capital targets. However this section should concentrate, not only on the rewards to potential investors, but also on the problems and risks that the business may face. It may be necessary to highlight the cyclical nature of sales or cash flow. It is important that the main risks facing the business are stated simply and objectively. If the owner-manager does not bring them out then it is certain that the potential investor will. Such risks might be, for example, 'that the technology is not protectable', or 'the meeting of sales targets is vitally dependent upon the recruitment of a regional sales force'. However it is no good simply highlighting the risks without stating how those risks will be minimised.

Detailed financial plan

A detailed financial plan for three years should be included with the business plan. This will include profit-and-loss estimates on a quarterly basis, cash flow analyses, monthly in the first year but quarterly thereafter, and annual balance sheets. Supplementary to the forecasts should be the assumptions on which they are based, in particular the build-up of the sales forecast. Investors are particularly interested in contribution and break-even analysis, since the break-even level is an indication of risk. Forecasts should also be treated to sensitivity analysis. This process involves making different assumptions which would vary the outcome of the financial plans. Typical variations would be based upon changes in sales targets or, for example, timing of cash flows. It is important to choose three or four main variables and to show the effect a variation in these would have on the financial plan. Most sensitivity analyses concentrate on timing, volume, gross margins and credit given.

Presenting a case for finance

The business plan is an essential element in presenting a case for finance. As such it is important that it well presented. This is not to say that the business plan should be overelaborate or expensively produced, but simply that it should be functional, clearly set out and easy to use. It is important that the plan has a table of contents. Frequently tabs are used at each section for easy reference. The use of charts, diagrams and graphs make detailed information more comprehensible. Most business plans that contain financial projections use a double-page layout for this information.

However the business plan is a necessary but not a sufficient condition for obtaining finance for a business proposal. The single most important factor in the eyes of any potential investor will be the personal qualities of the owner-manager and the management team that he brings along. Potential backers are looking for motivation, enthusiasm and integrity, but most of all the managerial ability and competence to make the plan actually happen.

To get a business to grow successfully requires a genuine desire to succeed, amounting almost to a need. The owner-manager must be able to motivate his management team so that they share that desire to succeed. Any entrepreneur must be willing to take risks – but only moderate risks that he believes he can overcome. The technical development engineer who has a good product idea but really only wants to build modified prototypes and is not interested in production and selling will not find any institutional investor willing to back him without his teaming up with others who have the qualities that he lacks. Enthusiasm and drive must, however, be tinged with a strong sense of realism in taking a market view of the business and its potential. Arnold Weinstock once said that all successful companies are run by people who understand the market.

Ability is important, and can be demonstrated to a potential backer by track record. Technical ability, along with patents, will protect the project from attempts by competitors to copy it. However a crucial factor that will convince potential backers that the plan will succeed is the ability of the management team. It is important that the business plan conveys the competence of the management team, not only directly by the inclusion of CV and so on, but also indirectly through the competence of the plan itself.

Once the business plan get through the initial sifting procedure, the presentation of the plan to backers will act as a further vehicle for demonstrating these qualities and convincing them of the competence of the team. First impressions are important, but demonstrated knowledge of the key areas in the business plan will go a long way towards generating the confidence that is needed.

A leading venture capitalist once admitted that, whilst discussions with the owner-manager centred on the business plan, the final decision whether or not to invest in him really was the result of a 'gut feel' a personal 'chemistry' between the venture capitalist and the owner-manager. At the end of the day that chemistry must lay the foundation for a long-term working relationship – a working relationship based upon substance and trust.

Nevertheless there are many ways of enhancing a presentation. It is always important to rehearse any presentation thoroughly. Among the elements of making the presentation successful it is often said that the owner-manager should manage the presentation with respect to his co-presenters. He should always emphasise market and management team expertise. In terms of style it is important to demonstrate the product or service as far as possible and to maintain eye contract with investors. Notwithstanding this, it is vital that the owner-manager and his team demonstrate a thorough understanding, familiarity and competence with respect to the business plan. Investors will want to spend some time simply getting to know the team members informally, at further meetings or even over dinner. And if the investment looks attractive . . . well, then it's down to haggling over the price.

Exercises

1. List the contents of a business plan drawn up:
   (a) for planning purposes within the firm,
   (b) for raising external finance.
2. Draw up a report for your superior in a bank outlining the criteria you recommend the bank to use in making a loan to:
   (a) a start-up,
   (b) an established small firm.
3. Write an essay on how computer-based systems can be used to help develop business plans.
4. Write a mission statement for a business idea that you explored in one of the exercises with Chapter 2.
5. Draw up a business plan for an idea of your own that you feel has some commercial potential. (See exercises in Chapter 2.)

CHAPTER 10

Small firms policy in Europe

Jim Dewhurst

SMALL AND MEDIUM-SIZED ENTERPRISES IN THE EC   198
ACCOUNTING VARIATIONS   201
EAST AND WEST EUROPEAN ACCOUNTING DIFFERENCES   202
CAPITAL AND FUNDING IN THE EC   204
LANGUAGE AND TRAINING   207
BUSINESS ATTITUDES   211
DIFFERENCES IN UK AND WEST CONTINENTAL
    CONTROL OF BUSINESSES   212
WEST CONTINENTAL TAKEOVERS AND MERGERS   212
TRAINING   215
REFERENCES   216

Small and medium-sized enterprises in the EC

Before looking at small firms and the policy of governments towards them, we need to discuss what we mean by a small or medium-sized enterprise (SME) in the European context. By the European Community's (EC's) principle of subsidiarity only those decisions which cannot sensible be made at member state level should be made by the European Community (European Union) itself.[1] Regula-

---

[1]The European Community (EC) consisted of the European Economic Community (EEC) – popularly known as the Common Market – and two other comparatively insignificant organisations – the European Coal and Steel Community (ECSC) and the European Atomic Energy Commission (Euratom). Under the Treaty of Maastricht the EC was renamed the European Union as from 1 November 1993. The EU, however, has continued to be referred to as the EC. In practice the terms European Community, the European Economic Community and the European Union, and their acronyms (EC, EEC and EU) are commonly used interchangeably, and they are so used here.

tions follow a similar pattern. Definitions of SMEs clearly fall within this remit, since otherwise it would be impossible to implement SME policy or to make useful comparisons across national boundaries without uniform standards. But the European Community has been an amalgam of member states. Historically each country has developed and used its own definition of small firms. Legislation has been passed, grants have been authorised and statistics produced using this parochial definition. Even within one country the definition has changed over time. In the UK, ever since the Bolton Committee (1971), emphasis has been placed on quantitative definitions. Thus the UK's 1985 Companies Act and the 1989 Act both used turnover, capital employed and number of employees. The problem with the former two is that inflation erodes both these measures. Indeed the 1989 Act, as we noted in Chapter 1, just increased the 1985 figures for these measures by some 40 per cent. The 1989 Act, which is still the relevant measure in this field, requires that, to qualify as 'medium', organisations must satisfy at least two of these conditions:

— a turnover not exceeding £8 million,
— a balance sheet total not exceeding £3.8 million,
— a number of employees not exceeding 250.

A more qualitative definition which emphasises independence, personalised management and market share does, in many ways, make more sense. The downside is that a subjective element is inevitably dragged in. The European Commission has recognised this and, after an attempt at a definition using money figures (which we give in Chapter 1), it has arrived at a quantitative definition which applies to all member countries. The Third Report of 'Enterprises in Europe', published by Eurostat, gives in Volume 1 these official definitions. Within the European Union therefore:

— micro enterprises are those businesses with less than ten employees,
— small enterprises are those with ten to 99 employees,
— medium-sized enterprises are those with 100–499 employees,
— large businesses are those with 500 or more employees.

Strictly, therefore, the term SME should only be applied to those businesses with employees in the range 10–499, and this restricted definition is the one that is properly used in all statistical work. It is clear, however, that micros are usually seen as SMEs in the general usage of the term.

These are simple criteria which do not need to take account of exchange rates, and are unaffected by inflation. They also correspond pretty much with generally accepted notions of micros, small, medium-sized and large enterprises. Accurate up-to-date figures for the numbers of businesses in the EC in each of these groups are hard to come by. The Second Annual Report of The European Observatory for SMEs, prepared for the EC's Directorate-General XXIII, estimated that in 1993 the EC had about 17 million SMEs. The number of large enterprises was put at 12,000.

The most recent, detailed, and *final* figures available are those by Eurostat for 1990. These show that in the (then 12) countries of the European Community (EUR12) there were some 14 million enterprises, employing 92 million persons: that is, 64 per cent of the EUR12 active population. Of the total number of enterprises 93 per cent were micros accounting for 32 per cent of total employment and 24 per cent of turnover. Small enterprises were responsible for 7 per cent of the total and more than a quarter of employment and turnover. There were fewer medium enterprises (only 0.5 per cent) and these accounted for 15 per cent of employment and 20 per cent of turnover. Finally there were then, as now, 12,000 large enterprises. They were the biggest employers with 28 per cent of EUR12 total employment, and they generated 29 per cent of total turnover.

Eurostat reported some interesting changes in the years from 1988 to 1990. First, the number of micro enterprises increased by 10 per cent, which was above the average. Micros also increased their employment figures by 12 per cent, but their increase in turnover was only 11 per cent, two points below the average. Second, large enterprises increased the number of their units, but only by 3 per cent. Their employment figures, however, were boosted by 12 per cent, and their growth, measured by turnover, was the highest at 22 per cent (deflated values). The increases for SMEs as a whole were below the average but they were more consistent for all the variables. Both number of units and employment increased by around 5 per cent, whilst turnover increased by 9 per cent.

From 1990 onwards the pattern changed somewhat. The Second Annual Report of The European Observatory for SMEs, as we have noted, confirmed that by 1993 the number of SMEs had risen to around 17 million. This pattern appears to be continuing. However it must be added that several national institutes have revised their methods of compiling data in recent years and particularly in the period 1988 to 1991. These methodological discrepancies at national level mean that any comparisons of absolute figures or derived statistics have to be made with great care. Since 1 January 1995 these problems have been confounded. On that day the European Union was enlarged to 15 countries by the inclusion of Austria, Finland and Sweden. These three countries have not used the standard business size classification common to the EUR12. In Austria the central statistical office has always used the establishment rather than the enterprise as the reference point. Further, only manufacturing industry and the civil engineering sector are covered in their figures. The size ranges used are 0–19, 20–99, 100–499 and 500 or more employees. In Finland data are not prepared on a basis that gives any easy comparison at all with EU figures. The Finnish contribution is of some importance in the enlarged community, however. The number of enterprises in Finland is approximately 1 per cent of the EUR12 total figure. Employment and turnover in Finland were 1.5 per cent and 2 per cent of the EUR12 figure, respectively. Sweden uses 0–19, 20–99 and 100-plus employees for its business size classifications. In 1991 employment accounted for 2.2 per cent of the EUR12 total size figure. Turnover, again as a percentage of the EUR12 figure, rose from 2.6 per cent in 1988 to 3.2 per cent in 1990.

Accounting variations

One of the advantages which follows from the adoption of a standard definition for a SME throughout the EC is that comparisons between member countries of numbers, distribution, growth and funding can readily be made. However analysing performance across the board also requires that financial figures have been prepared on a comparable basis. This has long been the goal of the European Commission. The provisions of the EC's fourth directive were generally taken on board in the UK in the 1985 Companies Act. But these provisions referred mainly to the presentation of final accounts. They did not deal with preparation of accounts, with standard accounting procedures or with standard disclosure provisions.

This problem is not confined to countries in the EC. It is worldwide. We start off, therefore, with the international scene, then deal with central and western Europe, before looking in a separate section, at the very substantial differences in accounting procedures between East and West Europe.

The Centre for International Financial Analysis (Cifar), a Princeton based institution, recalculated typical company reported figures from a number of countries using recommended common standards. The adjustments to net income were startling:

	per cent
France	+ 6
Germany	+44
Italy	+11
Japan	+12
Sweden	+60
Switzerland	− 8
UK	+ 4

Source: Cifar 1989 reports.

However even these figures must be treated with caution. The level of disclosure varies widely from country to country. Cifar reported that the most comprehensive and relevant data for industrial companies came from France, Ireland, Scandinavia (except Denmark), the UK and the USA. Below average disclosures occurred in Austria, Belgium, Denmark, Germany, Italy, Japan, the Netherlands and Spain.

Depreciation is the most widely varying item, with the economic life of an asset being treated as anything from five to 40 years. Good will is treated in a variety of ways. In some countries it is written off against shareholders' equity; in some it is amortised over periods ranging from five to 40 years. Failure to consolidate and the use of multiple classes of shares are other problems. All these add substantially to the existing difficulties in making comparisons as between countries, for figures such as income, cost of goods sold and, more importantly, performance ratios such as RONA (Return on Net Assets).

The traditional view in the UK has been that accounts in continental Europe have been prepared on a conservative basis. The Cifar figures given above did lend some support to this belief, particularly in the case of Germany. But this view is becoming increasingly outdated, though where punitive tax measures are more of a threat than equity markets this may still be the case. Nowadays in many areas new standards are increasingly being implemented throughout the EC. Generally assets are revalued upwards in the balance sheet and intangible assets are capitalised. Among the items which can still be treated in different ways are foreign currency transactions, joint ventures, off-balance sheet financing, such as leasing, and extraordinary items and long-term contracts. But generally throughout central and western Europe convergence of accounting methods and of accounts presentation is well on the way to a final consumation.

East and West European accounting differences

Command economies and market economies had different answers to the most fundamental industrial question of all, 'How many of *any* type of goods shall we produce?' The eastern command economy's answer was simple: 'Whatever the central state, in its wisdom, decrees.' But for a western market economy there is no decree laid down by the state. Its answer is that the 'right' number will be arrived at by the forces of supply and demand in a free market. And profit is the motivating force in that.

It is evident that moving from a command to a market economy has been a sea change and has presented many problems. Profit to centralists was a dirty word: but it was more than that. It was an unknown entity. So East European and CIS countries, when they entered into competition for markets with western businesses, have had to find out how to *measure profit*. Common costs, measurement of revenue, allocation of overheads, the preparation and presentation of accounts and GAAP (Generally Accepted Accounting Principles) have all been new and interesting concepts.

For a western SME which has invested in the East it has not been easy to make profits the value of which has been readily ascertainable. Getting profits out has been hard, too, but it has not been, as is still sometimes supposed, impossible. Dividend repatriation for foreign investors has just needed some ingenuity and effort. Barter has been used a lot. Barter practices will continue to exist as long as there is no truly free trade in money. The setting up of consortia (a pooling of companies for barter) has been used with clearing pools and centres for local hard currencies. Countertrade agencies – not much more than an elegant name for commercial organisations arranging cross-border barter – are still common in most European countries. The typical SME with little or no experience of the tricky business of barter will be well advised to use them. It is necessary, however, to give the goods or services offered a hard look. There needs to be a satisfactory answer to the question of why, if they are good bona fide products, they have not been sold on the open market.

Many East European countries wishing to encourage foreign investment have included tax holidays in the package of incentives they have offered to businesses. Tax has been a major problem. Some tax legislation is barely three or four years old. Generally it has not been tested by the Revenue in the courts, so its boundaries are uncertain. One of the difficulties has been that the concept of the separation of capital and revenue profits has not been grasped. There may be something that the West could learn here. Our proud tradition of accounting has relied heavily on the somewhat artificial distinction between these two. The modern tendency is away from 'high bookkeeping' towards a realisation that what really matters is cash.

In many East European countries local small business accounts still suffer from the original command economy's direction toward two major goals. The first was the traditional government requirement for statistical data for central planning. The use of a universal chart of accounts for reporting to government authorities was common. The second was for tax purposes. Accounting systems and procedures, though often limited to these goals, have generally been competent. Double-entry bookkeeping is common, too. There are, however, a number of major accounting differences from western and central European practice. Recognition of income is still mainly based on invoicing. The matching principle is not properly understood. The going concern concept has not been much used. Debtors are often not analysed by age. Provisions and contingency reserves may not exist. Stock is infrequently written off and is often overvalued. Book depreciation, as in the USA, is that prescribed in the tax regulations. Costing, until recently has been practically a no-go area and terms like 'cost of production' are not properly understood. As we noted earlier, capital and revenue profits are not separated. All leases are treated as operating leases.

All the above cause problems in understanding and control. One major weakness is the lack of accounting professions in the normal western sense. The idea of paying for an audit from an independent professional firm is still quite new. The former Yugoslavia had a competent central state auditing authority. This went against ingrained UK professional accountancy thinking. Nevertheless its advantages in terms of independence and impartiality are obvious: and the fact that it worked must give pause for some thought. Another common weakness is in MIS (Management Information Systems) and computer systems. The understanding of computer procedures is high, but the actual hardware is often, by western standards, archaic.

Marketing in eastern Europe and Russia has problems and barriers not met with in the West. In the EC the remaining barriers to cross-border trade have been demolished, but this is not the case for the ex-Comecon countries, which have no tradition of trading and dealing freely with other eastern bloc nations. For them any trade with other countries would have been laid down from above. They would do as they were told and no more. This lack of initiative and inability to make decisions are still common. With the removal of the central directive initiative is temporarily paralysed. One of the main practical problems in dealing with the CIS states, in particular, has been that of finding someone who has the power to deal with any business situation requiring a decision. The new political uncertainties only add to that.

Capital and funding in the EC

It has long been known that SMEs in the EC tend to get a much higher proportion of their funding from short-term finance than larger companies. For the major countries in the EC the difference is substantial. Nowhere is it more marked than in the UK. A 3i European Enterprise Centre report (1993), on the financing of enterprises in Europe shows that in France, Germany, Italy and Spain average small firms' figures for the percentage of short-term debt (overdrafts and short-term loans) in the total debt mix varied from 50 to 65. In the UK the proportion was a massive 76 per cent.

Loan finance

Since having long-term financing is always more risk-free and perhaps cheaper for the borrower, it seems certain that small firms are often forced into borrowing short. One reason is lack of collateral. Small firms has less net fixed assets in their total assets than have large businesses. Fixed assets are still the main form of security demanded by banks and other financial institutions. Small firms are also disadvantaged in relation to large companies by the cost of loan capital to them. All the evidence is that the additional premiums that small businesses have to pay over and above the rates demanded from typical large companies for their finance from banks run at about 1 or 2 per cent throughout the EC. In the UK, during the depression years and recently, there has also been considerable pressure for some relief from the volatility of interest rates. It is argued that small businesses borrow a high percentage of their funding on variable rates of interest and that therefore they are exceptionally vulnerable to government-induced changes in the cost of money.

On the face of it, a major source of funding for SMEs would seem to be trade credit. In the UK, for small companies, trade credit represents over 40 per cent of total capital and liabilities. The corresponding figure for large companies is around half of this. However much the same applies to trade debtors. The net gain to small companies in the UK of this apparently cost-free financing is therefore marginal. On the continent the evidence is that SMEs appear generally to receive less credit from their customers than they have to give to their customers. On the continent, too, small firms have to extend considerably more trade credit than larger firms.

Equity finance

The third major source of finance for SMEs is equity or venture capital. In the UK, ever since the Wilson Report of 1979, it has been known that small companies have a relatively small proportion of their assets financed by shareholders' funds, and this pattern appears to be continuing or even increasing. However, as with so many statistics for SMEs, categorisation or labelling may affect reported figures substantially, and conclusions drawn from them should bear this in mind. Owners'/directors' loans, for example, may be hidden in other balance sheet items. Across the EC, venture funding increased substantially in the years from 1987 to 1991. The First Annual Report, in 1993, of The European Observatory for SMEs gave figures for the proportion of venture capital funds in relation to GDP for member countries of the EC. The UK heads the list with 2.25 per cent, followed by Ireland and the Netherlands. The country for which venture capital is least important is Germany, where the proportion is less than 0.25 per cent of GDP. Greece, Italy and Denmark also show low proportions of risk capital. This same report drew attention to the fact that, across the EC too, most investment in venture capital in SMEs is concentrated on medium-sized firms rather than the smaller enterprises.

Many reports have drawn attention to the fact that venture capitalists, by favouring established companies and large investments, are aggravating the existing gap between small and large businesses. In the UK the absolute number of venture capitalists has been steadily reducing, and the number prepared to invest sums less than half a million pounds has fallen dramatically over the years. Development capital is their favourite form of funding. At the other end of the spectrum, start-up and seed corn finance are among the most difficult for a business to get. Only mezzanine capital ranks with these as the least easy to obtain.

Throughout the EC there has been a parallel decline in secondary stock market activity. By comparison with the USA, the informal venture capital networks and secondary markets in Europe are relatively undeveloped. To some extent the UK is bucking the general downward trend in smaller company flotations. Part of the reason may be an understandable desire to list in Britain rather in the USA on the smaller companies market there (Nasdaq). Some of the candidates in the UK for a new listing are not truly recent start-ups or even new or desirable companies. Some are the spawn of forced demergers. Some are forced issues made by operators taking advantage of the situation to push high-technology businesses into a listing that their past performance cannot properly justify. It may be, too, that the main reason for any upsurge in stock exchange activity in the UK is merely that Britain, the country which led Europe into the recession, is the country which has led it out.

Changes in the approach of banks

The other option for these firms in the UK is the traditional visit to the bank manager. It is still unusual for a British bank to take an equity stake in a business. On the continent it is much more part of well established policy. In Germany it is common. For the smaller SME, as we have noted, the equity capital alternative will not be available. For them the continued help and support of their bank is the only practical option.

Throughout Europe there is widespread unemployment. In 1995 UK unemployment was 8.2 per cent compared with 10 per cent in Germany and 12.2 per cent in France. Throughout Europe, too, there has been widespread agreement that the best way to combat this is by encouraging small businesses and start-ups. The pressure on banks to lend in the 1980s was enormous. Many banks obliged freely and some burnt their fingers. The apotheosis of this extreme approach was found, as one might expect, in America. In the USA one bank sent its loan officers into the field to operate on a range of new development businesses alongside a new freeway. The loan officers had to put a report into bank head office the moment they refused any loan in their area, and they had to give good reasons for their failure (as it was seen) to make the loan. Some were fired for lending too little. One bank, the Chicago Bank, fired officers who did not achieve their loan quotas. The Chicago Bank is now defunct and the easy lending practices of the banks in the pre-recession boom years were widely seen as totally inappropriate in the 1990s. One other factor, due to the recession, which has affected bank lending policy towards SMEs, has been the traditional heavy reliance on property for security. Private houses have been taken as collateral. Loans have frequently exceeded the present-day market value of the security. The overreaction by bankers to these problems has been marked and needs itself to be corrected. Fortunately throughout Europe the relationship between banks and small businesses is being worked out anew. Greater involvement by the bank with the management of the business has been suggested. Some consideration may be given to the possibility of equity staking by banks when looking at new funding. A longer-term lending relationship might be considered, with greater emphasis on fixed interest business mortgages. In all these British banks could well learn from the more flexible arrangements practiced in many countries on the continent.

Language and training

English is at once the most powerful and the most persuasive of the major western world languages. It is also the most annoying and frustrating. Throughout the world English is spoken as the mother tongue by some 300 million people. Another 300 million use it as their second tongue. Europe and Japan together form the main part of these second tongue users. It has been estimated that another billion learn English as a foreign language. In over 70 countries throughout the world English is either the official or joint official language. In part this is the heritage of our past imperialism. It has been a common pattern for many British colonies on their road to independence to start with English as their official language and then proceed to English, together with their own indigenous language, as joint official languages. A few are now dropping English. Nevertheless the quiet dominance of English as an official language is impressive. No other language comes close to it: the French language, with around half the English figure, is the only one in the same league.

It is important to understand the significance of these official language, taught foreign language and, particularly, second language figures. China is the largest country so far as first language is concerned. English is only second. But intra-China trade is of no interest to us. For inter-country trading a language which is understood by *both* parties is the thing that matters. English has been and still is that language.

English has a rival. In the European Community English and French are the two main working languages, and the determination of the French to protect their language is fierce. However in the technical committees of the EC (where much of the 'nitty gritty' is done) Germany predominantly holds the secretariat and some of the work there is in German. The predominance of German in this area, with French in second place, is a legacy of the initial setting up of the Community, with France and Germany as the two most powerful members, and Britain at that time not a member at all. However it is only in this area that German is powerful. If we try to assess the overall use within the Union of French, English and German, it is probably true to say that French has had, and still has, a very slight edge over English. Overall these two predominate.

Within the Community there is something very much like our own familiar north–south divide (perhaps more accurately north and south-east) in languages. This language division is between the 'Latin' languages of the south and west (French, Italian and Spanish) and the 'Teutonic' languages of the north and east (English, German, Danish and Dutch)

English in the Union

There is a clear political trend in European affairs which must operate towards enhancing the commercial use of English. The European Community at present has 15 members. With the one minor exception of Greenland, the Community's history has been one of majestic and uninterrupted expansion. The main reason for not easily accepting further approaches has been the stated belief that the Community has been growing so rapidly that a period of assimilation was neccessary. But this has passed. The free trade European Economic Area linking the EC and EFTA put the EFTA nations on the fast track towards full membership of the Community. There is a lesson to be learnt here: restrictions on foreign ownership of shares will go; the rich Nordic countries will be a new game area for UK acquirers.

EFTA countries have always used English extensively as a second language. The northern 'Eastern bloc' countries, and particularly Poland, continued to use English under Communist rule despite efforts to make Russian the compulsory second language. And in the Czech Republic and Slovakia English has recently made a resurgence in schools. English therefore has a very positive future as a commercial language in an enlarged Community. The industrial, trading and distribution possibilities are there. But the most important advantage of all will be gained if the new language of *communication* can be English.

The survival of commercial English

The need for language learning is self-evident. The argument, put forward in the past, against learning the foreign language was this: the mainland Europeans speak our language comparatively well; they have had to learn it because of the predominance of English as a second language; why waste such scant time and resources as an SME business manager will have in preparing for the late 1990s and beyond in this unnecessary way?

This is a silly argument born out of arrogance and lethargy. It is a delusion to think that the Dutch, Belgians and French learnt English as their tribute to the greater glory of Britain! They did so because it had been their common practice to learn a little of English and also the languages of their neighbours. But with the establishment of the Single European Market the growing advantages that this brought became self-evident. For that same Dutchman who talks to us so knowledgeably in our language can also speak some French and German. And it is not only English businessmen who like to be addressed in their own language.

Language education

Learning a foreign language is important. It is not just the benefit from being able to communicate on business affairs that matters, it is the confidence that comes from knowledge, and the good will that is established from appearing to take an interest. It follows that some ability in speaking a foreign language and in understanding foreign customs is a great deal better than none at all. Commercial classes or evening classes run by the local authority are satisfactory answers to this problem.

SME entrepreneurs wishing to build up an active involvement in a foreign country, and considering employing a graduate, should initially look for a student with a joint degree in languages and a course relevant to the work of the firm, whether this be engineering, transport, IT, science or general business studies. Failing this, small businesses should realise that it is far easier to train a language graduate in commercial skills than to take a student with some business qualification and train that student from scratch to a reasonably high level in a foreign language.

Secretarial staff

A somewhat similar approach should be used by entrepreneurs wishing to take on secretarial staff. The basic qualification necessary for a suitable secretary will be an ability to speak and write in the foreign language. Computer literacy is important, too. This will need to go beyond a simple skill in word processing. A capacity to deal with spreadsheets, databases, graphics, market analyses and so on is important. From the secretary's point of view it will be a help in finding a job to have attended a college in the vicinity which has build up over the years good contacts with potential employers. From the small business entrepreneur's point of view it will be a help to have taken part in the process. This need not involve any material commitment of resources. All that is necessary is an ongoing relationship with a local college.

Across Europe there is another trend. This is towards 'multilingualism'. As we have noted, European businessmen already have a far greater command of foreign languages, other than English, than have most British businessmen. The competitive advantage that this must give is great. On the continent around 5 per cent of total management training time is typically given to language training. This is far higher than in the UK. Unless something is done to reverse this situation the gap will widen. In the highly complex cross-border European commercial deals in the future, continental businessmen will use whichever language gives them the competitive edge. While it is still true that many important negotiations with foreign businesses can be carried out in English, and that takeovers and mergers are often organised by British financial institutions and nearly always use British takeover vocabulary, this situation is changing.

Many mainland continental businessmen are also more aware, and understanding, of other countries' habits and customs than are their counterparts in the UK. Perhaps a certain traditional arrogance still exists in British attitudes. In export marketing it is necessary to accommodate both behaviour and language with those of the customers. Businesses with existing contacts abroad will have staff who know about these matters. They can advise employees engaged in a new export drive directly, or they can put this information on file for later access.

Business attitudes

Repeated reference has been made to the different attitudes to management by UK businesses and by businesses on the continent. We see our attitude as the norm; certainly it is similar to that prevailing in the USA. But it is not universal. The Japanese consensus style, for one, is nearer to mainland Europe than it is to us. On the continent, in Japan, and in many other parts of the world, the situation is different. Key shareholders are more likely to be locked in. Often these shareholders are financial institutions such as, for example, the German universal banks. Such banks provide funds to large companies and to SMEs. They also do so at apparently lower rates than their counterparts in the UK or USA. But one person's gain is another's loss, and there is not much evidence that overall the net cost of capital in Europe is markedly different from that in the UK.

Mainland continental businesses do not lose shareholder confidence to quite so great an extent as in the UK if they do not report a rising profit figure each year and every year. They can and do take a longer-term view. As a direct consequence employees in these businesses, too, can take a longer view. They see themselves, and are seen, as part of the company, almost a community of friends. In many countries overseas the business is comparatively paternalistic in its approach. But this paternalism only applies to the business's own employees and shareholders. It does not extend to competitors. It does not prevent the business from being very aggressive overseas. The UK has been, as we shall note in a wider context later, the number one target for mainland continental predators.

These differences have been strongly drawn for emphasis. It is understandable that in a wider Europe they are beginning to disappear. Further most socially advanced UK SMEs use alternative methods in their business governance, such as profit sharing or share ownership schemes, to ensure worker participation. But the differences still exist. Entering Europe successfully without this understanding is like trying to win at American football without first finding out the local ground rules.

Differences in UK and west continental control of businesses

There are very substantial differences, too, between British and west European investment patterns and control of businesses. It is essential for any SME operating on the European mainland to understand these differences. They can be summarised as follows:

1. On the continent a much lower proportion of businesses are listed on stock exchanges than in the UK.
2. Many businesses on the continent, even some large listed companies, have been for many years, and still remain, controlled by families. Behind the scenes, with the details difficult for an outsider to discover, there are generally cross-holdings with other similar companies, or with banks, or with major shareholders. Generally there is a greater involvement by these parties in the strategic planning and management of the business than is common in the UK.
3. Most of the shares in UK companies, by contrast, are owned by financial institutions such as pension funds, building societies, banks, and unit and investment trusts. These institutions have a long tradition of non-interference in the domestic affairs of their investments (though the extreme 'hands off' approach has over the years been replaced by a more active involvement). Further there has always been one exception to this practice and that is when the company has substantial financial problems. In that case the financial institutions typically get together and play a dominant role in the restructuring.
4. In mainland Europe it is quite common for businesses to take a stake in another company which does not give them control. UK companies tend to want full control or at least a more active involvement.

West continental takeovers and mergers

On the continent almost all takeovers are still non-hostile. The 'get together' plan is agreed after long consultations and is implemented on a friendly basis. Most acquisitions are of private companies. Throughout the 1980s and well into the 1990s the UK was the number one target for EC cross-border takeovers. In 1990 the UK had nearly £14b. in value of its businesses acquired by businesses in the EC. This exceeded, by several times, the figures for Germany, France, Spain, the Netherlands and Italy. Each of these had around £2b. to £4b.'s worth of their firms taken over. The major acquirers in this period were Sweden, France and the UK, in that order. In 1993 there was a dramatic change. The UK moved up and for the first time headed, for a while, the league table of cross-border acquisitions involving European countries – a position that it has not been able to maintain.

The corresponding international figures are interesting. At the start of the 1990s foreign businesses were making net profits of around £7b. a year in the UK. By 1993, for every 100 workers in UK manufacturing, 13 were working for a foreign employer. This process of overseas infiltration into our economy has been going on for a long time. The USA and, more recently, Japan have been the main aggressors. A study commissioned by the Parliamentary Office of Science and Technology found that 'over the last 40 years the USA and Japan have each placed close to 40 per cent of their direct overseas investment in Britain'. However Germany has been moving up the league of European acquirers of businesses in the UK. In the 1992–3 period decisions by overseas-owned companies to invest in the UK still saw the USA in first place with 126 projects, but Germany was second with 51, pushing Japan, with 21, into third place.

The reverse process – that is, international investment by UK firms overseas – has always been helped by the high cash-raising power of the City. In the same period overseas direct investment by UK firms reached a massive 4.5 per cent of gross domestic product. This is a proportion exceeding that of any other European state. But as we have noted the UK then ranked low in the league of acquirers in the EC. It is evident that, with the great expertise that the UK has in the overall acquisitions game, and with the still powerful support of the City as a money supplier, and the growing communality of the EC states, the green fields of Europe are a fertile area for UK business growth. We can sum up this section by saying that, within the limited European area and also in the worldwide context, the UK economy has been one of the most open and non-parochial in all the world. As we come out of our recession there is a growing awareness of the potential benefits from sensible investment on the continental mainland. This is particularly the case for SMEs. In both eastern and central Europe the growth areas have been reported as being in the service rather than the manufacturing sectors. And the service areas are the prerogative of SMEs.

European takeover practice

Larger SMEs may well wish to expand by moving into Europe, but they need to know how to go about it in the different situation on the continent. A comparison of takeover and merger legislation and practice in Europe itself reveals some surprising differences. The UK market, as we have noted, has remained comparatively unrestricted and transparent. Indeed to many UK businesses playing the acquisition game it has seemed that the playing fields have not been level and that the goal posts have been of different sizes. Our own companies have been available for takeover on the open market, but companies in many countries on the continent have not been. Many European companies have been protected from takeovers by their two-tier boards, restricted voting rights, proscriptions on shareholdings above certain thresholds and institutional capital markets which do not easily allow the building up of large stakeholdings prior to a hostile takeover.

There are still many barriers to hostile takeovers on the continent. In France particularly, but also many other countries, the law and the application of the law by government departments often makes acquisitions by EC companies a long and difficult procedure. Acquisitions by non-EC companies are even more heavily proscribed. In Germany and the Netherlands their strong two-tier board system and their concern to protect employees' rights add to the existing problems in making acquisitions. Bearer shares are comparatively common throughout western Europe. In Germany it is normal practice for 'universal' banks to exercise their rights in these bearer shares on behalf of the companies with whom they are involved.

For UK aggressors the situation is bright. As we have seen, there is a mass of small and medium-sized family-owned businesses on the continental mainland. These are becoming more open to acquisition. Partly this is because of the slow but increasingly effective trend in EC merger legislation. More powerfully it is because these businesses are outgrowing a pattern which historically has existed too long. Many need new capital to survive. Some will have to go public to get it. There are increasing succession problems, too, for some of these firms, and most realise that in the coming, more competitive, single market of the late 1990s they need to be bigger to be more beautiful. Nevertheless the long tradition on the continent against hostile acquisitions and against outright ownership is still strong.

Mergers have often been seen as an appropriate answer to those problems, particularly for SMEs. They have, however, frequently run into difficulties. Mergers often appear to be good to both the prospective parties; but both sides to a merger see the new business as going the way they want it to, and with themselves somehow as still in charge. Rarely is there any such thing as a true merger. One party is almost always the boss. What is certain is that takeovers disguised as mergers almost invariably do not work out. Parallel with this practical problem with mergers is an accounting problem. In the UK

it has until recently been possible to choose between merger accounting and acquisition accounting. Merger accounting however, has
allowed corporations to use 'creative accounting' techniques to
enhance profits. The new UK accounting procedures will ensure that,
except in the rare cases of true mergers, acquisition accounting, in
which the newly purchased company is treated as an asset by the
acquirer, will always be used. What is certain, too, is that any
aggressive UK SME wishing to acquire, merge with or form an
alliance with a continental business should, before acting, be sure
both of its own real motives and of those of the other enterprise.

Training

British SMEs spend 1.29 per cent of their turnover on training. A 3i
European Enterprise Centre report (1992) gave this figure as part of
the results of their survey of over 10,000 SMEs in Europe. The
average percentage of turnover reported as being spend on training
in the other four countries covered in the survey was:

France	1.76
Germany	1.45
Spain	1.73
Italy	1.48

Britain therefore comes bottom of this table which gives the raw
results of this training survey, but these figures need to be seen in
the light of a number of other factors.

First French companies are required in any case by law to make
certain minimum expenditures on training. Second, the apprentice-
ship schemes are increasing the numbers in training in the UK.
Third, for many SMEs a significant proportion of training is done
internally by the businesses' own staff. In Britain 55 per cent of the
training was reported as having been undertaken in this way. In this
connection, too, the work of the UK's Training and Enterprise
Councils (TECs) is apposite. The UK government has done little to
encourage training through this route and the quality of the business
education supplied has not been good. The government's quasi-pri-
vatisation of training by the TECs has demonstrably not worked. The
TECs have been starved of money. Also they have not been well
supplied with the promised advice by directors and senior executives
from successful organisations. It should have been obvious that these
busy people would have neither the time nor perhaps the desire to
help SMEs with whom they generally have only tentative connections. Local Enterprise Agencies, set up in the early 1980s, found that

they had the same problems. Retired bank managers and elderly executives and academics are not always the best providers of practical up-to-date advice on business matters. Paradoxically retired executives seem to be successful in helping firms in eastern Europe. These 'grey panthers', to use the emotive term given to them by Sir John Harvey-Jones, or 'turnaround managers', in more officialspeak, have been much in evidence in Moscow, where the streets have been paved with consultants and experts. Perhaps the fact that many work on an expenses-only basis (or at any rate on a cost basis with very little added on for wages) provides a clue to their being sought after.

Throughout the world there has been, since the early 1960s, the phenomenon of 'jobless growth'. Germany, since 1960, has seen an overall growth of 122 per cent, but employment there has actually fallen by 15 per cent. In the UK the economy grew by just over 80 per cent, but employment fell by 6 per cent. Even in the USA employment has fallen behind growth. In the developing countries the situation has been even worse. The exception has been the Pacific basin region, and particularly Japan and its satellite economies in Malaysia, Singapore and South Korea. There the growth rates have been spectacular, but job creation has not lagged behind. These successful east Asian economies have three things in common. First, their governments have invested heavily in skills and education. Their workforces therefore move with changes in technology, rather than being displaced by them. Second, they have understood the need to support SMEs positively. In particular they have ensured that small businesses have received the flow of credit finance which they need for growth. Finally, in every case, a 'hands on' government approach has masterminded the implementation of these policies.

These successes have been noted elsewhere. In the USA there seems to be a determination to take the necessary positive action to help SMEs. There, 50 per cent of new jobs have been shown to have been created by small businesses. The investment credit packages and training measures will bring American practice into line with the modern Japanese-inspired approach. But of the world's three major trading areas, Europe still appears to be the most fragmented and backward in providing government initiative and help for training and education for SMEs, as well as appropriate financial support.

References

3i European Enterprise Centre (1992), *Report 3: Training Across Europe*, April.
3i European Enterprise Centre (1993), *Report 8: Financial Characteristics of Small Companies in Britain*, September.

The European Observatory for SMEs, First and Second Annual Reports (1993 and 1994) The Centre for Small and Medium Sized Enterprises, University of Warwick.

Case Studies*

---

*All case studies are intended for class discussion and not as examples of good or bad management practice.

The McArdle Syringe

This is a case about a business idea. The issue is whether the idea is really a business and how it should be exploited.

Questions

1. What further information is needed to evaluate the idea?
2. What further information is needed to evaluate the business opportunity?
3. What do you think about the market potential?
4. What options are available to exploit the idea commercially and what are the pros and cons of each option?
5. What would you advise Louis to do?
6. Draw up an action plan of the things he needs to do to make his decision.

Background

During 1991 there were over 12,000 reported 'sharps' injuries[1] from exposed needles in the USA. Between January 1989 and June 1991 there were 337 sharps injuries in one London teaching hospital alone. Many such injuries go unreported, so the full extent of the problem is not really known. However there is no doubt that, on a daily basis, medical staff using syringes for administering drugs or taking

This case was written by Ian Rae and Rifat Atun and based on material supplied by Louis McArdle.

© Copyright 1996 Ian Rae and Rifat Atun, The Management School, Imperial College.

[1]A 'sharps' injury is the same as a 'needle-stick' injury. It is an accidental injury caused by a needle.

blood are at risk of injury. The problem is that sharps injuries carry a risk of bloodborn infections such as Hepatitis B and HIV. Staff can be protected from the Hepatitis virus by immunisation but as yet there is no cure for HIV.

Recent well publicised reports of an HIV-infected surgeon working in a British hospital have stirred up anxieties about the transmission of HIV from patients to doctors and vice versa. In the USA in 1991 there was a great deal of publicity given to the case of a young female dentist who had accidentally pierced her hand after administering a dental anaesthetic and had contracted HIV from the infected patient. Such dire consequences are still very rare. For example, medical research carried out by the Royal College of Pathologists has shown that the risk of transmission from a single inoculation injury with HIV-positive blood is one in 275. However they can only become more common as HIV spreads.

The inventor

Louis McArdle is 28 years of age. He studied dentistry at Glasgow University before obtaining his fellowship in dental surgery at The Royal College of Surgeons of England in London. He has recently undertaken research into dental implants in San Francisco and is currently studying for a masters degree. Concerned about the consequences of sharps injuries, Louis came up with the idea for a new safer syringe.

At present a dental anaesthetic unit comes in three parts: (1) an anaesthetic vial which fits inside a cartridge; (2) the cartridge syringe, which is in two parts, the housing and the plunger; (3) the needle, which is screwed onto the syringe housing so that it perforates the vial. The plunger then pushes the solution out of the vial through the needle (see Figure 1).

The needle is initially sheathed by a plastic cover which is used to resheath the needle after use and prior to disposal. This is where many injuries arise. It is not uncommon, as the figures show, for people to stick the needle in themselves and thus create a possible source of cross-infection. Most standard syringes operate on a similar basis.

The new concept

The design contains two new concepts. Both the needle and the syringe have been redesigned to reduce the risk of needle-stick injury.

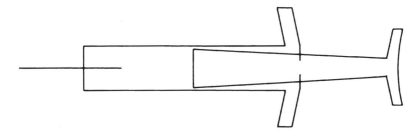

Figure 1   Existing anaesthetic unit (needle)

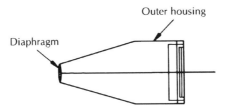

Figure 2   'New' needle: outer section

The needle

This is made up of two parts: (1) an outer sheath which protects the needle. This has a rubber diaphragm which the needle perforates when advanced (see Figure 2). (2) An inner section (block) which holds the needle and can move reciprocally within the outer sheath/housing (see Figure 3). When the inner section is advanced the needle perforates the diaphragm and is exposed, thus ready for injection.

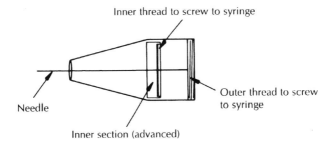

Figure 3   'New' needle: inner section

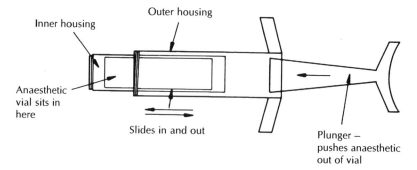

Three parts – al separate but come together.
1. Plunger.
2. Inner housing: The metal casing will contain the anaesthetic vial which is disposable. The inner section of the needle will thread onto this inner housing. The inner housing can be telescopically advanced and retracted within the outer casing.
3. Outer housing: This outer part contains the inner housing within it and allows the inner housing to advance and retract as above. The outer housing has an inner thread which screws onto the outer housing via the needle. The outer housing would have cut away panals down the length so as to observe the inner housing.

Figure 4   The 'new' syringe

The syringe

This is made up of three parts: (1) a plunger as before; (2) an inner housing; (3) an outer housing (see Figure 4). The inner housing sits within the outer housing and can be moved telescopically to increase the overall length of the syringe. The inner housing holds the anaesthetic vial.

When the needle and the syringe are put together the system works in the following way: The inner housing of the needle (containing the needle) is screwed onto the inner housing of the syringe. Similarly the outer needle sheath is screwed onto the outer syringe housing. Because both inner parts of the needle and syringe are fixed together they can be moved reciprocally back and forth within the attached outer housing and needle sheath (see Figure 5). The inner syringe housing can advance, at the same time advancing the needle through the diaphragm and exposing it, to allow the injection to be given. Once the injection has been given, the inner housing can be retracted manually and thus the needle is resheathed. The system can then be dismantled and the needle disposed of without risk of needle-stick injury.

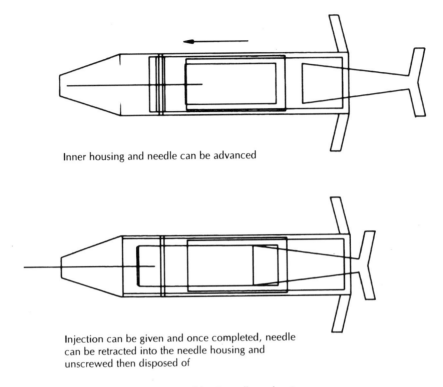

Inner housing and needle can be advanced

Injection can be given and once completed, needle
can be retracted into the needle housing and
unscrewed then disposed of

Figure 5 'New' needle and syringe

Protection of the idea

Before the invention could be exploited the idea had to be protected
under existing legislation to prevent it from being copied or simply
stolen. The most appropriate form of protection appeared to be by
way of patent. A patent would secure a monopoly right to the exclusive use of the invention for a maximum period of 20 years from the
date the application for the patent was filed. In order to be able to
discuss the syringe openly in public a patent application had to be
filed.

Not all inventions qualify for the grant of a patent. The Patents Act
1977 lays down that, to be patentable, an invention must:

(a) be new,
(b) involve an inventive step,
(c) be capable of industrial application, and
(d) not be 'excluded'.

To be patentable an invention must never have been made public in any way before the date on which the application for a patent is filed. The McArdle syringe met this criterion. The Patent Office say that an invention involves an inventive step if, when compared with what is already known, it would not be obvious to someone with a good knowledge and experience of the subject. In this context the McArdle syringe certainly appeared to be inventive. In order to be patentable an invention has to be capable of being made or used in some kind of industry. The McArdle syringe has the potential to be widely used by doctors, dentists, vetenarians and other medical practitioners. Lastly the syringe did not fall under one of the categories of excluded inventions. Excluded inventions are things such as scientific theory, the mathematical method or aesthetic creation.

The procedure for obtaining a patent is governed by the Patents Act 1977. The Act requires an application to be made in a particular way, using official forms. These are available from the Patent Office. The application must contain at least:

(a)   a request for a patent,
(b)   identification of the applicant,
(c)   a description of the invention, and
(d)   the filing fee.

An application cannot be given a filing date until all these items have been received by the Patent Office. Detailed drawings of the syringe were prepared and sent to the Patent Office with the application. The initial filing fee is £25. Later, at the search and application stages of the application, a further £130 is required at each stage.

Patent agents

Applying for a patent is a detailed, complex business. It is common for inventors to instruct agents to handle their patent applications. Provisional advice was obtained from agents regarding the patentability of the new syringe. Depending on the complexity of the invention, patent agents fees will usually amount to about £1,000. In order to minimise costs, Louis decided to file the initial application himself and instruct agents to deal with the more complex issues at a later stage. Within limits, amendments may subsequently be made to the application and with this in mind a filing date was obtained in September 1992.

To be patentable an invention must, amongst other things, be new and inventive. However, for an invention to have any prospect of commercial success, it needs more. For example, the invention may be new in the sense of filling a gap in the market. Alternatively the invention may provide a significant improvement in terms of cost, reliability or performance over other products already available in the same field. These issues were carefully considered and, if only from the safety aspect, it was felt that a market existed for the syringe. The healthcare industry was becoming increasingly safety conscious.

Commercial viability

To assess the potential of the new syringe it was necessary to look at the existing market. The various market segments had to be identified and the strengths and weaknesses of the market participants had to be gauged. The market breaks down into two segments.

Disposable, single-use syringes and needles

This is the large-volume, low-price sector of the market. There are some slight variations in the models but essentially there is very little product differentiation. The primary uses for such products are the injections of drugs and the taking of blood samples (phlebotomy). This segment of the market is particularly price-sensitive, with high-volume purchasers such as hospitals and district health authorities. In addition, there are more fragmented smaller purchasers such as general practitioners and pharmacies who tend to buy from wholesalers.

Single-use syringes sell for between one and ten pence each, depending on size and quality. The UK market is currently 125 million units per annum, with an expected growth rate of between 2 to 4 per cent. Becton Dickinson has 70 per cent of the UK market and its global sales are in the region of $2b. per annum. Bectons is a very large and powerful multinational company, as is typical of the major players in this market, such as Braun Medical and Sabre. There is also an increasing volume of cheaper generic syringes being produced in Korea and Taiwan.

The pre-filled syringe market

This segment of the market comprises two categories: pre-filled vaccines and injectable drugs. The UK vaccine market is approximately 6.5 million units per annum. The biggest seller is the flue vaccine, with sales in the region of 4.2 million units per annum at around £5.10 per unit. Other products:

Vaccine	Market size (millions)	Price (£)
Tetanus	1.0	0.8–1.0
Hepatitis B	0.5	11
Hepatitis A	0.3	12
Typhoid	0.2	12

There are other vaccines commonly used but they do not come in pre-filled syringes. The two biggest are the triple vaccine and measles, mumps and rubella, for which the UK market size is 5 and 2 million units, respectively, each year.

There are three real growth areas in this market segment, the first of which is the flu vaccine. The over-65s are particularly vulnerable and demographic changes have resulted in an increasingly ageing population. The flu vaccine market is expected to grow at approximately 10 per cent per annum. The second major growth area is the Hepatitis B vaccine which is being brought about by the need to immunise those at greatest risk, including health workers and the police. Thirdly, the Hepatitis A vaccine is being increasingly demanded by travellers.

As with the disposable syringe market segment, the players in this market tend to be large multinationals such as Merieux. They have a 60 per cent share of the UK flue vaccine market. Their other products include vaccines for tetanus, typhoid, rabies and meningococcal. Other players are Smithkline Beecham, Servier and Duphar Laboratories, all producing a range of products. These companies tend to manufacture the vaccine, with the syringe component sub-contracted to major manufacturers such as Merieux and Becton Dickinson.

It is highly significant that the aggressively acquisitive pharmaceutical company Medeva, led by B Taylor (ex-Chief Executive of Glaxo), is concentrating on this market which it sees as a growth area. Medeva has made strategic acquisitions in the market segments which include pre-filled vaccines (Evans) and pre-filled emergency drugs (IMS). With the acquisition of the Institut de Recherche Corbière it has established itself as a firm with a strong base in Europe and the UK.

Currently the majority of injectable drugs are sold as a powder and dilutant. The trend is towards pre-filled ready-to-use all-in-one syringes. This is particularly so for emergency drugs and dental anaesthesia. Potentially this is a very large market. The principal markets for such products are the emergency drugs used by doctors in hospitals and general practice. The present volume is around 700,000 units per annum, priced at between £1.50 and £3.50 per unit.

The drug companies are also selling their new products via custom-made syringes such as Glaxo's Imigran, which sells for £50 a unit. Glaxo subcontract the manufacture of the syringes to Becton Dickinson.

Opportunities

To develop the syringe himself Louis would have to either establish his own manufacturing facility or subcontract the manufacturing: either way, a high-risk, highly capital-intensive operation. With absolutely no experience in manufacturing, Louis believed that he would find it extremely difficult, if not impossible, to go it alone. Subcontracting would also be a problem, in that it is usually done in large volumes – not particularly appropriate for the small entrepreneurial start-up. Such a course of action would also involve the expense and time of developing a prototype. Each individual part of the syringe would require a separate injection moulding. Each moulding would cost approximately £10,000 to make. As the syringe comprises at least five separate parts, it was probable that costs would soon start to escalate and raising finance for the start-up would be a critical issue. It was anticipated that initial development costs could easily amount to £100,000 with professional fees, prototype costs and so forth.

Not only would getting production off the ground be a substantial task, but distribution channels would be extremely difficult to develop in the existing market-place. It would be almost impossible for the McArdle syringe to compete with the mass-produced single-use syringes which are inexpensive and sold in a price-sensitive market. Price is more of an issue than safety in this market and, as the new syringe would inevitably be more expensive, Louis doubted whether he could effectively compete against the existing products. It would be tough competing against the likes of Becton Dickinson on price.

More opportunities appeared to exist in the pre-filled vaccine market, but access to the drugs' would be necessary. Companies such as Glaxo and Smithkline Beecham, with their huge sales and marketing networks, hold an almost unassailable position in this market. These companies would probably deny access to the drugs for new market entrants. Louis was concerned about the high entry barriers for this market, but he was attracted by the possibility of achieving the higher returns and greater control associated with a start-up. Louis would have to bear all the risks, but would also take any profits.

A joint venture was another possibility. It could be undertaken with either a syringe manufacturer such as Becton Dickinson or, more realistically, with a drug company such as Glaxo. This would enable Louis to share the risk of the new venture and gain access to capital. However Louis still required his own capital, the extent of which would be governed by the deal. It would be necessary to sell the idea successfully to one of the major manufacturers. Once again, Louis had no experience of dealing with such companies. As with a start-up, raising capital was still likely to be a problem. In the current economic climate it was felt that it would be difficult to get bank finance without extensive security. Friends and family were a possibility. Venture capitalist rate start-ups as the highest risk and expect high rates of return. If an investor could be found, they would probably require a return of around 50 per cent compounded.

Some form of licensing agreement was also considered. In order to license the syringe it would still be necessary to develop a prototype model. The cost of doing this is substantial and the problem of raising capital still existed. A substantial attraction of licensing the syringe to a major manufacturer would be that it would take less time to take the product from concept to the market. There is less risk involved in licensing, but the returns are inevitably smaller. A 'one-off licensing fee plus royalties would have to be negotiated with any potential licensee and this might necessitate obtaining professional advice and incurring further expense.

With the patent already secured, there is little further cost involved in selling the idea. Certainly time would need to be spent on finding a buyer and negotiating a deal. Louis was concerned about this because he had no experience in dealing with such matters and had no direct contacts in the business. As with a licensing deal, there is likely to be a 'one-off' lump sum payment together with some sort of royalty arrangement. This option had the benefit of probably being more attractive to manufacturers as they could then retain control and develop the product further. Because of the limited risk involved, Louis was very interested in this option.

New developments

As a result of the extensive publicity given to the (possibly fatal) consequences of needle-stick injury, other new, safer products are beginning to appear in the market.

The Vacutainer

Developed by Becton Dickinson, this product is being increasingly used by hospitals and general practitioners. Essentially it enables the healthcare worker to safely remove the needle from the syringe with a reduced risk of needle-stick injury. It is for phlebotomy use only.

Safety-Lok

Once again this product has been developed by Becton Dickinson. It is simply a larger sheath which is placed over the needle for protection after use.

Newcastle needle

Developed by Newcastle General Hospital, this product has a protective sleeve on the needle which is drawn forward manually after use. This product has been patented and licensed to Coopers Needleworks to market in Europe. It is a major advance in design but the needle is still exposed prior to use.

The future

By June 1992 it appeared to Louis that the new syringe had great potential and he was keen to develop it further. However there were a number of uncertainties which still had to be dealt with. Firstly, would the syringe actually work? No working model had yet been produced. Secondly, if it worked, could it be made in sufficient quantities at an attractive price? Indeed could it be manufactured at all? How much was the syringe worth to a licensee or a buyer? Louis had no idea of its commercial value nor how he would go about arranging a joint venture, a sale or a licensing deal. Clearly, before the syringe could be taken further, these issues had to be addressed.

Claridges Restaurant

This is an actual business plan produced by someone who attended a Graduate Enterprise Programme. They required an initial loan of £35,000 and an overdraft facility of £3,500 to set up their restaurant. They obtained the money on the basis of this plan.

Questions

1. Overall, what do you think of the plan?
2. What areas do you think are weak and what areas would you request more information on?
3. What vital information is missing from this plan? Only when this is decided upon can any funding proposition be taken further.
4. Would you have lent them the money? If so, under what terms?
5. How much detail do you think should go into a plan
   - for internal purposes?
   - for the purpose of raising finance?
6. What do you think are the critical factors that will determine the success of this venture?

A business plan for Claridges Restaurant (partners: S.A & C.J. Claridge)

Contents
Executive summary
1 The business
    1.1 Introduction

1.2 Business mission
1.3 Objectives – short-term
1.4 Objectives – long-term
1.5 Key personnel
2 Markets and competition
  2.1 Selected market segments
  2.2 Market segments – growth and size
  2.3 Customer benefits
  2.4 Competitors
  2.5 Competitive strategy
3 Selling
4 Premises etc.
  4.1 General
  4.2 Key suppliers
  4.3 Quality control
  4.4 Staffing
  4.5 Wages
5 Financial data and forecasts
  5.1 Cash flow, profit and loss, accounts and balance sheets
  5.2 Financing requirements – loans, overdraft
Appendices: Curriculum vitae (not included)

Executive summary

Claridges Restaurant will be run as a partnership between Carolyn Claridge and Susan Claridge.

The 30-seat restaurant will offer a vegetarian menu and a non-vegetarian menu at lunchtimes and in the evenings. At lunchtime a special lunch menu will be provided offering snacks, vegetarian dishes, salads and non-vegetarian dishes for local business people, shopworkers and shoppers. The service at lunchtime will be quick, allowing for a high volume of customers.

In the evening the vegetarian menu will still be offered but a menu including popular dishes such as steak, chicken and fish will be well presented and served with a selection of unusual sauces and dressings. The market aimed for in the evenings will be young professional people between the ages of 18 and 30 years.

All the foods used in Claridges Restaurant will be additive-free and natural based. The lunchtime service will enable customers with a limited lunch break to enjoy their meal within the time they have, the restaurant being only a short walk or drive from where they work or shop. Car parking facilities will also be available. A full section of bar drinks and wine list will also be offered.

The forecast average spend at lunchtime is £2.80: no more than a pub lunch but providing an alternative to the noisy crowed and limited menus of pubs. The forecast spend in the evening is £10.50 including wine, which is well within the range of the young age group. Also provided in the evenings will be some live jazz and blues music such as piano or saxophone to provide fairly sophisticated background music and atmosphere.

In the first year we forecast a loss of £3,962, this mainly due to initial start-up expenses and high advertising expenses in order to attract customers at an early stage. In years two and three we predict a healthy profit due to a 10 per cent increase in sales each year and reduced loan interest in these periods. Because of the healthy cash position at the end of year 3 we would expect to be able to repay the outstanding balance on the loan at the end of year 4.

The overall objectives of the business are firstly to achieve and exceed sales forecasts to enable us to be operating at capacity, so that we can extend our opening hours to include morning coffee and afternoon teas. We would also aim to be able to employ several full-time members of staff and build up a team so that the partners can be clear of routine tasks and concentrate on day-to-day problems, meeting customers, mounting promotions and supervise the general running of the restaurant in order to build up the business further. After five years we would hope to set up a similar operation in another area.

The business will require an initial loan of £20,000 repayable over 5 years to convert the premises, equip the restaurant and pay initial administration fees. An overdraft facility of £3,500 will also be required according to cash flow forecasts to finance working capital.

By achieving forecasted sales in the first year, we would be able to repay the overdraft by the end of the year, and also pay the interest on the loan, enabling us to start repaying the loan in the second year of trading.

1   The business

1.1   Introduction

Claridge's Restaurant will be run as a partnership between Susan Claridge and Carolyn Claridge.

We have lived in the Beaconsfield area all our lives and through our own experiences and interest in the subject realised that there are no restaurants for young people to eat out in the evenings that provide a young, lively, fairly sophisticated atmosphere at prices young people can afford; that is a meal with wine for £10.50 or under. We also discovered, after conducting some preliminary market research, that there seemed to be a lack of someplace where people working or shopping in the area could go for a quick lunch or snack, spending only a couple of pounds on dishes other than filled rolls or sandwiches or the usual fried bar snacks.

1.2 Business mission

To start up and run a restaurant in the Beaconsfield area providing a menu biased towards healthy eating offering cheap lunches for local business people, shoppers and workers, and a varied interesting menu in a young, lively, sophisticated atmosphere for young professional people in the evenings.

1.3 Short-term objectives

To find and convert suitable freehold premises to a 30-seat restaurant with adequate kitchen, bar, dining, storage and car parking facilities. To build up a regular clientele and achieve forecasted sales by advertising and promotion and by the product itself; that is, friendly, efficient service and well cooked and presented food, resulting in a meal that is reasonable by being good value for money.

1.4 Long-term objectives

To be able to employ full-time members of staff to build up a reliable and conscientious team working in the restaurant, enabling the partners to concentrate on the day-to-day problems, to meet customers and suppliers, mounting promotions and supervising the general running of the restaurant in order to build and expand the business further. After five years we would hope to purchase a second premises in a different area and set up a similar operation.

1.5 Key personnel

Susan Claridge   Age 24
'O' and 'A' level qualifications in Food and Nutrition, BSc Hons Degree in Hotel, Catering and Tourism Management from Surrey University. Practical experience gained from a variety of establishments including pubs, pub restaurants, à la carte and fast food restaurants. One year industrial experience as management trainee at

Portman Intercontinental Hotel, London. Has worked in managerial positions at Wimbledon Tennis Tournament, Paris Air Show and Ascot Races. In April 1986 our business idea was accepted out of several hundred applicants for a place on the Manpower Services Commission-backed Graduate Enterprise Programme held at Cranfield Institute of Technology. This small business programme is sponsored by Arthur Anderson, BP, National Westminster Bank and the British Institute of Management.

Carolyn Claridge   Age 21
Catering experience from a variety of catering outlets ranging from institutional catering to pubs, wine bars and restaurants. She has run her own freelance catering business with a partner for the past two years, starting on the Enterprise Allowance Scheme. She has a good working experience of local suppliers, professional advisors and bookkeeping experience. Her partner, Caroline Burckhardt, Cordon Bleu-trained, will advise on menu planning and food presentation and costing as well as design or layout of kitchen facilities.

John Claridge
Financial advisor. Has run own successful engineering consultancy business for 15 years and has valuable experience in finance, VAT and bookkeeping.

Philip Hill
City and Guilds chef qualifications.
Has worked in 4- and 5-star London hotel kitchen in all sections.
Has 4 years' experience in assisting in the running of his parents' high-class restaurant in London.
Will be advising on general running of restaurant.

Peter Reid
Trained architect and surveyor.
Advisor on property and planning.

2   Markets and competition

2.1   Selected market segments

Segments aimed for at lunchtime
Shoppers – predominantly housewives aged 30–60 years.
Socioeconomic groups A, B, C1 and C2 living within a 10-mile radius of Beaconsfield.
Local business people – office workers and employees working locally. All age groups.

Local shopworkers – any age group.

Segments aimed for in the evenings
Young professional people in full-time employment, for example bank clerks, office clerks, trainee management, living and working in the area or commuting to London to work. Most have high disposable income to spend on eating and drinking out.

2.2 Market segments – growth and size

According to the Mintel Survey for Leisure Intelligence on eating out

> restaurant eating has fallen off among those over 45 years old and has conversely risen among the young. The young have now become almost as important a group of restaurant users as their elders. Reasonable prices, nice atmosphere and especially being in the mood for a particular type of food are all important among younger adults.

Mintel 'estimates that the market for eating out is worth around £3.5 billion nationwide' and the survey concludes 'the emergence of the youth market, together with the trend to healthier eating presents two potential target markets for eat-out operators in the future'.

Population figures for the South Bucks and Chiltern District based on the Registrar General's estimate predict that Bucks will remain the fastest growing country in the country, mainly owing to Milton Keynes and the Aylesbury Vale, both growth areas. Wycombe district had the largest population in the country and it is expected to continue to show growth in this area. The total population of 15–19-year-olds in the South Bucks and Chiltern District (10-mile radius of Beaconsfield) is 31,498.

We conducted a market research survey on 195 young people between the ages of 18 and 30 who were resident in South Bucks. Out of 195 asked 77.4 per cent said they thought there was a need for a budget-priced restaurant in the area. 30 per cent of this age range regularly eat vegetarian food. The largest percentage, 57.4 per cent, spend between £10 and £14 a head on a meal out in a restaurant. The most popular types of restaurant were steak houses, closely followed by wine bar bistros. 31 per cent eat out once a month, while 30 per cent eat out more regularly (once a week). The most popular socioeconomic grouping for people questioned was C1 – skilled workers; those with highest disposable income. For the lunchtime market we questioned 160 shoppers resident in the area, shopping at various shopping centres in Beaconsfield and surrounding villages and towns. 58 per cent of those questioned were housewives and 85 per cent said they felt there was a need for a restaurant providing quick snacks and lunches, both vegetarian and non-vegetarian. 61 per cent of those questioned ate vegetarian food at some time. 68 per cent said they were concerned about additives in the foods they ate. The most popular range for lunches out was between £2.50 and £3.50 (31 per cent).

We also questioned 72 companies in the area; 75 per cent said they employees ate lunch out at some time, the most popular venue being pubs; 66 per cent said they would use a budget-priced restaurant offering snacks and set lunches.

2.3   Customer benefits

Lunchtime
1. We can offer a snack lunch or a set meal which is an alternative to the usual filed rolls and fried pub lunches.
2. We will also be catering for the ever-increasing (see section 2.2) vegetarian and health consumers market by providing foods that are natural based and additive-free.
3. Our average spend at lunchtime is forecasted to be £2.80, which is no more expensive than the average pub lunch and considerably cheaper than most wine bar lunches.
4. The service provided will be quick and efficient to accommodate the average businessman's lunch break and a shopper's snack.

Evenings
1. We will offer the usual popular meat and fish dishes served with varied and unusual sauces, dressings and garnishes.
2. We will provide a fairly extensive vegetarian menu for the health conscious and for those who wish to be a little more adventurous.
3. Our average spend in the evenings is forecasted to be £10.50 including wine, which is considerably cheaper than the majority of restaurants in the area and consequently is good value for money.
4. The atmosphere in the evenings will be lively and sophisticated and this will be achieved by the use of live jazz and blues music and by friendly cheerful service.

2.4   Competitors

Primary competitors
These are restaurants that offer a similar product or service; examples are Browns and Sweeny Todds in Oxford and Maxwells in

Covent Garden, the major difference being the lack of vegetarian dishes provided on their menu. Instead they offer a wide selection of salads. The price, atmosphere and markets they serve are similar to those we are aiming for. The nearest outlets of this type are located in Oxford and London, that is 30 miles away.

The strengths of these restaurants are that they are well established, large and usually in prime sites.

Secondary competitors – strengths and weaknesses

STEAK HOUSES, such as Beefeater, Berni, Harvester

Strengths
Consistent quality of food and service within a known price bracket. Operate on a tried and tested formula. Branding very notable clientele (Source Mintel): men aged 25–64, mainly C1 socioeconomic group and business entertaining and families.

Weaknesses
No variation on menu or service. Limited menu, standardised decor, atmosphere unappealing to youth market.

CHINESE/INDIAN RESTAURANTS

Strengths
Appeal to consumers' taste for exotic foods and experiences. Part of the attraction is the feeling of being in a different world. Also meet the changing consumer preference for foreign styles of cooking. Usually late opening hours and takeaway provided.

Weaknesses
Menu limited to country of origin. Mainly meat-based. Fairly expensive in Beaconsfield area. Generally unsuitable at lunchtime. Many young people eat there for the late opening hours only.

WINE BAR/BISTRO

Strengths
Often have interesting alternative dishes on the menu, designer decor and a wide range of wines. Generally have a young appeal in the evenings, offering an informal atmosphere.

Weaknesses
Widely varying standard of food and service, often expensive for what is offered as food is used to create extra revenue above the sale of wine. Wines are often fairly expensive.

PUB RESTAURANTS

Strengths
Often have much character as part of old pub, reasonably priced, good location.

Weaknesses
Often only an extension of the pub. Food usually plain and simple and unimaginative.

FAST FOOD RESTAURANTS

Strengths
Speed of service, provide miniature meals, strong branding, heavy advertising campaigns. Brand loyalty, clean and fresh appearance. Mainly youth market.

Weaknesses
Limited, unvarying menu, standardised product, decor. Short stay only. Unlicensed.

2.5   Competitive strategy

(i)   *Price*
On the basis of market research, we have concluded that there is a gap in the market for a budget-priced restaurant.
   Prices are based on a general 30–50 per cent food cost.
   Priced as follows:

Starter	–	£1.50
Main Course	–	£4.00
Vegetables	–	£1.00
Dessert	–	£1.50
Coffee	–	0.50
Wine	–	£2.00
Average food		£10.50

However it is usual in catering to vary the food cost from one item to another:

Soup, starters, desserts and coffee	=	30% food cost
Main course and more expensive items	=	50% food cost
Wine and alcohol	=	50% material cost

   Therefore price is double the cost.

Dinner

Item	Price	Materials cost		Gross profit	
	£	£	%	£	%
Starter	1.50	0.45	30	1.05	70
Main Course	4.00	2.00	50	2.00	50
Vegetable	1.00	0.40	40	0.60	60
Dessert	1.50	0.60	40	0.90	60
Coffee	0.50	0.10	20	0.40	80
Wine	2.00	1.00	50	1.00	50
Totals	10.50	4.55	43.3	5.95	56.7

Lunch

Item	Price	Materials cost		Gross profit	
	£	£	%	£	%
Lunch dish/snack	1.80	0.54	30	1.26	70
Beverage	1.00	0.50	50	0.50	50
Totals	2.80	1.04	37.2	1.76	62.8

(ii)   *Promotion*

OPENING PARTY

To include local opinion formers; that is, councillors, local MP as well as the main potential customers. Also members of the press, senior marketing and sales people, advertising agents, travel and estate agents, bank managers and leaders of industry. For public relations purposes we should also invite our neighbours.

HANDBILLS AND POSTERS

In local shops, offices and industry.

PRESS RELEASE

In local newspapers.

'VALUE ADDED' PROMOTIONS

That is, free glass of wine with a meal during slack periods; one meal in ten free for special groups or complimentary birthday cakes for celebration parties.

SPECIAL PROMOTIONS

Seasonal menu changes and special dishes. Themes to mark dates such as St Valentine's Day, Wimbledon, Hallowe'en, Easter, Mothering Sunday. Themes based on particular types of food, for example French.

ADVERTISING

In regional and county magazines and in local papers.

LEAFLET DROPS

Handbills distributed door-to-door by local newsagents with the normal deliveries.

(iii) *Place*

Beaconsfield and the surrounding villages and towns comprise a pocket of wealth in South Bucks. The population is mainly made of:

(a) The elderly and retired.
(b) Middle-aged people, socioeconomic groups A, B, C1, C2.
(c) Their offspring who either:
    (i)   leave the area at the age of 18 for further education (educational standards being high, 12-plus still operates) and never return to the area for any length of time, or
    (ii) who stay living in the area and work locally or commute to London. A high number live with their parents as property prices are so high. Those that do rent or buy their own homes move out towards High Wycombe or Slough where houses are cheaper.
(d) Young families where the head of the household is a young executive moving up the socioeconomic scale and who will probably stay in the area.

Consequently the majority of the catering establishments operating at present reflect the affluent nature of the area. There are many high-class à la carte restaurants offering French, Italian and Chinese food, and fairly expensive Indian restaurants and pub restaurants. The steak houses are lower priced but have meat-based, limited menus, and are very standardised. Other affordable alternatives open to young people are the fast food restaurants: fish and chip shops, take-aways or pizza and burger restaurants located in the larger towns of High Wycombe or Slough.

We hope to be located in the Beaconsfield area and research has shown that at present there is no other restaurant offering a similar meal experience in this vicinity.

(iv) *Product*

THE MENU

We will offer a range of interesting starters, both vegetarian and non-vegetarian. The main course will be divided into vegetarian and meat-sections. Popular dishes will be included but will be served with a range of different and unusual sauces, accompaniments and garnishes. We also hope to offer a varied selection of salads and home-made desserts. As many as possible of our dishes will be home-made, using natural additive-free ingredients, for example wholemeal flour, brown rice, wholemeal pasta, vegetable fats.

At lunchtime we will offer a set price lunch with a choice of either starter and main course or main course and sweet, as few people require a three-course lunch these days. Offered also will be salads and snacks such as jacket potatoes with wholesome fillings.

All bar drinks will be available and a selection of wines offering a choice of French, German and Italian wines. We would also like to provide a selection of home-made fruit-based wines.

DECOR

The main colour scheme will be black, cream and green and these colours will be used in the restaurant decor, on the menu, logo, adverts and leaflets.

The black and cream colour scheme will give a sophisticated appearance to the restaurant, being neutral colours and thus fairly discreet. The green will add colour, warmth and freshness and will be introduced by the use of plants and greenery.

ATMOSPHERE

Lunchtime

Busy atmosphere with fast service and high volume of customers can be enhanced by the use of fast tempo music playing softly in the background.

Evenings

Slightly more relaxed atmosphere but still lively, with live jazz blues piano music or saxophone music as background, also providing a centrepiece attraction.

3 Selling

In-house sales

(a) *The food* – our most powerful sales weapon will be the food itself; attractively presented and displayed, it should help sell itself, e.g., salad bar, self-service, table or counter.
(b) *The menu* – which will be attractive, clear, easy to read and understand and honestly priced with no hidden extras.
(c) *Service staff* – should have friendly, welcoming, helpful attitude

– they can boost sales by asking the right questions at the right times. Can be achieved by thorough training and selection.

(d)   *Extras* – aperitifs, starters, extra vegetables, desserts, wines, coffees, liqueurs, brandies, cigars are all potential sales and need to be actively sold.

(e)   *Service* – this itself can help sell a restaurant; right length of time between courses, efficiency, etc.

(f)   *Changes and novelties* – new dishes, new ideas, new table decorations. Point of sale literature to draw attention to changes, e.g., table cards, bulletin boards by the entrance, poster in the window.

4   Premises

4.1   General

Type
Preferably a freehold premises with planning permission or already a catering establishment.

Our father will purchase the freehold of a property and will charge us rent for operating our business from there.

Location

SUITABILITY FOR MARKET
In a secondary location, easy to get to with passing traffic and shops and businesses close by. Preferably away from residential areas because of parking and noise constraints. Must be located within a workable distance from suppliers.

ACCESS
The entrance must be clearly visible to encourage 'change' trade. Rear entrance is needed for deliveries, staff access, refuse removal. Fire regulation authorities require clear access and exit routes. Clear access to car parking facilities for customers and staff is also needed – one space per table plus two spaces for staff are generally required

Size
The four main areas of space needed are:

> Seating of customers
> Food preparation
> Storage
> Other – delivery, guest WCs, rubbish, office space

For a 30-seat restaurant:

Area	% of Total	Sq. ft.
Dining	50	450
Food preparation	20	180
Storage	10	90
Cleaning/wash-up	7.5	67.5
Guest cloaks	7.5	67.5
Staff WC	5	45
	Total	900 sq. ft.

This is allowing 11–14ft per person for table service at medium price.

A space of 8ft 6in. square is needed for a square table and four chairs in a medium sized restaurant. This gives a 2ft 6in. table space for chairs and room to pass. Main traffic routes should be at least 5ft wide – fire regulation authorities specify this.

Design and decor
Ideal shape is rectangular with walls in a ratio of 3:5 and service doors on a long wall.

Attractive features such as fireplaces, natural wood or brickwork are also desirable. Flooring would be carpet tiles, wooden restaurant furniture, lots of greenery and plants. Kitchen – floors tiled. Walls around stoves lined with stainless steel or tiled. Wash up area tiled – easy to clean.

Services
Gas, electricity, water, drainage, sewage, WCs, ventilation, space heating, water heating, refuse collection.

Maintenance
Would largely be carried out by my father, but on leased equipment there is usually a maintenance and service agreement.

4.2 Key suppliers

Butcher – H. A. Price & Sons: good quality butcher, have traded with previously.
Dairy goods – local dairy
Fruit and vegetables – local greengrocer
Wholefoods – 'Beans and Wheels' (local wholefood and healthfood co.): free delivery service.
Dry goods cleaning materials – Booker Cash & Carry
Equipment – various

4.3   Quality control

(a)   *All recipes will be tested initially*
  (i)   to give a standard recipe to work to;
  (ii)   so customers are given a constant product;
  (iii)   so food costs can be checked exactly;
  (iv)   so different ingredients and different qualities can be tested;
  (v)   to enable us to specify accurately the raw materials to be purchased;
  (vi)   to test one yield of each batch of ingredients;
  (vii)   to help decide the portion sizes for each item;
  (viii) to establish the waste on items in preparation and cooking.

(b)   *Portion control*
  (i)   to help control food costs accurately;
  (ii)   to enable preparation of portions in advance.

Method
Use of standard-sized scoops, ladles, serving dishes, plates, bowls, etc.
Use of pre-portioned food, e.g., gateaux.

(c)   *Checking of deliveries*
Check for – quality,
              portions,
              size, e.g., eggs, steaks,
              damaged goods.

4.4   Staffing

Initially my partner and I will be the only full-time staff in the restaurant with perhaps one casual staff in the kitchen and one in the restaurant. On weekend evenings this may be increased to two in each area, depending on trade.

4.5   Wages

£2.00 per hour for 4-hour shift lunchtime an 5-hour shift evening 6.30–11.30 p.m. Plus tips.

5 Financial data and forecasts

5.1 Cash flow for first year: assumptions

1. Sales forecasts based on a 30-seat restaurant in Beaconsfield area. Sales figures high in first month because of opening advertising campaign, opening party and initial curiosity.
   Second month figures lower as traditionally February is a quiet month in catering. Peak time is in 12th month (December) owing to Christmas.
2. Drawings @ £50 per week each,
   National Insurance is included in the wages figure.
3. Food and drink purchases @ 40% of sales
4. Rent is based on our father's mortgage repayment on freehold premises @ 15% interest on £100,000 = £15,000.
5. Rates estimated to be £3,000 p.a.
6. Wages @ £2.00 per hour.

4-hour lunch shift
5-hour dinner shift

Based on employing part-time kitchen help for the first 6 months on Friday and Saturday evenings and one week-night, also Sunday lunch

= 3 nights	=	15 hours
1 lunch	=	4 hours
		19 hours @ £2.00
	=	£38.00 per week
	=	£152.00 per month

After six months we would hope to employ a restaurant helper as well; both kitchen and restaurant staff would be employed for Friday and Saturday nights and Sunday lunch, only cutting out week-night help.

2 nights	=	10 hrs × 2	=	20 hours
1 lunch	=	4 hrs × 2	=	8 hours
				28 hours @ £2 per hour
			=	£56 per week
			=	£224 per month

7. Loan interest on a £20,000 5-year-term loan @ 14% interest = £2,800.
8. Loan repayment delayed until 2nd year.
9. Overdraft interest worked out on the highest overdraft figure for the quarter @ 15% interest.

Monthly cash-flow statement for first year of trading including VAT excl. income tax

	Mth 1	2	3	4	5	6	7	8	9	10	11	12	Total
Receipts													
Rest. sales	4,830	2,968	4,088	5,096	5,628	6,160	6,902	7,378	7,854	8,064	8,120	8,498	75,586
Total receipts	4,830	2,968	4,088	5,096	5,628	6,160	6,902	7,378	7,854	8,064	8,120	8,498	75,586
Payments													
VAT (payment)			930			1,321			1,732			1,933	5,916
Accountants' fee												500	500
Repair costs						200							200
Petrol/motor expenses	100	100	100	100	100	100	100	100	100	100	100	100	1,200
Drawings @ £50 p.w.	400	400	400	400	400	400	400	400	400	400	400	400	4,800
Food & drink purch. @ 40% of sales	1,932	1,187	1,635	2,038	2,251	2,464	2,760	2,951	3,141	3,225	3,248	3,399	30,231
Heat & light			350			350			350			350	1,400
Rent	1,250	1,250	1,250	1,250	1,250	1,250	1,250	1,250	1,250	1,250	1,250	1,250	15,000
Rates	250	250	250	250	250	250	250	250	250	250	250	250	3,000
Tel. & post.			100			100			100			100	400
Advert. & printing	200	200	200	200	200	200	200	200	200	200	200	200	2,400
Wages gross	152	152	152	152	152	152	224	224	224	224	224	224	2,256
Sundries	100	100	100	100	100	100	100	100	100	100	100	100	1,200
Capital costs						200							200
Loan interest @ 14%	233	233	233	233	233	233	233	233	233	233	233	233	2,796
Overdraft int. @ 15%						247			203				450
Total payments	4,617	3,872	5,700	4,723	4,936	7,567	5,517	5,708	8,283	5,982	6,005	9,039	
Opening bank bal.	1,293	1,506	602	(1,010)	(617)	55	(1,352)	13	1,703	1,274	3,356	5,471	
Surplus deficit	213	(904)	(1,612)	373	692	(1,407)	1,385	1,670	(429)	2,082	2,115	(541)	
Balance c/fwd	1,506	602	(1,010)	(637)	55	(1,352)	33	1,703	1,274	3,356	5,471	4,930	

Balance carried forward 4,930

Profit and loss account for year 1

	£	£
Sales (net of VAT)		65,727
Less cost of sales		
Opening stock	500	
Purchases	26,288	
Less closing stock	(500)	
Cost of sales		26,288
Gross profit		39,439
Less expenses		
Planning permission	50	
Accountancy fees	700	
Solicitors' fees	600	
Advertising	3,400	
Printing	200	
Heat & light	1,400	
Insurance	500	
Motor vehicle expenses	1,450	
Sundries	1,400	
Repairs & maintenance	2,347	
Depreciation	2,652	
Telephone	400	
Drawings	4,800	
Wages & N.I.	2,256	
Rent	15,000	
Rates	3,000	
Loan interest	2,796	
Overdraft interest	450	
		43,401
Loss before tax		(3,962)

Opening balance sheet

	£	£
Fixed assets		13,060
Stock	500	
Cash	1,293	
		1,793
		14,853
Loan		(20,000)
		5,147
Represented by:		
Expenses to date		5,147

Balance sheet as at end of year 1

	£	£
Fixed assets:		13,260
Less depreciation		(2,652)
		10,608
Stock	500	
Cash	4,930	
	5,430	
Loan creditor	(20,000)	
		(14,570)
		3,962
Loss in first year of trading		3,962

Quarterly cash-flow for second year assumptions
1. Assume sales increase by 10%
    10% increase in sales   =   £ 7,559
    Therefore total sales
    for second year   =   £75,586
                                £83,145

First year quarterly sales figures

Jan. Feb. March	Apr. May. June	July. Aug. Sept.	Oct. Nov. Dec.
Total sales 11,886	16,884	22,134	24,682
22% increase 14,501	30% inc. 19,079	8% inc. 23,905	4% inc. 25.670
	= £83,155 = 10% overall increase		

2. Assume costs increase by 3% (rate of inflation)
3. Drawings increased from £50 per week each to £60 per week each
                            =   £480 per month
                            =   £1,440 per quarter
                            =   £5,760 p.a.
4. Capital costs doubles for extra equipment = £400
5. Loan repayment   =   £20,000 over 4 years
                            =   £5,000 per year
                            =   £416 per month
                            =   £1,248 per quarter
6. Loan interest calculated @ 14% on outstanding loan at end of each quarter.

Cash flow for third year assumptions
1. Assume sales increase by 10%.
2. Assume costs increase by 3%
3. Drawings increased to £70 per week each
                            =   £140 per week
                            =   £560 per month
4. Wages increased by 5%.
5. Capital costs doubled for extra equipment
                            =   £800
6. Loan repayment still £1,248 per quarter paid at beginning of each quarter.
7. Loan interest calculated @ 14% on outstanding loan at end of each quarter.

Quarterly cash flow statement for second year of trading

	Q1	Q2	Q3	Q4	Total	3rd year
Receipts						
Restaurant sales	14,501	19,079	23,905	25,670		91,471
Total receipts	14,501	19,079	23,905	25,670	83,155	91,471
Payments						
VAT (payment)	1,135	1,493	1,871	2,009	6,508	7,159
Accountants' fee				515	515	530
Repair costs		206			206	212
Petrol motor expenses	309	309	309	309	1,236	1,273
Drawings @ £60 p.w. each	1,440	1,440	1,440	1,440	5,760	6,720
Food & drink purchases @ 40% sales	5,800	7,632	9,562	10,268	33,262	36,588
Heat & light	360	360	360	360	1,440	1,485
Rent	3,862	3,862	3,862	3,862	15,448	15,913
Rates	772	772	772	772	3,088	3,183
Telephone & postage	103	103	103	103	412	424
Advertising & printing	618	618	618	618	2,472	2,546
Wages	581	581	581	581	2,324	2,440
Sundries	309	309	309	309	1,236	1,273
Capital costs		400			800	800
Loan repayment	1,248	1,248	1,248	1,256	5,000	5,000
Loan interest	656	613	569	525	2,363	1,663
Total payments	17,193	19,946	21,604	22,927	81,670	87,209
Opening bank balance	4,930	2,238	1,371	3,672		6,415
Surplus deficit	2,692	(867)	2,301	2,743		4,262
Balance c/fwd	2,238	1,371	3,672	6,415	6,415	10,677

Balance c/f

Profit-and-loss accounts

	Year 2 £	Year 2 £	Year 3 £	Year 3 £
Sales		72,309		79,540
Less cost of sales				
Opening stock	500		500	
Purchases	28,924		31,816	
Less closing stock	500		500	
		28,924		31,816
Gross profit		43,385		47,724
Less expenses				
Accountants' fee	515		530	
Repairs	206		212	
Motor expenses	1,236		1,273	
Drawings	5,760		6,720	
Heat & light	1,440		1,485	
Rent	15,448		15,913	
Rates	3,088		3,183	
Telephone & post.	412		424	
Advert. & Printing	2,472		2,546	
Wages	2,324		2,440	
Sundries	1,236		1,273	
Loan interest	2,363		1,663	
Depreciation	2,732		2,892	
	(39,232)		(40,554)	
		(39,232)		(40,554)
Profit for year		4,153		7,170
Retained earnings b/f		(3,962)		191
Retained earnings c/f		191		7,361

Balance sheet as at end of years 2 and 3

	Year 2 £	Year 2 £	Year 3 £	Year 3 £
Fixed assets:		13,660		14,460
Less depreciation		(5,384)		(8,276)
		8,276		6,184
Stock	500		500	
Cash	6,415		10,677	
Loan	(15,000)		(10,000)	
		(8,085)		1,177
		191		7,361
Represented by:				
Retained profits		191		7,361

Break-even calculation

Total number of meals sold in 1st year	=	10,660
@ average price of £6.65	=	£70,889
Cost of one meal	=	£2.90
Therefore total cost of meals	=	£2.90 × 10,660
	=	£30,914
Therefore gross profit	=	£70,889 − £30,914
	=	£39.975

$$\text{Gross profit margin} = \frac{GP}{Sales} \times 100$$

$$= \frac{£39,975}{£70,889} \times 100 = 56.4\%$$

Overheads (fixed costs) for 1st year	=	£23,600

$$\text{Therefore break-even turnover} = \frac{Overheads}{G.P.\ Margin} \times 100$$

$$= \frac{£23,600}{56.4} \times 100$$

$$= £41,845$$

$$\text{Break-even gross profit margin} = \frac{Overheads}{Sales} \times 100$$

$$= \frac{23,600}{70,889} \times 100$$

$$= 16.7\%$$

5.2 Financing requirements – loans, overdraft

In order to find the initial requirements of the business we would require the following financing:

1. Long-term loan (5 years) £20,000
    This loan will be used for:
    (a) Purchase of restaurant, bar and kitchen equipment,
    (b) Initial solicitors and accountancy fees,
    (c) Purchase of dry goods and bar stock,
    (d) Pre-opening advertising.
2. Overdraft facility (short-term) of £1,500.
    This facility will only be required for the first six months of trading to finance necessary working capital requirements.

Breakdown of loan expenditure

	£	£	£
Loan			20,000
Expenses			
Planning permission	50		
Solicitors	600		
Accountant	200		
Advertising	1,000		
Printing	200		
Insurance	500		
Tax and insurance	250		
Sundries & extras	200		
Restaurant repairs & maintenance	1,628		
Kitchen repairs & maintenance	519		
Expenditure items		5,147	
Capital additions			
Van	2,000		
Restaurant equipment	7,833		
Kitchen equipment	3,227		
		13,060	
Stock		500	
Cash remaining		1,293	
		20,000	

John Jederman

John Jederman is made redundant and is trying to decide between two options: (1) setting up his own business; (2) taking up an offer of writing, lecturing and tutoring at a local college.

Question

What would you advise him to do, and why?

John Jederman

John Jederman (JJ), aged 47, is married with two children aged 17 and 19. The elder child has left home; the younger has a place at Essex University. JJ has a cottage at St Neots, 18 miles from Cambridge. He has a CNAA degree in Business Studies. For the last three years he has been a temporary lecturer in marketing at the local technical college in the Commercial Studies department. Cutbacks there have meant that they can no longer employ him. Prior to this job he was employed for nearly ten years in a small toy manufacturing business run by an owner-manager. JJ worked in the sales department and with an assistant covered the whole of England and Wales. For the last three years he had also assumed some responsibility for manufacturing and design and the owner-manager regarded him as his 'second in command', so JJ was most upset when his employer announced, somewhat abruptly, that he was getting on in years and wished to retire, was selling the business, and that all the staff would be dismissed. JJ tried to purchase the business himself, but was unable either to raise enough money, or to persuade his employer to keep the business going.

Before his employment with the toy manufacturer, JJ had a short-term commission in the Army's Supply and Transport branch. Nearing the end of his service, he had been assessed for his leadership and personal qualities, and a comprehensive report made out. This report was based on 'in-depth' interviews with a battery of army psychologists, and also on reports from his senior officers. Some parts of the report (a copy of which was given to JJ) were concerned only with army matters and have been omitted; the relevant parts to this case study are shown in Appendix A.

JJ is now considering two propositions. They are:

1. To set up a new company, 'Funlines' to innovate and market low-priced impulse gift lines. His detailed proposal, shown in the form of a business plan, is outlined in Appendix B.
2. To take up an offer of writing, lecturing and tutorial work in retail management and business studies at the Cantab Correspondence and Tutorial College, based near Cambridge. This would involve him in:
   (a)   writing notes for BTec, Host, Start-up, HNC, ONC, GCSE and also new degree courses in retail and marketing management, and business studies generally.
   (b)   lecturing at the correspondence college most days and some evenings a week.
   (c)   tutorial and assignment checking work for students.

A copy of the contract offered him is shown in Appendix C.

John Jederman now sees himself as being at the parting of ways. Whichever course he pursues has to be successful or, at the least, secure and satisfactory, since, with his fiftieth birthday approaching, he will soon be too old to change. Once committed, he will be on board, a single track tram!

JJ decided to spend some time in testing his personal desires, interests and needs, as he sees them, in a variety of complex forms, against those provided by each of the alternative forms of employment. He is aware that his attempt to quantify these factors could be criticised as being 'very subjective', and he is aware too that the main benefit arises from the increase in self-awareness that must come from working through this exercise. His wife has already made her opinion quite clear. Based on her experience of him in his previous two jobs she comes down firmly on the side of the correspondence college post. Tutoring, writing and lecturing are all forms or work which are congenial to him, she says. JJ wonders if her view may be subjective too, influenced perhaps by the big disparity in the amount of time he will spend at home with each job.

On the all-important questions of salaries, JJ is unable to make any clear distinction between the two jobs; both appear to offer about the same. He realises, however, that so far as risk is concerned there is a substantial difference. This factor is included in the test.

JJ completed the test (Appendix D); he was as honest with himself as he could be, and he was mildly surprised at the result. Prior to taking the test he had been quite certain, in his own mind, that his strong preference was for setting up the 'Funlines' business.

Appendix A: extracts from report on Lieutenant J. Jederman

Leadership and initiative

That this officer has latent leadership qualities is not in dispute. We have only to refer to an occasion when his unit was on loan to the Malaysian government and engaged on bringing up sensitive supplies to government troops in Negri Sembilan. A small group of aborigines, drunk on a local brew made from palm trees, successfuly raided his supplies. Lieut. Jederman on his own initiative walked to the aborigines' camp, talked to the leader, quietened him down and returned with the supplies.

However we have to add that in our opinion it was the situation which itself brought out the action from Jederman. In other circumstances – for instance, when his unit was relaxed and at rest – it seems that Jederman reverted to a passive role and indeed control of the unit appeared to pass to Jederman's Sergeant, NCOs and other ranks.

This position is paralleled in other situations where initiative needs to be shown. If there is a clear need for initiative, Jederman will supply it. If no initiative is manifestly demanded, Jederman is not forthcoming. He is not good at foreseeing likely trouble, and taking a firm line in advance.

Dominant/submissive roles

Jederman takes orders easily provided he has confidence in his commanding officer. Weak or uncertain leadership from above throws him into some confusion. He likes clear directives and clearly delineated areas of authority. Again, paradoxically, once it is evident to him that he must act on his own, he does so very effectively. It is on the borderline that he has problems.

Junior NCOs generally regard Jederman as fair, and easy to work with. There is some evidence that they may on occasion exploit his good nature, but the extent to which they are allowed to do this is limited. On the occasion ... [here follows another long military example of his 'easy-going' attitude].

Personal qualities

Jederman is easy to get on with, friendly, generally of a sunny disposition, liked and respected by his peers. Occasionally he goes through bleak periods. In such circumstances he tends to retreat into his own company, though he will talk over his problems with his friends. He always does seem to have one particular friend with whom he spends most of his available time.

Intelligence

Jederman scores highly on both quantitative and (to a slightly lesser extent) on non-quantitative, lateral thinking-type tests. His raw IQ score is high, around 146.

Ambition

Jederman is ambitious and seems prepared to put himself out to gain the necessary qualifications and experience to go higher. We rather doubt, however, if Jederman has the necessary qualities of ruthlessness to reach the very top. He can be ruthless and very determined when placed in a situation where this is clearly demanded. In other situations he takes a more passive role. In the final analysis he probably lacks much of the killer instinct. It is this which makes us question whether he is suitable for promotion much beyond the ranks immediately above him. [It was this comment, more than anything else, which made Jederman decide that – although a permanent commission has been offered to him with promotion to the rank of Captain – he would be better not to accept, and that he should take his chance in 'civvy street'.]

Appendix B: 'Funlines' proposed business plan

Introduction

This plan has been compiled by the founder of the proposed business.

It relates to a proposal to establish a business involved in the innovation and marketing of low priced gift lines.

The purpose of the plan are:

(i)   to determine and demonstrate the viability of the proposed business;
(ii) to enable the business to present a case for financial support to bankers;
(iii) to act as a basis for control in the proposed business.

Statement of goals

(i) *First year of operation*
To generate sufficient profits to enable me not to drop much on the standard of living I currently enjoy with a salary circa £15 000 per annum and to provide a return on initial investment of 40 per cent. As demonstrated in the (profit and loss account), this would require a turnover of £200 000 and pre-tax profits of £17 000 would be generated.

(ii) *Second/third years of operation*
By retaining profits within the business to increase turnover by the end of year three to £300 000 per annum with the subsequent increase in profit and return on investment.

Environmental factors

The major market is seasonal and therefore depends on reasonable weather during the summer months with the subsequent high/low level of tourism.

As will be discussed later, competition within the industry comes chiefly from importers and it is felt that there are three main trends which have developed over the last two to three years:

(i) It would appear that we now have to accept an exchange rate of around £1 sterling/$1.60 (US dollars) and almost all relevant sources of supply for importers trade in US dollars. Furthermore, all international sea freight rates are charged in US dollars and they obviously form a major proportion of the landed cost of imported merchandise. In addition, UK Customs and Excise duties are charged on a percentage basis of £ sterling landed cost and due to the two factors mentioned have effectively increased in cash terms.

(ii) The major sources of supply are in the Far East and are very dependent on the US market, which has been and is currently very depressed. Due to the subsequent drop in revenue, the Far Eastern manufacturers will not spend money on developing new ideas and the market 'cries-out' for something different.

(iii) Imported goods have been subject to quota arrangements with HM Customs and Excise but are now subject to EC quotas.

Existing market

The traditional avenues of trading, that is, manufacturer or importer/wholesaler/retailer have been almost totally eroded in the gift trade and the importer generally deals solely with the retailer.

The customer is usually to be found in a holiday centre, which may be a coastal or recreational centre, and he wants a quick turnaround from the product. His normal mark-up would be around 100 per cent on cost.

Table 1   Locations of major importers

Location	Turnover	Number of product lines	Number of representatives
Newcastle on Tyne	£6m	2,000	10
Leeds	£8m	4,000	20
Southend on Sea	£3m	4,000	15
Harlow, Essex	£5m	3,000	15
Scarborough	£1m	1,500	6
Leeds	£2m	1,000	4
Weston-Super-Mare	£1m	1,000	3

Competitive analysis

The competition would come almost totally from importers who are buying their products mainly from Pacific basin sources. They are in size between £1 million to £8 million per annum turnover and are geographically spread around England, the location of the major ones being shown in Table 1.

They market mainly through trade shows held between early December and late February when they take initial orders, and then during the season through a network of self-employed agents or representatives. As can be seen from Table 1, they operate on a product range varying from 1000 to 4000 items.

The representatives of customers at the trade shows vary from professional buyers to owners to managers, depending on the type of outlet.

The pricing strategy of the competition is generally to add 50 per cent to 55 per cent to landed cost, although this can reduce for very large buyers.

The competition

(i)   Their strengths:
       Significant financial muscle;
       Bulk buying, so low unit costs;
       Established representatives/agents,
       History/tradition.
(ii)   Their weaknesses:
       Lead times on imports;
       Total dependence on imports;
       Currency fluctuations;
       Dependence on Far Eastern ideas;
       Import tariffs, quotas;
       High overhead content.

The marketing plan

(i) *The target market*

The products fall within the cheaper end of the gifts category and are therefore always liable to change, improvement and whims of fashion, and are generally in an impulse-buying situation. It is common at the cheap end of the gift trade for products to have a three-year product cycle. The products have been targeted on the child/adolescent segment and the buying motives are self-consumption and gifts for others.

The market worth for any particular range of products is virtually impossible to evaluate although the total gift market must be considered extensive. The magnitude of this proposed operation is therefore unlikely to upset the present market. Probably the most important factor in the market is the seasonal nature of demand.

The UK market may be segmented geographically as follows:

(a)   England
(b)   Ireland
(c)   Scotland
(d)   Wales

I have decided to ignore the Scottish and Irish markets and concentrate on the English and Welsh outlets, of which I already have some knowledge.

The market may then be segmented as:

(a)   Coastal
(b)   Inland
     (i)   Major tourist attractions, i.e. zoos, etc.
     (ii)   General gift boutiques/greetings shops.

The coastal market, while being spread over the period June; July and August is, in fact, highly concentrated in the six-week period of the school summer holidays.

The inland tourist attractions, whilst still being seasonal, have a six-month trading period.

The general inland gift shop covers a twelve-month trading period with the occasional peak, for example, at Christmas.

The market may then be segmented by customer:

(a)   Credit-worthiness
(b)   Location

(c)   Size
    (i)   Large national multiples, for example, John Menzies, W. H. Smith.
    (ii)   Larger centralised outlets, for example, West Midlands Safari Park.
    (iii)   Smaller single gift shops.

I have decided that owing to the limited resources available financially, payment by my customers is paramount and I will therefore aim at those with the ability to pay quickly. The location will be primarily inland to extend the operating season and fall into the medium-size retail outlets.

(ii)   *Marketing mix*

(a)   PRODUCT
The gift trade in this country tends to follow trends that are innovated and established in the USA. The nature of the product necessitates being first in the market and therefore the US market must be studied very closely for developments.

The product will be six lines designed for a children's market and retailing for a maximum of £2.99. Inside this limit the psychological price barriers are 99p and £1.99.

The product offers a differential advantage over competitor's products in quality, display at point of sale, exclusivity and servicing of customers.

(b)   PRICE
The retail prices are as discussed above. The normal retail mark-up is 100 per cent on cost and I must, therefore, aim my products at 50p, £1.00 and £1.50.

Normal trade terms will be net 30 days, but in the line with the proposed policy relating to financial limitations it is proposed to give a substantial discount, say 10 per cent, for payments within seven days. This discount can satisfactorily be included and 'lost' in the initial mark-up.

(c)   PLACE
It is my intention to deliver the initial orders personally to improve customer contact and service. Repeat orders, because of lower quantities and light-weight products, will be mailed.

It will be unnecessary to carry stock initially as orders will only be placed to match orders previously taken by me. After the initial product input, estimates will be made as to the likely repeat level. An extremely reliable source of information on this score will be the zoos and safari parks where reasonable trading levels are reached two months before the coastal trade begins. Their results will be researched and forward orders placed as appropriate.

(d)   PROMOTION
A number of intended initial customers are already well known to me, and in that sense little promotion is necessary and can be done by telephone or letter.

It is my intention to hire a suitable showmobile during the initial selling period to introduce my products to the customer. This, I believe, is preferable to trade shows because of the limited market I am aiming at, and it increases convenience to customers. Once the product is introduced to the customers orders for replacement stocks can be from the catalogue, by letter or by telephone.

(iii) *Controls*

Because of the seasonal nature of the business it is felt that the twelve months fall into six distinct categories with three different types of control. The six categories are *summer selling, summer deliveries, summer repeats, winter selling, winter deliveries* and *winter repeats*. Because the goods are initially sold on display stands the control would be numbers of stands sold and then in the delivery period, number of stands delivered. The control during the two repeat periods must be level of percentage repeats by product line.

(iv) *Costs*

The costs of the first year's marketing operation will be time, travelling and subsistence. These will be incurred annually during January, February, June, July and August each year. The costs in the first year has been estimated at £8000 for motor vehicles and £3000 for subsistence.

The manufacturing plan

(i) *Product development*

All manufacturing will be subcontracted out due to the variety of products being sold. A manufacturer for each type of product will be located and the product developed in conjunction with him.

(ii) *Facilities*

An acquaintance owns and operates a warehousing/despatch service in Burton-on-Trent and my intention, at least in the short term, is to use this service to enable me to have more time to devote to the marketing of the product. The only facilities necessary, therefore, will be an office and this will be located at my home in order to have the necessary back-up from my wife.

(iii) *Organisation*

With manufacturing and warehousing subcontracted, only marketing, product development and administration will have to be handled. I will personally handle product development and marketing, leaving my wife to deal with administration matters.

(iv) *Costs*

Owing to the pricing structure of this proposal and of my customers, manufacturing costs must be a maximum of 25 per cent of retail price. Any product failing to meet this specification will not be considered.

Warehousing, as previously discussed, will be subcontracted also, at a cost of 5 per cent of turnover. Insurance cover for stock only and delivery of goods will be at my expense.

All office facilities are already available at my home and therefore the only real cost will be the extra telephone expenses incurred.

The financial plan

(i) *Capital*
The directors of the Company will be:

(a)   the founder as Managing Director;
(b)   the founder's wife as Director and Company Secretary.

It is estimated that the two directors will each invest £2,500 in Ordinary Share Capital. It is projected that a further funding of £32,000 will be required in the first year. See cash flow forecast (Table 2).

(ii) *Cash flow*
The cash flow forecast attached shows the total funding necessary. Because of the different types of funding available, interest has been excluded. Funding is at a maximum mid-year. This pattern would be repeated in subsequent years.

(iii) *Break-even analysis*
A break-even chart of the first year of operation is included (Table 3). This is based on the assumption that costs of goods, stands, warehousing, cash discount and postage are variable costs and that all other costs are fixed.
Because of the relatively high fixed overhead content of costs the break-even point is rather high. However, little cash has to be injected initially until orders are forthcoming from customers.

(iv) *Profit-and-loss forecast*
A first year profit-and-loss account is attached (Table 4). This shows that even at this relatively low level of turnover a satisfactory return on investment is made in the first year. It is felt that the level of turnover is easily attainable and that the volume is restricted only by the need to limit financial borrowings.

(v) *Financial projections*
The costs in this project are relatively simple to project and control. The key to success and to control is the sales turnover. Careful gauging and monitoring of turnover will be carried out on a daily basis.

Key fundamentals to the business

(a)   Sources of new ideas both in the introductory stages of the business and later to stimulate customers and expand the customer base.
(b)   Location of reliable competitive suppliers with whom a continuing mutually profitable arrangement can be developed.

Table 2 Year 1: cash flow

	Jan	Feb	Mar	Apr	May	Jun	Jul	Aug	Sep	Oct	Nov	Dec	Total
Sales	–	–	20	55	35	20	30	25	9	2	2	2	200
Receipts (net of discount)	–	–	5	30	30	25	40	30	25	12	5	3	205
Outgoings													
Purchases (incl. VAT)	–	–	15	25	20	15	30	5	3	2	–	–	115
Stand costs	–	–	3	3	2	–	–	1	1	–	–	–	10
Warehousing	–	–	1	3	2	1	2	1	–	–	–	–	10
Variable costs	–	–	–	–	1	1	1	1	–	–	–	–	4
Fixed costs	8	4	4	4	4	4	5	4	3	3	3	3	49
VAT	–	–	–	–	–	7	–	–	3	–	–	–	10
Monthly totals	8	4	23	35	29	28	38	12	10	5	3	3	198
Monthly movement	(8)	(4)	(18)	(5)	1	(3)	2	18	15	7	2	–	7
Cumulative	(8)	(12)	(30)	(35)	(34)	(37)	(35)	(17)	(2)	5	7	7	7

Table 3   Year 1: break-even analysis

	£000s
Sales turnover	200
Fixed costs	49
Variable costs	134
Net profit	17

Contribution per £1 sales: $\dfrac{66}{200} \times 1 \dfrac{100}{1} = .33$

Break even point: $\dfrac{£49,000}{33p} \times = £148,000$

Table 4   Year 1: profit-and-loss account

	(£000s)	
Sales	200	
Less discounts allowed	20	
		180
Less cost of sales		
Goods	90	
Stands	10	(100)
		80
Variable expenses		
Warehousing	10	
Postage	4	(14)
		66
Fixed expenses		
Salaries and wages	23	
Leasing	5	
Motor vehicle costs	8	
Telephones	2	
Printing and stationery	2	
Subsistence	3	
Artwork	4	
Sundries	2	(49)
Net profit		17

(c) Operational plan to utilise the existing customer base.

(d) To utilise fully the financial resources available without putting the business at risk.

(e) To continue to improve the profit as forecast in year one by the measures in (a) and (d) above and increase the return on initial investment to 100 per cent per annum by year three.

The research and development plan

(i) Product development must be an ongoing task with regular introduction of new lines. It is intended to maintain the same restrictions in price range as this is the market/product field with which I am familiar. All developments will be made with this in mind. The search for new product ideas may involve visits to centres of innovations for gifts such as the USA, Italy, Taiwan and Korea.

(ii) As increased funds become available the market must be expanded to cover a larger percentage of the prospective customers known to me. The larger customers mentioned in the market segmentation may then be attacked.

(iii) The net development must be to aim at a higher market share in the area of the market defined as the target market without putting the company at risk either financially or in terms of resources.

Appendix C: contract between Cantab Correspondence and Tutorial College (hereinafter CCTC) and John Jederman

1. CCTC will pay John Jederman a yearly salary of £15,000, payable monthly in arrears, together with certain additional fees and commission payments for writing course material as shown in items 2 to 7 inclusive below.

2. CCTC will pay £1,500 for the preparation of new degree course material in retail and marketing management. This is an advance on commission which will be at the rate of 5 per cent on sales of the two courses from now onwards. It is agreed that the advance on commission shall be paid within the period of 30 days after receipt of the material for the course.

3. Annual Statement of Fees and Commissions. During the month of December in each year, CCTC will submit a statement containing the following information in relation to the twelve months ending on the preceding 30th September.

    (i) The fees (net VAT) received by CCTC during the twelve months from students taking the courses for which you have written the material.

    (ii) The percentage of those fees due.

    (iii) The advances, if any, made in the course of the previous twelve months.

    With each such statement CCTC will remit the amount shown on the statement.

4. Duration of Agreement for Commission Payments. The agreement for Commission Payments will continue for the duration of the course. The course shall be deemed to come to an end when CCTC, on reasonable, substantive grounds (for example course no longer required because of

major syllabus change withdrawal of subject, replacement course needed to meet radical changes in the syllabus, course inadequate for current examination requirements, etc.) decides that the course is no longer to be marketed by CCTC.

5. Course Maintenance. Following publication of the new course(s) and (subject to the rights of termination set out above) it is required that you:

 (i) rewrite and update the lessons, tests and specimen answers of your course(s) whenever modifications are required by changes in the law or practice or by alterations in the applicable syllabus or in the regulations of the examining bodies.

 (ii) rewrite for CCTC every December, or earlier if necessary, any modifications which you believe should be made to the lessons, tests and specimen answers of your course(s) in readiness for the following academic year.

6. Annual Report/Rewriting/Revision Fee. For the services to be provided under Paragraph 5 of this agreement CCTC will pay an annual retaining fee of £500. This payment is additional to any commission due under item 2.

7. Copyright. It is agreed that copyright in the course materials be vested in CCTC.

8. Holidays with pay. Three weeks are allowed per year in addition to statutory bank holidays.

9. Sickness or injury pay entitlement. The salary of a member of the staff less any national insurance benefits to which he/she is entitled will continue to be paid in full for a period of up to 3 months due to illness or injury in any period of twelve months. Beyond that, payments or part payments shall be at the discretion of CCTC.

10. Superannuation arrangements. Monthly-paid members of staff are required to join the CCTC pension fund.

11. Period of notice. Three months, to expire at the end of the calendar year.

12. Retirement. Members of the teaching staff will retire at the end of the calendar year in which they reach the age of 65 years, with the option to retire at any time after the age of 60.

13. Residence. Members of staff are required to live within a reasonable distance of their place of work.

Appendix D: Psychological test results

Factor (1)	JJ's views (2)	Corresp. assigned weight (3)	Funlines			CCTC		
			JJ's assessment (4)	Corresp. factor (5)	Weight × factor	JJ's assessment (6)	Corresp. factor (7)	Weight × factor
Pay								
Risk	Unhappy at risk	6	High	-8	-48	Moderate	-4	-24
Capacity to earn more	Required to be available	4	Many	+5	+20	Some	+3	+12
Fringe benefits	Appreciated	3	A few	+1	+3	Not available	0	0
Conditions of work								
Human contact	Essential, but happy with periods on his own	5	Variable	+2	+10	Sometimes lonely	-2	-10
Monotonous/variable	Likes variety	3	Little	-2	-6	Some variety	+1	+3
Travel								
At work	No 'nights away'	2	Some nights away	-2	-4	None	0	0
To work	Unhappy with too much	2	A lot	-5	-10	Some	-2	-4
Hours of work	Dislike of 'office' hours	3	None	0	0	Some routine	-4	-12
Weekends	Required to be free	3	Not always free	-2	-6	Always free	0	0
Holidays	Important	4	Wintertime only	-1	-4	Any time	0	0
Job satisfaction, etc								
Job satisfaction	Very important	10	Good	+4	+40	Fairly good	+3	+30
Integrity	Important	8	Some	-2	-16	Satisfactory	0	0
Humanity/toughness	Dislike of hard dealing	5	Toughness	-4	-20	Satisfactory	0	0
TOTAL					-41			-5

Hightech Components

Roger Lacey is looking for new challenges. He is ambitious to see Hightech Components grow but without losing the qualities that have made it successful.

Questions

1. What has made Hightech successful? What is its competitive advantage?
2. Does it occupy a market niche, as Roger thinks?
3. What are the pros and cons of the growth options Roger is considering?
4. What course of action would you have recommended?

The decision

In the spring of 1987, Roger Lacey sat down in his office in Hampshire to take stock of his company and its prospects for the future. Hightech Components Ltd had been trading for over ten years. During that time its sales had risen from less than £100,000 to a figure close to £2 million. With cash in the bank, mounting profits and orders for up to four years ahead, Hightech was a success by anyone's standards.

Roger recalled having read once that the problems caused by success in business were actually more difficult to resolve than those of failure. At the time he had smiled wryly to himself. I should have those problems, he had thought. Well, now he had. He had set out

This case was written by Tony Kippenberger under the direction of Paul Burns.
© Copyright 1996 Paul Burns.

to build a unique type of business in the electrical components business, in which product range and quality combined with personal service would confer an advantage that his competitors would be unable to match. Now that he had achieved that goal, the question he had to confront was: where to next? How could the business grow and flourish without losing those very qualities that he believed were responsible for its success?

Precision systems

In 1971, Roger Lacey was working as a sales representative in the electrical engineering industry. One morning, he received an enquiry from a company called Precision Systems Ltd. The managing director of the company asked him to put forward a proposal for some assorted products which included electromechanical assemblies. When Lacey returned with the proposals, a few weeks later, the managing director of Precision Systems spent some time working through the proposal with him. At the end of the meeting, he asked for more information on additional items.

On the third visit to the company, Roger was somewhat taken aback when the managing director asked him out for lunch. He was even more startled when, in Roger Lacey's words, 'It became apparent that he knew full well that I had a beaten-up Ford Cortina 1600 around the corner and he knew my exact salary – £1,500. It was obvious then that he was not interested in our proposals but that he had been interviewing me "on the job" with a view to recruiting me. He offered me a salary of £3,000 a year and a Ford Granada before I had even asked what the job was. He wanted me to start on 1 September as his replacement because he was moving to become the holding company's European sales manager.' Roger accepted the job.

Until then, Precision Systems Ltd had been UK agents for an American company, Inland Motor. Inland Motor were manufacturers of high-quality precision servo components. They had decided to take over the UK company and turn it into a full time office.

'After I was taken on by the Americans, I went to America for a couple of months to get some accounts and product training. When I came back, I was quickly thrown into Scandinavia for the odd month, and everywhere else, while supposedly having control of the London office at the same time.' Roger was not very impressed by what he found: 'That office that I took over was predominantly machine tool-oriented. Orders and contracts tended to be done on the back of cigarette packets. From the office in London, I had control of the company's representatives in Scandinavia and some other parts of Europe. There was one particular representative in

Scandinavia who I had to visit for periods of two to three weeks at a time. Every time we went to see a customer together, he started asking as many questions as the customer. It became a bit galling. I was on a small salary, but he drove a Rolls Royce and went back to stay on his boat every evening! And yet the guy could not close a sale without someone like me around.'

Roger soon found other areas, apart from machine tools, where sales of the company's products could be expanded. These were mainly defence equipment, robotics and computer peripherals. At Roger's initiative, this part of the business grew in importance and, in 1975, the operation was split. Roger moved to Reading, with a secretary, to look after the new business areas he was developing. The rest of the office stayed in London, still handling the machine tool industry.

Soon after he opened the office in Reading, he received an offer from Racal Electronics to join them as their European sales manager. He was pleased by the offer, but decided that it was not the opportunity he was looking for. The disparity between the high level of earning and poor technical knowledge of Inland Motor's representatives in Europe had left a deep impression on him. He had been thinking for some time of a means by which he could move into a position where he acted as the company's agent. The Racal offer acted as a spur. After discussing things with his wife, Roger flew with her to the USA and saw the parent company. 'I went to America to talk to them about Racal's offer, not to get more money out of them, but to discuss where we, as a company, were going. They asked what would make me stay, so I said that I wanted to start my own representative company, which at that time was a unique concept in the UK.'

Starting up

Roger proposed that Inland Motor should set him up in his own business as its sole agent in the UK for the products and markets he was handling in Reading. This was a reversal of the policy that the company had adopted in taking over Precision Systems. However Roger Lacey explained why they considered it: 'It was a spin-off operation, in an area where they didn't quite know what the potential was and where I believed I did.' The company said they would think about it and let him know. He and his wife took a fortnight's holiday in the USA, unsure what Inland Motor's reaction would be.

When they got back in touch with Inland Motor, the answer was 'Yes'. Roger and his wife flew back to England to start their own business. He recalls how unprepared they were. 'On the aeroplane we discussed what we could call the company – we had a list of 18 names and about fifth on the list was Hightech Components. But we did not know how to register the company and we did not know what financial deal to put together. From my American training we know we had to produce a cash flow projection and we needed to prepare and analyse budgets and forecasts. I did not know how to do it for British banks. I needed a good accountant to help, not one of these back street guys who was a bookkeeper.'

So I went to the Inland Revenue who recommended two or three people. I then went to the banks – the local branches of Natwest, the TSB, Midland and Barclays – and I asked them who they rated. The only common name to come out of all of this was one chap, David Preston from Hugill & Co. I went along to see him and we sorted out a package.' Roger had no money to pay him, but David Preston agreed to take on the business as an investment in the future. Of the three names for the new company which Preston checked, only Hightech Components was unused. It was a name for which the company was to be offered a lot of money in the future.

In its first year, 1976, Hightech Components Ltd achieved a turnover of £93,000 and made pre-tax profits of £18,000. Roger was in business.

Roger's concept

For some time before he had approached Inland Motor, Roger had been struck by the possibilities of taking the usual method of working as an agent or representative a stage further. He had not been impressed by Inland's European agents: 'They worked from home. You went back to their flat and their wives answered the phone. I thought that an agency could be run in a much more pro-fessional way. The ideal goal would be to have your own conference centre and your own method of putting on seminars. It would be to have people selling the products who knew what they were talking about, so that the same person could talk to the buyer and the chief engineer. Technical knowledge, selling skills and a knowledge of costing would be brought together in the sales function and put under one umbrella in a small unit. That was the goal.'

While he knew that the right product was important, he also knew the importance of people: 'The key was the right products as well as the right people and the right atmosphere to enable those people to succeed. Quality in the product and service from the people should go hand-in-hand. Business schools always go for the bottom line, but the importance of people must be appreciated.'

The products Roger intended to sell were advanced servo components for closed loop control systems.* He planned to offer engineers
the full range of products, including drives, controls, position and
velocity transducers and amplifiers. This meant the company could
offer an engineer all the servo components that he needed to build
systems.

Hightech's growth and development

Roger and his wife set up their company in 1976 with an initial share
capital of £500. Although Roger's wife was a 'sleeping' director he
was proud of the fact that she had always owned half the shares:
'None of this 49 per cent business; in marriage you've got to trust,
haven't you?'

The first employee was a secretary to provide support while Roger
was 'on the road'. The second employee was Graham Horner, who
joined the company in 1978. Thereafter the company grew at the rate
of one extra employee each year. In 1980, the company looked for
new premises and bought a house, previously occupied by solicitors,
in Tadley, Hampshire. The name was changed to Servo House and
the company adopted the slogan 'Servo House of Great Britain'.

Hightech started in 1976 with a customer base of only 10 accounts.
By 1981 this had grown to over 100 and by 1987 to over 200 active
accounts. Roger observed that Hightech 'followed the predictable
path of an expanding business. Turnover went up in nice, gradual
steps.' By 1987 it was around £2m.

Turnover £000s	1976	1977	1978	1979	1980	1981
	93	280	420	591	593	593

Turnover £000s	1982	1983	1984	1985	1986	1987
	908	985	1,840	1,750	2,188	2,000

(These figures do not represent sales volume, as over 50 per cent of
sales are direct orders on overseas suppliers).

In 1984 the company moved to a higher level of sales. As the size
of order grew, so did the likelihood of surges in turnover. Up to
1985, the company's largest order had been $300,000 worth of com-
ponents, yet in that year this was broken on three occasions. Another
reason for fluctuations was that there was no set order cycle. A

Servo: of a system in which the main mechanism is set in operation by a subsidiary
mechanism and is able to develop a force greater than the force communicated to it.

number of large orders might either repeat at 18-month intervals or all come together in the same year.

Turnover in 1986 was over £2m. and by the beginning of 1987 the company had the largest backlog of orders it had ever had. Although the traditional order fulfilment period for this type of equipment was 14–20 weeks, Hightech had started to obtain orders which were spread over four years. The forward order book looked very healthy.

Product applications

The company was an approved servo component supplier for a large number of military, aerospace and industrial applications on land, sea and in the air. Among the companies it supplied were British Aerospace, Dowty, Ferranti, Ford, GEC, IBM, Plessey, Racal, Rolls Royce, Smiths Industries and Thorn EMI. It was also an approved supplier to the Ministry of Defence.

Roger was enthusiastic about the variety of applications: 'We are involved with a new throttle control for British Aerospace. It is a unique application and, at the moment, it is still specified for the new European fighter aircraft. We supply components for the Sea Harrier. For the radar in the front of the aircraft we drive and position each plate for the Ferranti radar system. We also supply the motors that drive all the British Navy periscopes and we supply components for the guidance systems on missiles and torpedoes. Space applications is another area for us. We do all the motors that go into the solar ray drives that keep the satellite pointing at the sun for its energy. Another typical programme for us involves remote control vehicles used for surveillance work. Again, we supply components for the on-board control systems.'

Competitive advantage

The components offered by Hightech were manufactured by five companies. The company was the exclusive UK agent for three divisions of Inland – Speciality Products, Defence Products and the Sierra Vista Division. It was also the exclusive UK agent for three other American companies – Inductosyn International, Sequential Electronic Systems Inc and Airflyte Electronics Company. The only non-American company for whom it had exclusive rights was Thomson CSF of France.

In the UK, Hightech Components faced limited competition. A number of domestic UK companies made drives, motors and controls, but few of them offered the comprehensive range of components that Hightech made available to its customers. In Roger's view, Hightech's ability to sell a mix of components and a wide variety of options put the company in a strong selling position. For instance, when Hightech started to build up a market in direct drive motors, some UK companies sought to compete, but it was very difficult for them to succeed because Hightech was able to offer around 20,000 different options, whereas the UK companies could only produce a limited number of designs. In some areas, Hightech was in a particularly strong position. For example, in controls, the company had the exclusive UK agency for a small range of products that were made by one company in America and for which there was no second source anywhere.

Hightech used these unique products as one element in its selling strategy. Once a purchaser had an application for one component, the company had a sufficiently broad, but homogeneous, range of products to offer a complete set of complementary components. Only three or four UK companies produced part of the range offered by Hightech and nobody produced the full range.

Roger was clear about the continuing growth potential of his business: 'I think we have got quite a long future ahead of us, even with our original product lines. If you are with big enough companies like Inland Motor, who are a $30 million company, they are constantly creating new technology themselves, so they are creating our tomorrow for us. As long as they keep creating, we are OK. The thing to avoid in the "rep" business is being tied into a company that has a good product one year, but never reinvests.'

Sales and marketing

One of the problems which the company faced was that it appeared to do a disservice to British industry by being an importer of foreign components. Roger had clear views on this: 'We don't have it on our conscience because we actually create employment and wealth in Britain. The projects we are involved in are better because of the technology that we provide. An example of this is British Aerospace. Instead of their having to compete in America with old-fashioned motor technology, we can supply them with lighter components which give better control so that they can go in and compete against the Americans. If they buy from us in ex-works dollars there is no UK mark-up; we sell at the same price as US domestic. So they have a big advantage, because they can buy the same product as their American competitor, at the same price, from us.' Hightech believed that approximately 50–60 per cent of its components were re-exported in British-made products.

The company worked hard at turning Roger's original concept of selling into reality. In his view, the need for technical competence was even more important than ever before. 'If you are going to see the engineer you have got to know the subject that you are talking to him about. What engineers hate these days are salesmen who say, "Oh, I must ask the chief engineer back at base and I'll get back to you".' If they have invited you there they want you to be able to handle their enquiry there and then. When we visit customers, we carry an incredible amount of material with us. We have samples, books and all the technical charts with us. We are prepared to camp out at a customer when we are with him and we offer almost a free consultancy service because what we are doing is coming up with suggestions of how to solve his problems by using our products. It is a different method of selling with the buyer: he is just worried about price and delivery. The engineer is worried about performance. A great deal of our work is military and the buyer is not particularly price-conscious.'

The company used seminars as an important part of its selling effort. At Servo House in Tadley, Hightech had a fully equipped exhibition, seminar and conference room which seated 55 people. Using titles such as 'Advancements in modern servo-component technology', Hightech offered these seminars either in-house or at the premises of client companies. All the customer's engineers were invited and, because the seminar was free, many companies wanted their staff to attend. Roger knew the benefits of this method of selling: 'It gives us access to anything from 20–30 engineers who, in normal selling time, it would take three to four weeks to reach individually. So it's a very economic way of selling. When we do a seminar at a customer's premises, we always leave a huge book of product specifications in the company library for future reference!'

Rather than advertise, Roger and his staff devoted time to writing technical articles for magazines. Because they did not charge for writing them, most magazines put in Hightech's name. The only advertising space the company bought was in the trade reference manuals used by engineers looking for Hightech's type of equipment. The company only exhibited once or twice a year, preferring to spend time on direct customer contact.

What the company did do was produce high-quality sales literature. It tended to use bright colours which would stand out on an engineer's cluttered desk. 'Colour has a great effect on people. If you have brightly coloured literature they tend to think that you have got a reasonable image. Image is very important for us. A lot of people order from us who have never seen us. If it costs at least £30 per visit to see a customer, you should spend at least £5 if you are only going to write to him. It other words it has to be good high-quality material – it is not worth economising. All too often, if you write to a company for information, all you get is a compliment slip with minimum information. But if someone writes back to you and takes time over your enquiry and encloses a bit more information, which company are you going to be interest in? It's worth the extra effort to be one step ahead.'

Roger saw customer service as a matter of doing some fundamental things. 'Normally we make sure that we read his request properly. If he asks us to do certain things, such as to provide a written quote or a telex quote, we do it and keep to his time scale. We usually reckon to follow up with a phone call very rapidly after sending a quote. I think that is the secret, to make it easy for him. Give him what he wants, but also, before you send the price back, do a bit of market research with him as to why the quote has come in, what the project is for, whether there is any competition. If there is, you want to know who it is because it gives you an idea on pricing.' By operating in this way, the company achieved a conversion rate of enquiries to orders of around 15 per cent. The industry average was believed to be about 5 per cent.

In terms of pricing, Hightech had a standard price list. Although the company was prepared to negotiate from time to time, Roger was very conscious that their product range tended to be at the top of the market: 'We are expensive but we give high quality and we don't make any concessions. We are not embarrassed by the fact that we are high price. Our products tend to be at the Jaguar and Rolls Royce end of the market. With the sort of technology and quality of our products we are in a particular market area. That is where we live and we are unashamed to be there. Virtually none of our products is priced below £100 and generally the price is several hundreds pounds and upwards. We are in really high precision, servo system components.'

'We try to make profit on every single order, even one-offs. When we started we were prepared to take the odd lost leader but we don't know. I give the guidelines and I decide what profit margin we are aiming for. We try to get that wherever possible. But if we are involved with competition, there is a point where we will not go below a certain percentage. Basically I look for a minimum profit margin of 15 per cent.'

Company structure

It was company policy not to reveal the size of its staff. It was a source of some entertainment to Roger that some competitors believed that Hightech employed around 40 people because of the level of service that they provided. the company actually employed only eight people and the structure was relatively simple.

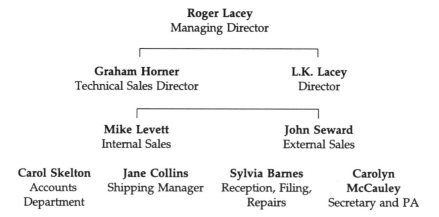

Graham Horner, the Technical Sales Director, reported directly to Roger Lacey. Mike Levett and John Seward reported to Graham Horner.

Carolyn McCauley acted as secretary and PA to both Roger and Graham and managed personnel matters. She also handled hotel bookings, exhibitions and seminars.

Sylvia Barnes acted as receptionist at Servo House, was responsible for filing and handled all repairs and rejects. She also acted as secretary for Mike Levett and John Seward.

Jane Collins was Shipping Manager, responsible for all imports, documentation and despatch. Her target was to earn her salary in savings on shipping costs.

Carol Skelton, who had been with the company for seven years, was the company accountant and was responsible for producing the monthly management accounts.

Roger saw the company structure providing four different functions. Graham Horner, Mike Levett, John Seward and himself fulfilled the sales function. Jane Collins and Sylvia Barnes provided an order progress function. Carolyn McCauley and Sylvia Barnes supplied secretarial services and Carol Skelton provided the accounting back-up.

People

In line with his original concept, Roger recognised the importance of people to the operation. 'We have never gone for regional salesmen.

We have everybody operating from here. We have people who are all self-starters in their own right. We tend to go for interesting people who don't run with the crowd. If you given them a task to do, just leave them to get on with it. If they don't, then you change the person. I think most people enjoy the freedom.'

The company had a bonus scheme for employees which had been in operation since the early 1980s. Roger Lacey was a firm believer in its importance: 'I regard profit-sharing as the icing on the cake, as the reward for that extra effort. In effect, it is a bonus based on our level of profits. When I started the scheme, I listed a number of reasonable points that I would consider before deciding how much people got. These were: time keeping, tidiness both in dress and own office area (in keeping with the sales environment), the 'natter factor' – time lost through excessive private conversations inside working hours – extra hours worked above normal, willingness to assist others as a team, personal approach to work, thinking about the well-being of the company, genuineness of sick leave, consistency throughout the year (not in the last two months of the year) and intrusion of private life into office day – private phone calls and so on. When I issued a note on this to the staff, I made the point that it assumed that the company was making a profit. No profit – no profit sharing.'

Because he was away from the office a good deal, Roger Lacey had to rely to a certain extent on 'gut feel' to decide on the profit sharing allocation. The scheme was linked to a series of appraisal interviews which he conducted towards the end of each year. These interviews lasted for around three hours each and, because they were so intense, he could only manage two interviews a day. Apart from putting in the effort of appraising people properly, Roger Lacey believed that any such scheme must be worthwhile: 'It has to be generous, otherwise it is not worth doing. The range has gone from the lowest ever at £350 to as high as £2,500 at the last review.'

Import procedures

Because all the company's sales were met by imported components, the method of meeting orders was a critical element in the company's operation. Orders were met in one of two ways. Roger explained: 'If we are buying from America there are two methods of handling a sale: ex-works or CIF. Ex-works is when a customer buys in dollars and is invoiced direct from the USA. We still handle all the order paperwork and monitor it and the order still comes here, but the invoice goes direct to the customer from the USA. When the customer pays, we get our commission.'

However some customers don't appreciate what dollars are, and they want a pound sterling delivered price, to the door. In that case we supply on a CIF basis – that is, carriage, insurance and freight. The good arrive in the UK, the import duty is paid and the goods are relabelled at point of entry and sent direct to the customer. We are then invoiced from America, we add on the import duty, we pay the freight costs and we invoice it all to the customer. This means that it goes on our bought ledger and we have to get the money.'

The decision about whether to try and put an order through as an ex-works or CIF order tended to depend on size. The company worked on the basis that any order worth more than £25,000 should be an ex-works dollar order so that the suppliers took the risk. This limited Hightech's exposure to a maximum of £25,000. However, if companies such as GEC wanted to place pound sterling CIF orders, these rules were stretched. Each new customer was subjected to a credit check as a matter of routine but in general the type of company who order high-quality, high-price components was a low-credit risk.

Both methods of fulfilling orders had advantages. Roger Lacey summed these up: 'One gives you funding and one less bother. Our largest suppliers do like us to get a bias towards the ex-works, so that they do not have too much money going through our books, thus further increasing the amount that we owe them. Our turnover figures are not the same as our sales figures. They comprise only the CIF contracts and our commissions. The ratio. tends to be in the order of 60/40: 60 per cent ex-works and 40 per cent CIF.

Finance

Inevitably, Hightech owed its suppliers considerable sums of money at any one time and this could be as high as £350,000. An original credit limit of £100,000 had been passed as the business had grown and the additional £250,00 had then had to be covered by a bank guarantee. Hightech's suppliers had agreed to share the cost of the guarantee because it meant that, if Hightech was unable to meet its commitments, the suppliers would still be paid by the bank.

Until 1984 Roger and his wife had needed to provide personal guarantees. Given the sums of money involved, this was a considerable commitment. Roger was relieved that these were no longer necessary: 'Now that we don't have to give directors' guarantees, at least we know that our house cannot be seized! If something went wrong and the bank had to sue us, it is the company's assets which are now at stake.' Roger appreciated the bank's help in this area: 'We have always paid our bills on time so we have never had a problem with the bank. What they do like to see, each month, is a copy of our receivables. In the 11 years we have been trading we have only had two bad debts. They were very small. We had an amusing situation with a company in High Wycombe which went down the tube, owing us something like £18,000. As soon as we got the letter in the post, I went straight over that afternoon but found no-one there. Eventually I tracked the Receiver down. He was at the offices of the guy who wanted to buy the company. I walked in and they asked what the problem was. Over a cup of coffee I explained, saying that the company had gone to the wall owing us £18,000 and the goods must still be in the stores. The Receiver said that he was not bothered by things like that. I told him I was not leaving without an answer. He said that they were having a meeting. As that did not bother me, I said that he'd have to throw me out. Anyway he sent someone to look in the stores and sure enough, there were our goods. I took them back! The only thing we lost on that was our mark-up. We sent the motors back to America and the other bits back to France and I think we lost about £3,000 on the deal in the end.'

Computerisation

In early 1985, Hightech decided to computerise its entire operation. The company's customer base had grown from ten in 1976 to nearly 400, and there was a constant turnover of accounts. This increase in the volume of work had meant that the paper-based progress system which the company used was under serious strain. In addition, the increasing range of products which the company offered meant that, with between 30 and 40 orders being completed in busy weeks, the chance of human error was increasing. This was particularly so because the use of model numbers to specify products meant that typographical errors could result in the despatch of the wrong item.

A firm of computer consultants was employed. After six months' study, they recommended that Hightech install a networked computer system. At the time, networks were still relatively uncommon in Britain, so the consultants recommended an American firm. Roger rang Inland Motor to ask them to run a check on the company for him in the States. He was shocked by the answer. Inland's enquiry revealed that the recommended firm was technically bankrupt and on the point of going into liquidation. Hightech refused to pay the consultant's fees. The plans for computerisation were now seriously delayed and so Hightech turned to the National Computing Centre and found that a government scheme vetted computer consultants who could help small businesses. A further study was completed within three months and resulted in Data General being recommended as the hardware supplier.

Hightech then had to decide through whom to buy the equipment and which software house to use. A tender went to three companies and the smallest, a company called TML from Marlow, won the contract. Roger Lacey and some of the Hightech staff worked over Christmas and wired the entire building. Every room contained plugs and sockets so that terminals could be installed anywhere and everywhere. TML wrote the software system. The total cost was £80,000 of which £35,000 was spent on software development.

The enquiry system

The new computer system integrated the management of each enquiry, from first contact through to receipt of order. It contained a complete filing system providing detailed information on product numbers, supplier codes, supplier references and other relevant facts. When an enquiry was received, and there was an average of between 40 and 50 new enquiries each month, the person receiving the enquiry would allocate a number and enter the details on his terminal. Included in the details would be the date on which action was next required. At the same time, a corresponding paper-based file was opened. The computer then acted as a prompt for further action. Each morning, Mike Levett, in charge of internal sales, logged into his terminal and was provided with a detailed list of which enquiries were due to be followed up. The paper-based files, which contained background information such as correspondence, would then be passed to the person whose initials were on the enquiry, ready for action to be taken. If anyone was absent, Mike Levett would initiate whatever action was necessary himself.

The computer also provided a 'visit schedule'. When members of staff were making sales visits, the computer was able to isolate additional customer contacts in the same geographic area and provide a progress check on each order or enquiry from all those customers. This mean that sales visits were made as efficient as possible and that the person calling on clients knew the exact position on all the current business in hand. The system also kept a complete dossier on all orders placed with suppliers so that it could be checked quickly about the status of all customer orders.

The paper-based files were colour-coded. Standard enquiries were kept in orange folders but special 'blue chip' enquiries were kept in blue files. To merit being classed a blue chip, an enquiry had to meet certain criteria, not necessarily financial. These could include large quotations, technical difficulties, a prototype enquiry, an important project tender against competition or an enquiry which suggested a new potential market area. In order to avoid excessive use of the blue chip status, anyone, including Roger Lacey, who wanted to give blue chip status to an enquiry had to persuade at least one other member of the sales team of the merits of doing so.

Once an enquiry had blue chip status, it got priority treatment. There was an unwritten rule that, if a blue chip file was seen sitting on someone's desk, he was likely to be asked why he was not taking action on it. As a result, all the staff made sure it was dealt with quickly and returned to Mike Levett. Blue chip enquiries, therefore, flowed rapidly through the system and the necessary action was always given priority over other work.

When an enquiry was converted into an order, the paper-based file was closed. However the order system fed back into the computer so that when a client range it was possible to access immediately, either by the company or by project, the position of the order.

Project allocation

Project allocation was often made on the basis of the person who received the original enquiry. However, while each of the people involved in sales was technically qualified across the range of products, each of them had a degree of speciality knowledge and interest which generally influenced allocation. For instance, Graham Horner tended to pick up the more technically complicated and larger contracts. If a large contract became particularly political or very price-sensitive, it would usually be handed over to Roger.

Regular customers preferred to deal with their usual contact and in many instances a very close relationship became established. Other customers were happy to deal with any of Hightech's staff because, over time, they had got to know all of them. It also meant that customers could have an instant response to their enquiry from whoever was available.

There was also a good deal of interchange within the allocation system. Often a new enquiry would be transferred, as the project progressed, from the person who originally received it to someone else. This happened when someone was away on business or on holiday. At such times the flexibility of the system and the computer back-up meant that anyone else could maintain the progress-chasing function. On other occasions, projects which had started from a telephone enquiry would be transferred from the person who took the call to another member of staff who was making a sales visit in the customer's area. There were some large projects in which all the sales staff became involved over time.

Roger was very pleased with the way the system worked: 'We have an informal, flexible system which works well because we have a good team. It might seem inefficient, but it means that we are all involved in different parts of it. If someone is on holiday then someone else can carry on with their project. The person who picks it up then has the customer coming back to him rather than the guy who first dealt with it. Some other organisations are not so flexible – if the guy is away for a month the enquiry just sits on his desk, awaiting his return.'

The combination of the flexible allocation of work and the computerised progress system impress clients. It also had a lighter side. When clients visited Servo House they discovered how they got such instant service. Roger Lacey gave an example: 'A very good customer of ours had been planning to visit us for ages. He always asked the most awkward questions but he was convinced that all of us had superb memories. When he saw the computer he knew how we did it! It allows us to make very good use of time. When he rang on one particular order we could quickly scan all his other enquiries and tell him what was happening on the quotes he had asked us for. It also meant that we could ask how proposals we had put to him were going. It's very effective as well as being economic, because we don't have to call the customer back.'

Roger was very anxious to avoid any move to a more geographic or regional sales organisation. He believed that the flexibility that Hightech's system offered provided the best type of customer service. 'The thing that controls everybody is the file and whoever has that controls the project. Because we all live from a central filing system, by definition we all have to be here and use the files and the computer. It would be difficult to do it any other way, because we do rely very much on the interaction between people, the flexibility and the fact that we all get on. There is always the danger that we might tread on each others toes, but it hasn't happened yet.'

A move to a more focused sales operation, based on product categories, was also ruled out because Hightech's ability to sell additional components on the back of the original specification was an important part of the sales technique. 'We sell servo systems; we are not just distributors of individual products.'

The way ahead

Roger was ambitious. Having reached the £2m. turnover level, he wanted to expand the business even faster. As an aid to focusing his thoughts on the prospects for the future, Roger briefly listed, on a pad in front of him, the policies he was determined to maintain in order to continue the existing high level of earnings:

- to remain as a supplier rather than manufacture, doing what we know best;
- to retain the clean 'Habitat' image which marked the company out in a traditionally 'dirty industry';
- To preserve the culture of the organisation – tightly-organised, informal, and highly committed to quality and service;
- to stay at the top end of the market, always seeking to sell the best in technical innovation.

He then added a note on some of the options available to him:

- to focus on existing customers, trying to increase the unit value of sales and the quantity of repeat business;
- to go all out for new customers;
- to increase the range of products, perhaps by acquiring additional agencies for overseas manufacturers;
- to take on an agency in another European country;
- to cut back on some areas which had lower volume or profitability;
- to diversify, on our own, or through innovative joint ventures such as the mechanical arm project with Southampton University;
- to sell out: offers and approaches were now running at two or three a year.

There may well be more, Roger reflected. The question is: which of these are best for Hightech? What will take all of us in the direction we want to go without sacrificing what we've worked so hard to build?

Epilogue

After must thought, Roger came to the conclusion that Hightech had found a comfortable market niche for itself and that this might be endangered if he expanded the company too far, too quickly. He decided to continue much as before and to try to curb his personal desire for growth, which he realised came from his inherent entrepreneurial drive rather than an analysis of Hightech's opportunities. Roger decided that incremental growth was best for Hightech, growth based on finding new customers but also making the most of the excellent relationships they already had with their existing customers. He decided:

- Not to sell out. He was not ready for that yet.
- Not to diversify. This presented too many risks.
- Building on the strength of his sales team and the relationships they had, he would try to increase sales to existing customers. To help with this strategy he decided to try to find new companies to represent in the UK. They would have to offer complementary products and be acceptable to the companies Hightech currently represented – particularly Inland Motor.
- To continue looking for new customers, particularly outside the defence sector. However he decided not to change his marketing strategy, which seemed to be working well.

In 1991 Hightech opened a £500,000 extension to Servo House, increasing the available office space from 3,000 to 6,000 sq ft. The extension was self-financed. By that time the Hightech team had grown to ten.

By 1992 Hightech had over 300 active accounts and turnover had topped £3m. Hightech was now representing two new companies; Astro Instrument Corporation of the USA, which produced a unique brushless motor gearhead range that produced very high torque, and PMI Technologies of the USA, a sister company to Inland Motor producing a low inertia printed circuit motors.

In April 1994, Kollmorgen Motion Technologies Group, owners of Inland Motor, purchased the assets and liabilities of Hightech Components. Roger Lacey became Director of European Business Development at Kollmorgen, responsible for improving the company's market penetration in Europe. Graham Horner took over as managing director of the now renamed Kollmorgen Hightech Ltd. It was a friendly takeover.

Consetec Ltd

This is a case about a rapidly growing company that is only eight years old. The owner-managers want to achieve further growth but also feel uneasy about being too tied in to one market sector.

Questions

1. What are Consetec's strengths, weaknesses, opportunities and threats?
2. What do you think of the industry in operates in and what are the company's competitive advantages?
3. How do you think the owner-managers have handled the growth of the company?
4. What are the company's options for growth in the future? What are the pros and cons of the different options? Which would you recommend?

Background

Consetec Ltd is a small but rapidly growing computer systems hardware and software design company. Their area of expertise is the design of High Integrity Safety Systems (HISS) which use 'redundant' technology based on the programmable logic controller (PLC). Consetec acts as a Systems Integrator (SI) whereby systems are integrated and customised to meet a particular need. Consetec deal in the design and integration of control system and equipment. The key strength of the company is that it writes the software used to drive these systems and these PLCs form the 'brain' of most modern control systems. In the petrochemical market, Consetec provides mainly fire and gas safety systems and emergency shut-down (ESD) systems which utilise technology at low and intermediate levels. These require specialist technology and expertise.

The company experienced rapid growth during the period 1990–92 which has made obsolete the company's business plan written in 1990. The company has concentrated on the petrochemical market where demand for HISS has benefited from the unfortunate Piper Alpha disaster in 1988. However Consetec's directors feel uneasy about 80 per cent of their business being derived from this sector and are considering new markets for the development of the business.

Consetec was set up in 1984 by three ex-British Aerospace employees, Dan Burnell, Peter McKay, the technical director, and Bob Hanson. They had the idea of developing and marketing an electronic navigational plotter. Initially the venture was part-time and drew on expertise from the group's contact network. A further two engineers, Bruce Pollard and Jack Pearce, soon joined the group. Jack worked full-time on the project. At this time John Booth and David Proudfoot of Falcon 2001 Ltd, a major control systems supplier, became involved. The initial capitalisation was £32,000 all of which was provided by the founders.

The original idea did not take off. The company needed to gain advanced orders to finance the development of the project. Without a working system the idea was difficult to sell and the time leads involved would have caused severe cash flow problems. It would have necessitated an injection of venture capital or grant assistance, such as a DTI Smart Award. John Booth and David Proudfoot realised the potential of matching the groups' programming expertise to the demand which existed for bespoke software for PLC and control systems generally. They provided Consetec with work through Falcon 2001 Ltd on a subcontract basis. Consetec grew steadily between 1985 and 1990. Jack Pearce, one of the full-time engineers, left in 1987 because he could not cope with the overload of work which happened from time to time and the need for him to deal with customers directly.

The company has moved premises four times to its current site and the constant work overload continues as a way of life as the company expands. The company now employs 49 full-time people and there are plans to move again soon, which will undoubtedly cause additional stress.

Peter McKay, one of the founders, has had a great influence from the beginning on the company, particularly upon its technical focus. The arrival of David Proudfoot in 1988 as the Technical Applications

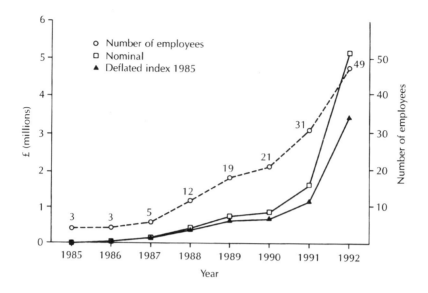

Figure 1   Consetec turnover, 1985–92

and Sales director saw a period in which the company won larger orders. The major influence, however, has undoubtedly been the appointment of John Booth as chairman in early 1990. Figure 1 demonstrates the accelerated growth from 1990 onwards. John Booth brought with him considerable business experience, having founded Falcon 2001 in the early 1970s, and was responsible for the development of electronic HISS in the oil and gas production industry. He had many contacts in the petrochemical sector and was well respected in the industry. He sold 75 per cent of Falcon and moved to Consetec after the 'time bar' imposed at the time of the sell-out had expired. The growth of Consetec since his arrival full-time illustrates the value of personal contacts and reputation in industrial markets. During this time the petrochemical sector declined, while Consetec's order book to the sector was growing. Some of the increased sales came from direct contracts rather than acting as subcontractors through companies like Falcon 2001 Ltd.

Control of the company has remained decentralised, with no individual holding more than a quarter of the shares:

	%
John Booth (Directors)	22
David Proudfoot (Director)	18
Peter McKay (Director)	22
David Wright (Secretary)	11
Others (Company Engineers)	27

Decision making has traditionally been by consensus and the directors have co-operated without significant incidents marring the development and cohesion of the company.

Appendixes 1 and 2 show the balance sheets for the eight years to 1992, the performance ratios and the growth in numbers employed by Consetec Ltd. There is no long-term debt and 100 per cent of the equity is held by the directors and employees. The business has been financed through retained earnings and is financially healthy. The directors are confident that outside finance could be attracted should the need arise.

The management believe they have the knowledge, experience and contacts to get the business to grow further, especially in the petrochemical sector. They have achieved financial independence through organic growth with no external ownership and potential control problems. Their research shows that the industry is experiencing growth of about 7 per cent per annum. Success in the petrochemical sector will provide the resources for their further expansion and medium-term plans.

While the industry is fragmented and in the early stages of development, economies of scale have yet to become a significant competitive weapon and the smaller company can thrive. In the petrochemical sector ICS hold the dominant market share and price cutting by them has forced Consetec to improve operational efficiency to win orders at a lower margin and still survive. Consetec are proud of their product development abilities and feel that they have the expertise and innovative abilities as well as the engineering competence to stay ahead of the competition. Strong network relationships have been formed with major PLC suppliers (GE–Fanuc) which can be further exploited.

However it is recognised that there is a very heavy reliance on the petrochemical market. Only two directors are involved in the marketing decisions of the firm, and there is no recognised marketing plan. A problem exists that the initial system definition or job evaluation is carried out by only two directors, thus limiting the number of leads that can be processed. This bottleneck is seen as a constraint to growth. The financial planning, project evaluation and financial risk avoidance skills are also weak within the company.

The company experienced overtrading in 1991: it tended to chase turnover at the expense of margins. It is difficult to turn business away, but Consetec are aware not only of their reliance on the petrochemical sector but also that the type of business which they are picking up is changing their focus away from core activities. Cash flow problems have resulted from time to time, owing to the increase in overseas orders, adverse payment terms and fluctuating exchange rates. There is a need for enhanced management skills in this area.

The basis of competition is also shifting within the petrochemical sector and becoming more aggressive. As a result of the widening business base there is an increasing need for more staff to interact with customers. There is a need to deal with the dissatisfaction felt by technical staff, who do not appreciate having this additional responsibility, and morale is low. An additional problem is that new commercial managers who are being recruited are initiating changes which are upsetting the managers of long standing. It is feared that continuing the pace of change without consultation and involvement may result in managers leaving the company.

#131;Internal management and control issues have tended to dominate directors' time. In order for growth to continue, directors have decided to set up systems for gaining access to better internal information to help with budgeting and control of the company. This will have an effect on the working environment of the project managers and engineers.

The customer base in widening, resulting in personnel taking on more responsibility. Staff supervision is reducing and engineers are having to take on more commercial decision making. A restructuring is taking place which will identify more commercially astute engineers, who will become business project managers, and the predominantly technically competent will be called technical project managers. While this is in response to the changing role requirements it is also recognised that staff motivation and development is important. The creation of new positions which cater for individual competencies as well as company needs is considered to be one way of achieving this.

Consetec is technically innovative and uses product development as a competitive strategy. The company is considering more than one market for its products. Forward integration by major PLC suppliers to exploit certain higher value-added areas of the control system value chain is a possibility. This would lead to increased competition through price cutting, but it could also be an exit opportunity for Consetec's owners.

The market

Consetec's market can be described as the electronic control systems industry. The scope and therefore the size of the market is difficult to define but, by looking at various sources of secondary information, the company estimates that the instrumentation and control and automation industry in the UK is between £3.1bn. and £3.6bn. in 1991 and has been growing at 7 per cent per annum. (sources: GAMBICA and Business Monitor Reports). The electronic instrumentation and control market, which is closer to Consetec's market, was valued at £1.79bn. in 1991. This category can be further subdivided between large companies, with more than 500 employees, and small companies employing less than 500 employees.

Large companies £1,218m.
Small companies £572m.

Total £1,790m.

The European market for process control instrumentation was then $6.4bn. and was estimated to rise to $8.06bn. by 1996 at 1992 prices. This represents 6 per cent compound growth. The breakdown by country (source: Frost and Sullivan, 1992) is as follows:

UK	12%	Italy	10%
Spain	5%	France	15%
Benelux	9%	Germany	27%
Scandinavia	11%	Rest of Europe	11%

Strongest growth is in Spain (estimated $378m. by 1996) and Germany (estimated $2.19bn. by 1996).

The UK market in 1992 is $768m. or £404m. Using the business monitor information, the UK smaller companies process control systems market is £130m. This compares with £78m. for the petrochemical market (source: Programmed Business Development, 1992). The US process control software market is estimated to be $104.4m. (source: Automation Research, 1989) and is predicted to grow at 21 per cent per annum. Use of control systems is being increasingly recognised as providing manufacturers with real benefits.

Recession in the UK may delay investment by manufacturing industry in plant. In order for Consetec to survive, it will need to find new opportunities. It is hoped that the company will be 'tooled up' and ready to take advantage of an upturn in the economy or a legislative change which would force producers to invest.

The pharmaceutical industry

One option for Consetec is to diversify into a different segment of its market. The company has commissioned some research into the possibility of penetrating the pharmaceutical industry, which is generally regarded as recession resilient. UK pharmaceutical manufacturers increased output by 5.7 per cent in 1990, when the rest of UK manufacturing output declined by 1 per cent. The non-cyclical nature of the market is mainly due to the long R&D period which reinforces a longer-term view throughout the sector. The UK industry is ranked fifth in the world in terms of output value, and is the third largest exporter of pharmaceuticals, which in 1990 brought in trade surpluses of £1.1b. The key characteristics of the industry are that:

- it is highly regulated;
- it enjoys patent protection-based monopolies;
- it has stringent safety testing; and
- there is no direct marketing of ethical pharmaceuticals.

The industry is moving away from an emphasis on R&D and marketing towards increasing manufacturing efficiency. EC reports indicate that the industry is operating at only one-half to two-thirds capacity, which equates to £450m.–£750m. in lost revenue. With EC legislation likely to demand increased product standards and reduce national differences while maintaining prices, there is likely to be some manufacturing plant rationalisation. Over 75 per cent of pharmaceutical manufacturers in the UK are located near to Consetec in south-east England.

The Association of British Pharmaceutical Industry (ABPI) reported that £338m. was invested in process plant in the UK between 1988 and 1992:

Glaxo	£240.00m.
Pfizer	£ 40.00m.
Fisons	£ 30.00m.
Smith/Kline Beecham*	£ 17.00m.
Sandoz	£ 6.50m.
Ciba-Geigy	£ 3.75m.
Regent Laboratories	£ 1.00m.

(*£1.8m. of which as spent on a controlled production line.)

There are seven different hardware suppliers (PLCs) of which Siemens and Texas Instruments are the best known. For the software-driven proprietary supervisory systems, only IBM and DMAC are well known across the industry sector.

A system is usually sourced through an external supplier. It is rare for a company to develop an in-house system, and it is more usual for these to be modifications of a standard package. The key factors influencing the buying decision as to the choice of system supplier are shown in Table 1, with a relative score to indicate their significance.

Table 1   Importance of buyer characteristics

Characteristic	Weighted score
Support service	18
Financial stability	18
Management ability	13
Quality assurance	12
Track record	
System engineering	7
Stature/presence	3
Process engineering	1
Price	3
Experience with large projects	0

The respondents to the research commissioned by Consetec were asked to compare the company with ten competitors in terms of technical capability, quality of service and price. The perceptual maps (Figures 2–4) show their relative performance.

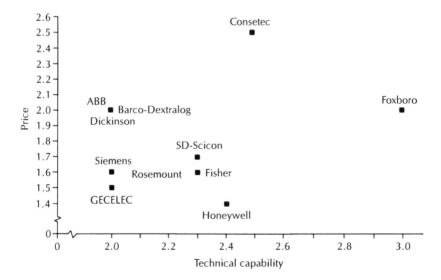

Figure 2   Price versus technical capability

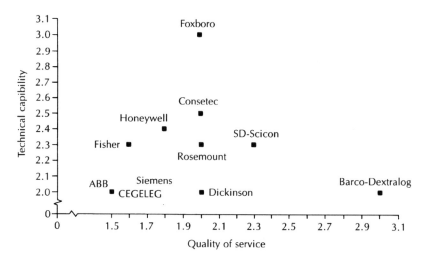

Figure 3   Technical capability versus quality of service

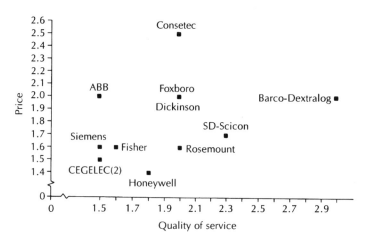

Figure 4   Price versus quality of service

Appendix 1: Consetec Ltd, financial accounts history

	1985	1986	1987	Year end (31 January) 1988	1989	1990	1991	1992	1987–92 average
Turnover	3,715	38,927	149,970	411,434	744,542	868,767	1,664,249	5,163,673	1,770,533
Cost of sales	0	0	0	201,421	444,754	448,468	1,006,608	3,826,451	1,185,540
Gross profit	3,715	38,927	149,970	210,013	299,788	420,299	657,641	1,337,222	584,993
Admin. expense	3,096	28,197	126,693	128,081	227,963	347,187	478,422	765,589	389,448
Other income	0	501	3,527	3,002	8,348	8,410	1,520	16,078	7,472
Op. profit (PBIT)	619	11,231	26,804	84,934	80,173	81,522	180,739	587,711	203,016
Interest paid	0	0	34	718	231	0	2,623	3,848	1,484
PBT	619	11,231	26,770	84,216	79,942	81,522	178,116	583,863	201,532
Tax	186	3,369	7,891	23,520	21,132	22,083	46,052	182,933	59,144
PAIT	433	7,862	18,879	60,696	58,810	59,439	132,064	400,930	142,388
Fixed assets	0	2,488	18,657	30,407	32,636	32,460	28,707	111,847	47,211
Stock	0	0	0	0	0	0	35,000	513,067	109,613
Debtors	1,468	32,801	50,694	138,176	195,322	354,988	673,637	1,388,473	550,139
Bank & cash	1,107	21,172	35,075	35,071	49,731	58	28,569	63,437	35,373
Current assets	2,575	53,973	85,769	173,247	245,053	355,046	737,206	1,965,077	695,126
Creditors	1,171	43,716	65,988	67,382	101,002	132,410	372,308	1,144,115	363,443
Deferred tax	0	3,555	8,143	23,750	21,141	22,987	46,052	182,232	59,052
Overdraft	0	0	1,086	22,617	6,831	24,855	7,335	9,429	14,213
Current liability	1,171	47,271	75,217	113,749	128,974	179,352	425,695	1,335,776	436,709
Net current assets	1,404	6,702	10,552	59,498	116,079	175,694	311,511	629,301	258,417

Appendix 1: Continued

	1985	1986	Year end (31 January) 1987	1988	1989	1990	1991	1992	1987–92 average
Total net assets	1,404	9,190	29,209	89,905	148,715	208,154	340,218	741,148	305,628
Long-term debt	1,074	0	0	0	0	0	0	0	0
Share capital	2	1,000	1,000	1,000	1,000	1,000	1,000	1,000	1,000
Share premium	0	0	1,140	1,140	1,140	1,140	1,140	1,140	1,140
Retained earnings	328	8,190	27,069	87,765	146,575	206,014	338,078	739,008	303,488
Total liabilities	1,404	9,190	29,209	89,905	148,715	208,154	340,218	741,148	305,628
No. of employees	3	3	5	12	19	21	31	49	26

Appendix 2. Consetec Ltd, Financial ratios and trends

	1985	1986	Year end (31 January) 1987	1988	1989	1990	1991	1992	1987–92 average
Ratios									
Liquidity	2.20	1.14	1.14	1.52	1.90	1.98	1.65	1.09	1.63
Current	2.20	1.14	1.14	1.52	1.90	1.98	1.73	1.47	1.72
Gearing (%)	325.45	0.00	3.72	25.16	4.59	11.94	2.16	1.27	0.09
Profit margin	0.17	0.29	0.18	0.20	0.11	0.09	0.11	0.11	0.13
ROCE	0.44	1.22	0.92	0.94	0.54	0.39	0.52	0.79	0.64
Stock turnover							47.55	10.06	11.52
Debtors turnover	2.53	1.19	2.96	2.98	3.81	2.45	2.47	3.72	3.09
Net assets/turnover	0.38	0.24	0.19	0.22	0.20	0.24	0.20	0.14	0.20
Turnover employee	1,238	12,976	29,994	34,286	39,186	41,370	53,685	105,381	54,782
Profit/employee	206	3,744	5,354	7,018	4,207	3,882	5,746	11,916	6,554
Capital/employee	468	3,063	5,842	7,492	7,827	9,912	10,975	15,125	10,266
Trends (per cent)									
Debtors		2134.40	54.55	172.57	41.36	81.75	89.76	106.13	98.31
Creditors		3633.22	50.95	2.11	49.89	31.10	181.18	207.30	94.32
Turnover		947.83	285.26	174.34	80.96	16.68	91.56	210.27	114.77
Real growth turnover		888.52	272.95	163.28	72.50	8.02	75.05	193.08	102.39
No. employees		0.00	66.67	140.00	58.33	10.53	47.62	58.06	62.91
PBT		1714.38	138.36	214.59	-5.08	1.98	118.49	227.80	111.56

Rollerdoors Ltd

This is a case that illustrates the incremental approach to financing adopted by small firms. Rollerdoors was set up as an importer of doors and developed into a manufacturer. As it grew, so too did its need for finance. This case allows you to explore the sources of finance open to a smaller company.

Questions

1. What do you think of the way Rollerdoors was financed?
2. Would you recommend any changes in the bank's approach to Rollerdoors?

Introduction

J.M.G. Rollerdoors Limited was established in the UK as an owner-managed business in the mid-1980s. It is mainly concerned with the provision of roller doors for domestic and industrial garages. It is also engaged in the provision of remote control devices and corresponding fittings to make these doors open and close automatically. When established, Rollerdoors was involved in the importing of doors and plants for sale into the UK market, either to individuals or to construction firms.

Financial structure

At start-up the firm was funded completely through internal equity. The owner-manager invested £30,000 to set up the business and parental family contributions amounted to a further £20,000. In anticipation of significant delayed payment problems, particularly from customers in the construction industry, the business was able to establish an overdraft facility of £50,000 with its bank. It received eight weeks' trade credit terms from the suppliers of doors and parts. Its terms of credit was invoice were 30 days.

Initial trading conditions

With minimal marketing in Yellow Pages and local newspapers, Rollerdoors attracted sufficient customer interest to break even. Because of the competitive pricing of the doors and parts owing to the strong value of the pound sterling at the time, the order book began to grow quite rapidly after six months' trading. Given the volatility of the pound sterling, however, and uncertain economic conditions in prospect, attention was focused on means of avoiding dependence upon imported materials.

The need for a domestic manufacturing facility

The obvious means of avoiding the vulnerability of dependence upon overseas suppliers was the construction of a domestic source of supply. In short it was decided to explore the feasibility of building a plant in the UK. Having visited the overseas suppliers of doors and parts, the owner-manager was aware of the requirements for plant equipment in order to set up a domestic outlet. She was also aware of the sources of the plant and equipment which was required. This was not available in the UK and would also, therefore, need to be imported. Its cost would again be dependent upon the value of the pound sterling at the time of payment.

Financing the plant

A fully functioning plant could be constructed for around £120,000, given the prevailing value of the pound sterling. This was too small to be of interest to formal sources of venture capital, even though the owner-manager would have welcomed some external equity participation, along with the additional decision-making and strategic support that this might bring with it. Contact was established with the local enterprise agency in an effort to find an individual investor who might be interested in joining the business and providing the equity injection which was required. Although negotiations were undertaken with several 'business angels', these tended to be time-consuming and ultimately unproductive. J.M.G.'s owner-manager found that the business angels who would have been suitable in the context of her requirements wanted to take too high a stake in the business, given the amount of commitment and efforts that she had already had to put in over the previous year to establish a going concern. After six months it was decided to forgo further attempts to raise external equity, and discussion were held with the bank manager. The business had a short but established track record and had been making profits for the previous 12 months. The bank offered a three-year term loan of £100,000 contingent upon a further £20,000 injection of personal or family equity, a floating charge on the business and a personal guarantee based on the owner-manager's house.

Although she could accommodate the collateral requirements and equity additions of this arrangement the owner-manager of J.M.G. Rollerdoors Limited could not entertain the short-term repayment profile required by a three-year loan. She used a variety of financial projections to illustrate why some form of repayment and interest rate holiday would be necessary while the business accommodated the adjustments cost of moving from selling imported doors and parts to constructing a plant and manufacturing their own. The bank was unable to offer this kind of flexibility.

Changing economic conditions

The firm was established in the south east and by the end of the 1980s the first portents of recession were beginning to hit the construction industry. The flow of orders became less predictable and there was also a growing problem with delayed payment. Over the next six months business was sufficient to break even, but the firm suffered from a number of non-payments. Several of the construction firms which they supplied had gone into liquidation with little prospect of any payment since the firm J.M.G Rollerdoors Limited was well down the list in terms of priority for the creditors to the companies which had folded. Banks became more wary of providing greater debt in general and increasingly bank managers became more experienced in dealing with the needs of small businesses in recession. Indeed Rollerdoor's bank had established an 'intensive care unit' to look after those whose long-term viability seemed moderately assured but who risked going into liquidation owing to short-term cash flow and liquidity problems.

J.M.G. Rollerdoors Limited's owner-manager argued that the need to set up an independent manufacturing plant was now greater than ever since there was increasing uncertainty about the value of sterling. She argued that a direct purchase of the requisite plant and equipment should be made in order to achieve a good price before sterling fell. She also argued that with recovery predicted by many (inaccurately as it transpired) it would be important to have the plant up and running in the event of recovery and an increase in demand. These arguments were accepted by the bank, contingent upon the provision of more security in the form of one of the parental houses. The firm decided against the possibility of a term loan under the loan guarantee scheme because of the interest surcharge that this carried and also what it perceived as excessive bureaucracy in the application process and the associated time that this might involve.

The plant was purchased and constructed in 1992, although the firm hit considerable liquidity problems as a result of unforeseen delays in making the plant operable. These delays were accommodated by a short-term increase in the overdraft facility provided by the bank, secured by the new factory and the plant and equipment therein. (The factory was rented and therefore the security referred only to the plant and equipment.) By 1993 improvements in the trading conditions in the construction sector, although intermittent, provided a sufficient order book and enabled the firm's owner-manager to take a relatively confident and optimistic view of the future. As a result she has taken steps to increase the production level of the business by running a small shift system and employing a further six people, making the total labour force 15 full-time staff.

Rough Rider Seating plc

Rough Rider Seating (not the true name of the company) is an example of a successful management-buy out.

Questions

1. What do you think of Rough Rider's prospects at the time of the buy-out proposal?
2. What are the advantages of a management buy-out?
3. Would you have financed the deal?
4. What do you think of the deal structure? What is the purpose of the convertible, cumulative, redeemable preference shares?
5. What risks did the buy-out team face?
6. What risks did ECI face?

1 The proposal

At the end of 1983, ECI Ventures were approached, via the merchant bank, Kleinwort Benson, by three senior managers from the UK subsidiary of Beacon Inc., a large, quoted, US engineering company. Beacon had earlier that year merged with another US engineering corporate. The new senior management of the parent company had been undertaking a detailed review of all its businesses. In the autumn of 1983, the US parent had announced that it intended to rationalise its international operations and that Rough Rider Seating

---

(RRS), including its UK, continental European and Australian manufacturing and distribution facilities, would be put up for sale.

The three UK managers had approached their parent company and suggested a management buy-out (MBO). They believed that RRS Europe, while recently having made losses, was poised to reap the benefit of substantial recent investment in both new products and improved engineering facilities. ECI and Kleinwort Benson were approached to support a purchase valued in total at £7.7m.

2 The business

RRS produced suspension seating for the works vehicle market, primarily trucks and tractors, in addition to construction equipment. The parent company was formed in 1935 and set up a UK subsidiary in 1963, followed by a Belgian subsidiary in 1967. Selling primarily to the 'original equipment manufacturers' (OEM) market, and including most of the largest car, truck and agricultural vehicle manufacturers among their customers, RRS was seen as the worldwide market leader throughout the 1960s and 1970s.

The UK and continental European operations, RRS Europe, grew rapidly in the 1970s but faced a chronic shortage of capital for investment to expand production facilities, despite demand continuously exceeding supply. This scarcity of capital was a result of the US parent's commitment to a heavy domestic acquisitions programme. The purchase of a controlling interest in the original US parent company and its international subsidiaries in 1976 by Beacon did not improve this situation and further funds for new investment in Europe were not sanctioned until 1980.

Unfortunately, by 1980, RRS Europe had inevitably lost market share to aggressive competitors, primarily two German companies. Products were seriously outdated and cost levels reflected the lack of investment in modern production facilities. The decision in 1980 to build a new manufacturing facility in Carlisle, which replaced four smaller and outdated production sites, came too late to prevent serious erosion in the performance of the company and, more importantly, a material loss of RRS Europe's credibility with major customers. These problems were compounded by the investment in expanded production facilities being made at a time when the UK was in the middle of an economic recession. Since 1979 European demand for trucks and tractors had slumped significantly, resulting in a sales decline of over 20 per cent for RRS Europe's products.

Efforts in 1981 to improve the UK situation by investing in a new product range of advanced seating models for trucks, tractors and vans were proving expensive. The new factory was also experiencing significant commissioning problems as the production staff struggled to become familiar with the new equipment and layout of the larger factory. The arrival of a new managing director, Ralph Seddon, in 1982 helped stem immediate losses as a result of his introducing a vigorous cost-cutting programme. However the merging of the US parent company at the beginning of 1983 once again resulted in a moratorium on new investment in Europe. The confirmation that RRS UK and all European and Australian interests would be sold by late 1983 added yet one further challenge.

However, by 1983, the concept of managers becoming part-owners of their former business divisions and subsidiaries through the vehicle of MBO was becoming increasingly widely known and practised in the UK. Accordingly Ralph Seddon (aged 42) in co-operation with the operations director (Chris Harold, aged 36) and the financial director (Ted Marley, aged 36) sought and received permission from their US parent company to launch a management buy-out.

3   The management team

Ralph Seddon, an American, had spent all of his working life in the engineering industry both in the USA and, latterly, the UK. While trained as an engineer, he was uncommon in his grasp and belief in the importance of marketing. He had a good track record of managerial accomplishments and was known to be highly regarded by RRS's major customers.

Chris Harold was a well qualified and progressive production engineer. Harold had been responsible for the introduction of the new production facilities in the UK including two sophisticated 'robot' welding lines. He, likewise, had a good industry reputation.

Ted Marley had started his career as an accountant in the UK car industry and had joined RRS UK four years earlier becoming the financial director in 1980. He was widely familiar with both UK and US financial reporting requirements.

The team showed an unusually good balance of skills. While not including a marketing/sales professional, this responsibility was included within the experience and interests of Ralph Seddon, who became chairman and managing director of RRS Europe. Importantly the team members knew each other well and appeared to work effectively together.

4   The deal

The managers proposed to buy from Beacon Inc. all activities excluding RRS (USA), a company exclusively servicing the US truck market. A sales and distribution agreement was to be signed with Beacon Inc. which gave RRS Europe worldwide marketing agreements, excluding the US and Japanese markets. Immediately after the MBO, the new company would consist of the following:

- United Kingdom – manufacturing and assembly site (225,000 sq. ft), 226 employees.
- Belgium – manufacturing and assembly site (61,000 sq. ft), 84 employees.
- Sweden – distribution and marketing office, three employees.
- Germany – regional sales office, two employees.
- France – regional sales office, two employees.
- Australia – regional sales office, two employees.

The £7.7m. financing package was to be used to finance the following commitments:

- Purchase of RRS Europe from Beacon Inc. (£6.0m.)
- Factory closure in Belgium (£0.7m.)
- Increase in working capital (£0.5m.)
- Additional capital expenditure (£0.2m.)
- Interest charges (£0.3m.)

The purchase of RRS Europe was at a 40 per cent discount on net assets which were valued at around £10 million.

5 Deal funding structure

Although subject to change, it was proposed to fund the deal between ECI Ventures and Kleinwort Benson with the management contributing £100,000 of ordinary shares for 51 per cent of the equity. The concluded agreement was as follows:

Ordinary shares	
Management	£100,000
ECI Ventures	£ 50,000
Kleinwort Benson	£ 50,000
Partly convertible, cumulative, redeemable preference shares	
ECI	£450,000
Kleinwort Benson	£450,000
Subordinated loan from Beacon	£1,600,000
Kleinwort Benson loan & overdraft	£5,000,000
Total	**£7,700,000**

Table 1   RRS Europe trade performance, historic and projected

	Turnover	Op. profit	Op. margin (%)	Net profit[*]	Net margin (%)
Performance (£000s)					
1979	10,808	370	3.4	46	0.4
1980	10,625	309	2.9	187	1.8
1981	7,728	(1,464)	(18.9)	(3,021)	(39.1)
1982	7,779	(1,976)	(25.4)	(3,700)	(47.6)
1983	8,303	(1,062)	(12.8)	(2,509)	(30.2)
Projected (£000s)					
1984	9,400	(370)	(3.9)	(1,285)	(13.7)
1985	11,300	930	8.2	638	5.6
1986	12,100	1,246	10.3	994	8.2
1987	13,300	1,563	11.7	1,403	10.5
1988	14,500	1,926	13.3	1,906	13.1

[*]The net figures included non-recurring costs, which in 1984 will amount to £0.7m. following the closure of the Belgian factory.

Beacon's 12 per cent loan would be paid back in tranches starting from 1986. ECI and Kleinwort Benson would initially hold 49 per cent of the equity (ordinary shares), with their final share depending on the subsequent performance of the MBO. Kleinwort Benson intended to reduce their loan commitment, which was secured on the Carlisle property, by a sale and lease-back arrangement. As was expected, this subsequently realised £4.5m.

6   Historic and projected performance of RRS Europe

Table 1 gives the trading performance of RRS Europe up to the proposed MBO, and its projected recovery as an independent business. The projected sales costs were the same, apart from adjustments relating to the cost of financing the MBO, as those that the UK management submitted to Beacon's board prior to the proposed MBO. The recovery plan was based on the dual objectives of increasing sales volume/market share and unit cost reduction together with a reduction in fixed overheads. Validation of the expected cost reductions was to be included in the due diligence undertaken by the operating accountant.

The optimistic sales forecasts with a 25 per cent increase planned in both 1984 and 1985 were the result of RRS Europe introducing new products in all market segments. These new products either had recently been launched or were in the process of final acceptance testing by major customers. Major customers including Ford Tractor, International Harvester, Iveco and General Motors had confirmed the attraction of the new products and indicated that the projected sales increases were achievable. However, in order to realise the intended sales, it was critically important that RRS Europe ensured that its costs remain attractive against its German competitors.

Variable profit margin, which was the main marketing management tool for product costings, was forecast to improve by 2 per cent in 1984 and 2.1 per cent in 1985. These cost improvements were in large part conditional on the closure of the Belgian manufacturing plant and the transfer of production, valued at £2.4m. sales value per annum, to the more efficient UK site. This transfer would also help reduce non-variable, overhead costs which also put the Belgian factory at a disadvantage.

7 Market size and forecast

RRS Europe sold direct to the major OEMs as well as maintaining a European distribution network for the after-sales market. Customers were serviced by seven sales regional managers and engineers plus two further technical vehicle installation staff. (Table 2).

Management expected to see an increase of over 40 per cent in annual sales in these markets over the five years from 1983. Key buying factors in the industrial seating market were deemed to be (in order of importance):

Table 2 Western Europe: historic and projected sales of suspension/de luxe static seats (thousands of units)

Year	Heavy trucks	Ag tractors	Industry & construction machinery	Forklifts	Total
1979	220	400	95	55	770
1980	210	350	90	50	700
1981	195	315	80	45	635
1982	180	280	65	40	565
1983	185	290	70	45	590
Projected					
1984	195	320	78	48	641
1985	220	330	85	57	692
1986	235	350	90	63	738
1987	250	360	100	68	778
1988	280	380	110	75	845

- price, quality, delivery and performance,
- name/reputation,
- unique technology/product innovation,
- breadth of product line,
- service,
- warranties,
- financing,
- national preference.

The two most serious competitors to RRS Europe were both independent German companies. Isringhausen in the truck market and Grammar in the agricultural market. Both firms were strongly established in the large German market and were expansionist. They each benefited from scale economies through the production of high volumes of standard modular products.

8   Strengths and weaknesses of RRS Europe in 1983

Strengths

1. Competent and well balanced management team which was already showing a positive impact on the fortunes of RRS Europe.
2. New product range on the verge of large-scale commercialisation, and apparently attractive to OEM buyers.
3. Modern and well equipped UK manufacturing plant able to take the planned increase in output. Labour force was disciplined and only weakly unionised. Financial controls were tight, which was consistent with UK parent's management style.
4. Sales forecast was deliberately conservative in line with the US parent's policy of only allowing positive variance. At the time of the MBO, RRS Europe was running 13 per cent ahead of sales budget for 1984/5.

Weaknesses

1. Industrial seating market was heavily reliant on sales to powerful OEMs, which could result in significant pressures on future margins.
2. Future growth of sales was dependent on OEMs' policy of outsourcing products manufactured by RRS Europe.
3. Demand for seatings was derived from the market for trucks, tractors and so on. The truck market was improving, but both

trucks and tractor markets show long-run, cyclical trends.
4. The two remaining European (German) producers were both private firms with strong finances and established market positions. They both competed strongly on price.
5. The US vendor was a potential competitor in Europe if an infringement agreement was not reached.
6. The risks of problems in closing the Belgian plant had not been fully clarified or quantified.
7. The future fortunes of RRS Europe were strongly conditional on the effective team work and continued commitment of the three key managers.

9   Project outcome

The buy-out was successfully concluded in the summer of 1983. A partner from ECI Ventures, Martin Makey, who had been instrumental in effecting the deal, became a non-executive director (and latterly chairman) of the new company. On completion of the purchase, the Belgian manufacturing operation was closed and all production was relocated to the Carlisle factory.

The three managers fully lived up to the commercial expectations placed on them by the external investors. The period to 1988 was to see a record growth in sales and profitability achieved by RRS Europe (see Table 3). The sale of the Belgian factory, as projected, resulted in a substantial reduction in overheads and operating costs. The management also introduced a number of advanced engineering developments into the Carlisle factory, the most important of which was to commit to 'Just in Time' production processes. Research and development into new product lines was continued, resulting in the launch of a number of new suspension units, seating models and related accessories after the buy-out. The directors also sanctioned

Table 3   *RRS Europe: actual results, 1983–8*

	Turnover	Profit (loss) before tax	Earnings per ordinary share (p)
1983	6,195	(1,926)	(19.4)
1984	9,063	(775)	(8.4)
1985	14,028	682	6.2
1986	14,564	579	4.5
1987	16,722	958	8.0
1988	22,261	2,122	13.0

the purchase of two related acquisitions: a manufacturer of gas springs and shock absorbers, and an electrical control equipment supplier for RRS Europe.

By 1988 RRS Europe exported two-thirds of total production, with Western Europe accounting for 87 per cent of sales. The remaining sales were primarily to Australia and Eastern Europe. OEM customers in trucks, agricultural machinery and construction equipment continued to remain the largest customers for RRS Europe's expanded product line, which now included seven separate product ranges and more than 400 final variations.

While the figures showed a remarkable level of sustained performance which significantly exceeded the business plan, the investment had not been without some problems. In particular the relationship between two of the key senior managers became increasingly fraught after the death from cancer of Ted Marley in 1986. Marley had acted as balance and mediator between the two other senior executive managers, Seddon and Harold. The differing personalities, management styles and career objectives of the two directors had been such as to result in an increasingly overt level of hostility between the two men. The untimely death of Marley had removed the most effective brake on their mutual antagonism. Concerns over the long-term effect of this situation on the morale of the management team and the likely deleterious effect on trading performance led the institutional investors to ask for the resignation of Seddon as executive chairman and managing director. After protracted negotiation, Seddon agreed to this request, including the sale of his shares. Based on the 1988 profit forecast, Seddon's 19,166 'A' ordinary shares were valued at £1.6m. This sum was jointly underwritten by ECI Ventures and Kleinwort Benson.

10   The flotation of RRS Europe plc

At the end of 1988, RRS Europe gained a full listing on the London stock market. 3,994,881 ordinary shares of 5p each at 135p per share were placed by Robert Fleming & Co. Ltd. This placing represented 34 per cent of the enlarged issued share capital of 11,488,511 ordinary shares. 2,513,400 of these shares were from the existing shareholders, with the remainder representing a new issue of ordinary shares by the company. The two institutional investors sold 1,673,000 ordinary shares and, following the placing, retained 3,406,800 ordinary shares in the company. The institutional shareholders' equity holding was thereby reduced to 29.7 per cent of the enlarged ordinary shareholding.

The market capitalisation of RRS Europe at the placing price was £15.5 million. The forecast price/earnings multiple at the placing price was 7.8 times (on a forecast tax charge of 11.3 per cent) and 10.8 times (on a forecast tax charge of 35 per cent). Forecast earnings per ordinary share of 17.3p and 12.5p were based on forecast and notional tax charges, respectively. Forecast figures were based on a consolidated profit on ordinary activities before taxation for the year ending 31 December 1988 of not less than £2.05m.

The flotation generated £1.6 million for the company. This additional funding was used to strengthen its capital base and improve liquidity. £213,000 was used to redeem one-third of the institutions' cumulative redeemable preference shares by the end of calendar year 1988, which was a requirement of the original financing package. Nearly £1m. was used to eliminate the group's overdraft.

11   Returns to the institutional investors

Over a four-year period, ECI Ventures provided £698,000 of finance as lead investor and received proceeds and income totalling £1,295,000. The annualised internal rate of return on Rough Rider Seating (Europe) to ECI was 74 per cent.

Franchising: Evaluating the Profit Potential of a Franchise Opportunity

The case gives you guidance on how to evaluate the profit potential of a franchise opportunity by looking at a fictitious company, Fastprint, and comparing it to two other companies: Fastfood and Gamesters.

Questions

1. What do you think of Frastprint's potential?
2. What additional questions would you ask the franchisor?
3. Would you recommend John Smith to take up the franchise?

The Franchisee

At the very minimum you will expect the franchisor to give you a breakdown of the capital you will be expected to provide, and what it will be used to buy, and a projected profit-and-loss account, perhaps showing different results according to the level of sales achieved.

Initially two examples taken from pulicity brochures are shown; they are from the instant print area and from fast foods. As can be seen from a comparison of the two documents, Fastprint have provided a far more detailed breakdown, and one that is far more helpful to the potential investor. It would be almost impossible for the franchisee to make any adjustments to the Fastfood capital requirements without substantial further enquiries, whereas he or his professional advisers can immediately see where Fastprint's estimates might be unduly optimistic or pessimistic. Moreover Fastprint specifically state that prices are exclusive of VAT, whereas Fastfood leave the investor in the dark as to whether VAT would also have to be financed.

However, it is probably unfair to judge franchisors solely on the basis of information included in their publicity brochures; the franchisors have their business to protect and, as they are dealing with individuals who have at least some entrepreneurial spirit, there is a risk of their costings being used by someone else to set up independently. This possibility cannot be eliminated, as anyone who is being asked to part with a fee should demand a detailed breakdown first, but it need not be made too available to the general public.

Assuming that the franchisor has got the start-up costs right, in many cases he is in a position to put the franchisee in touch with sources of finance. If the franchisor has made arrangements with a bank for the provision of loans then there is some assurance that the proposition has been examined and approved (or at least not rejected) by someone with some experience – an important point when the franchisor is not one of the old established or household names.

It is important to have a clear idea of the start-up costs and capital requirements of a franchise, if only because these are going to be a prime determinant of the franchise chosen.

Fastprint Inc

Inventory & capital requirement for a typical base unit

Equipment		£
Offset machine (*see note 1*)	5,000	
Camera/processor	1,625	
Guillotine	1,225	
Cash register	475	
Electronic composer	4,425	
Sundry finishing	500	13,250

Building and furnishings (*see note 2*)
  Shopfitting
  Heating
  Electrical
  Decor
  Signs

Office stationery	
Furniture	
Carpets	8,000
Legal fees	1,000
Franchise 'package' fee	
Property fees	
Architect fees	
Launch promotion	
Training	
Sundry corporate items, etc.	5,600
Licence fee	3,900
Training course expenses (accommodation and travelling)	400
VAT (reclaimable)	3,425
Estimated total capital investment	35,565
Less finance leasing	13,250
Estimated initial capital requirement (*see note 3*)	22,315

VAT shown above is calculated against Equipment, Licence Fee and Franchise Package Fee. All other amounts shown are VAT-exclusive. VAT is recoverable with first VAT return and can then become working capital.

Notes:
1. A reconditioned offset machine may be available at a reduced price.
2. Building costs are based on a shop unit not requiring major construction work. Undeveloped sites will involve a corresponding higher outlay and a property premium may also be required.
3. Licensee's drawings during first year will be required in addition.
While every effort has been made to ensure that the information contained in this statement is accurate, it is intended only as a guide and will vary in each case according to the condition of shop, proposed geographic location and the individual circumstances.

Fast food inc

Capital requirement breakdown	
Shopfitting	£25,000
Equipment	£11,000
Franchise fee	£2,500
	+VAT
	To be paid on
	singing contract

We have taken a shop with a turnover of £2,000 per week as an example. There is no such thing as an absolute average shop and this breakdown is only given as a guide. Prices quoted are correct at time of printing. Franchise fee includes on-site opening assistance and training. There will be an opening publicity campaign which will cost in the region of £800.

Gamesters

The potential franchisee wants to make, if not a fortune, at least a living. The downside of the increased security and reduction of risk that are the attractions of franchising is that the potential rewards are likely to be lower. In order to consider the problems of interpreting the predictions given by franchisors, it may be useful to consider a fictional example constructed from various brochures:

Gamesters Ltd

	£	
Capital outlay:		
Shopfitting	12,000	
Equipment	4,000	
Stock	10,000	
Franchise fee	3,000	
Sundries	1,000	
	30,000	
Profit forecast:	£	
Sales	52,000	
Cost of sales (45%)	23,400	
Gross margin	28,600	
	£	£
Gross margin		28,600
Expenses:		
Franchise royalty (5%)	2,600	
Advertising fund (2%)	1,000	
Wages and NHI	11,000	
Rent, rates, insurance	5,000	
Light & heat	500	
Postage and telephone	400	
Motor and travel	700	
Accountancy	600	
Depreciation	1,500	23,300
Net profit		5,300

The franchisors stated that the predicted sales figure of £1000 per week was a conservative estimate and, given that the business (selling and repairing computer games) would more than break even in the first year, the franchisee could expect a healthy return in subsequent years, if the growth in demand for electronic leisure goods continues.

The prospect looked reasonable, and the franchisee went ahead, financing it as follows:

	£
Own capital	10,000
Loan from parents	10,000
Loan from bank	10,000
	30,000

plus £2000 of his own which provided his initial cash for working capital.

Towards the end of the first year, it became apparent that all was not well; he was running close to the limits of his overdraft facility despite achieving the predicted sales. The only two courses of action appeared to be either to run down his stocks, or to replace his skilled employee with a less able part-timer. Either of these would probably cause sales to deteriorate, and Gamesters would rapidly complain about the damage to their corporate image.

This sort of situation is often caused by a misunderstanding of the term 'break-even'. There are, in fact, three break-even points which should have been calculated in order to assess the financial viability of the business:

1. The operating break-even. The business *has* achieved the operating break-even, considering this as follows: out of every pound's-worth of sales, 45p goes straight out on the immediate cost of goods sold, leaving 55p towards other expenses. The franchise royalty and the advertising fund, which vary directly with sales, take out another 7p, so the other, fixed, costs must be met out of the remaining 48p. These fixed costs total £19,700, so £19,700÷0.48 or £41,042 sales are required to break even.
2. The cash flow break-even. Unfortunately the operating costs do not include all *cash outflows* from the business and, as detailed, do not allow for bank interest or repayments of principal; nor do they allow for drawings for the franchisee and his family to live on. Assuming bank interest at 14 per cent and repayments averaging £2,000 a year, £3,400 is being added to the costs; and if a minimum living expense is estimated at £5,000 then the break-even becomes (19,700+£8,400)÷0.48 or £58,750, which is not being achieved. Even if depreciation is eliminated as not involving cash flow (though the assets will eventually have to be replaced) the break-even is still £55,625.
3. 'Desired return' break-even. This is a rather more nebulous concept, but in the present case the following would probably be taken into account:
    (a) The figure should allow for some interest on the loan from his parents, which he would feel morally, if not legally, obliged to pay – allow £1,400 (as to the bank).
    (b) Had he been able to invest his own capital, it would have earned interest; allow £12,000 at 10 per cent = £1,200.
    (c) Had he been working as an employee, he might have earned, say £9,000 a year rather than the £5,000 drawn.

To keep things simple these figures do not allow for taxation on profits but, of course, depending on personal circumstances, tax may be due.

Further comments on the print franchise

Looking at an actual forecast, again taking Fastprint as one of the most detailed and realistic estimates, there are still some shortcomings: John Smith (an actual individual, though not of that name) having some experience in printing and design, considered taking out a Fastprint franchise, but eventually decided to go it alone. However he found the predicted costings he had been given useful, and prepared his business plan on the basis of them. He obtained finance from the bank under the loan guarantee scheme. Now, after about 18 months' trading, he is in severe financial difficulties because of cash flow problems, and the business could fail in the next few months.

Doubtless Fastprint's would say that this merely proves that he should have had the strength of the franchise company behind him, but it is instructive to see where his costs differed from those predicted. First, the cost of sale figure was too low. Recent increases in the price of paper, especially, meant that the £13,000 needed to be increased by 50 per cent to £19,500. Advertising was about £400, telephone £1,000, sundries £900. The rent, rates and insurance figure was underestimated by £3000 (the figure might have been adequate outside London, but not within; a central London location would have involved an even higher figure). Given that the capital requirements breakdown gave a leased assets figure of £11,000, the 'machine rentals' at £840 seems extremely low. On a four-year contract, £2,800 was regarded as realistic. On the other hand, £1,500 was regarded as a more realistic figure for depreciation, given that the fixtures and fittings were estimated at £7000. Obviously, this would, to a large extent, depend on how quickly the franchise fees and licence fee were written off. This would not, however, affect the cash flow position.

If Fastprint's figures are adjusted for these amounts, the profit of £83,360 reduces to £1,800; and this, it should be remembered, is an operating profit, not taking into account repayments of capital. It is not clear to what the interest figure refers, but if it is a bank loan, then the repayments will presumably be fairly substantial. Nor has anything been allowed for living expenses. So, allowing new fixed overheads of £30,700 and a lower contribution rate of 62.5p, operating break-even would represent sales of £49,120 and cash flow break-even correspondingly higher, depending on loan repayments and personal circumstances.

Had he been a franchisee, John Smith would also have had to pay the royalty and marketing fees of £5,200, which would have turned his profit into a loss of £3,400 and his operating break-even sales would have been £58,500. Whether the franchisee could avoid this would depend on the franchisor's policies – is he allowed to raise prices, or are they fixed? Can he open for longer trading hours? Can he stock sidelines of higher mark-up goods? All these questions need to be answered before signing the contract.

Projected operating statement for an established fast print shop

	£ 1,500	%	£ 2,000	%	£ 2,000	%
Weekly average sales						
Sales	78,000	100	104,000	100	156,000	100
Royalty 5%	7,800	10	10,400	10	15,600	10
Marketing services fund – 5% (see note 1)						
Cost of sales	19,500	25	26,000	25	30,000	25
Gross profit	50,700	65	67,600	65	101,400	65
Overheads						
Wages	16,000		20,800		32,200	
Advertising	750		900		1,600	
Free beverages and music	300		400		700	
Heat and light	1,100		1,300		1,900	
Postage and stationery	350		450		650	
Motor and travel	1,100		1,200		1,800	
Repairs and renewals	1,900		2,400		3,000	
Telephones	700		800		1,100	
Sundry expenses	750		1,000		1,500	
Rent, rates and insurance	7,800		7,800		7,800	
Interest (HP)	1,320		1,320		1,820	
Machine rentals	840		1,560		2,800	
Depreciation	3,040		3,040		3,700	
Bank charges	150		350		400	
Accountancy fees	750		900		1,200	
Total overheads	36,850	47	44,220	43	62,170	40
Net profit (see note 2)	13,850	18	23,380	22	39,330	25

Notes:
1. Marketing services fund is guaranteed to be spent entirely on advertising and marketing services to promote and develop the service in accordance with clause 7(a) (ii) of the licence agreement.
2. These figures should not be construed as representations of profits of any specific franchise, nor as any assurance that a new franchise will in fact make a profit.

Short Engineering (A)

Short Engineering is buying a Dutch company called Pelumbo and Donald Dunsinane is going over there to meet the staff and 'sell' the deal to them.

Questions

1. What are the questions you think he is likely to be asked?
2. Do you think he is right to use M. Presnic as an interpreter?

General introduction

Short Engineering had been in several locations in the south Midlands since it started business in 1971. It saw itself principally as a satellite business supplying components to car manufacturers. It tried to survive the motor industry's recession years and the increasing competition from other supplier by concentrating on parts for specialist manufacturers, including car kit producers. However in the early 1980s sales dropped considerably. To try and save the business Donald Dunsinane, a 'company doctor' with a proven record, was brought in as chief executive. As part of the deal he became the major, but not the controlling, shareholder and he was given control over operations and planning.

Overseas sales had always contributed a small but generally increasing part of total sales. For a long while Short had had a direct export involvement with Pelumbo, a business situated near Enschede, in Holland, close to the border with Germany. Pelumbo was a family business with some 45 employees. It was run in rather a lethargic way by an owner-manager who, by the late 1980s, was near retiring age. Most overseas sales had been channelled through this business. Pelumbo had been used as an agent and distributor in an attempt to capture a share of the market in that area.

When he started work in 1986, Donald Dunsinane set about reducing the number of employees. When he took over Short were employing about 450. By 1990 the staff numbered 370. Dunsinane offered job shops, outplacement counselling and generous redundancy payments. By the early 1990s he had a slimmed down staff force with whom he enjoyed good relations, and a steadily increasing cash balance at the bank. He had also increased total annual sales from around £6.5 million to £8.5 million.

In 1993/4 the domestic market showed signs of further slowing down. Dunsinane felt that he had already secured as large a part of the home market as was practical, and that no further substantial cost reductions could be made. He decided that the time had come for a bold expansion into Europe. This would mean acquiring limited manufacturing facilities. Pelumbo had these. Dunsinane also knew that Pelumbo's owner was not averse to selling. In February 1995 the board of Short supported Dunsinane in his proposal to acquire Pelumbo.

Donald Dunsinane was a working engineer by profession. He had obtained an MBA degree the hard way through a local Distance Learning MBA course. On any showing he was the driving force behind Short's success, though he would have been the first to admit that Geoff Pearson, his finance director, and the only other executive director, had been a formidable right-hand man. He gave Geoff considerable freedom of action and relied heavily on his judgement. On several occasions Geoff had pulled him up short when he had tried to put through some of his wilder ideas. On this occasion he decided to put Geoff in general charge both of the takeover and of management control at Pelumbo.

The 'sell' to the new employees at Pelumbo

At the informal, weekly, Friday evening meeting between Donald Dunsinane and Geoff Pearson the main item for discussion was the 'sell' to the staff at Pelumbo. The deal with Pelumbo had been finalised. Both men agreed that it was essential for Donald, as chairman, to go across to Enschede, address the employees there, tell them about the benefits that being a subsidiary of Shorts would bring, discuss their anxieties, allay their fears and, generally, as Geoff put it, 'get them on our side'. Geoff had jotted down a few brief notes which he handed to Don:

1. Interpreter. Which one?
2. Short. Its strengths. Mention turnover, profit (we will have to be a little careful about that; we do not want to give the impression that we are overendowed with the good things of life which they can have unlimited access to), pension scheme, labour turnover figures.
3. Advantages of being a subsidiary of a larger organisation:
   - increase in sales, access to a wider market;
   - better supplies, lower cost of sales;
   - economies of scale;
   - technical help;
   - stability, capacity to ride out a temporary local recession;
   - welfare, pension, retirement benefits; opportunities for promotion to senior posts overseas;
   - better funding.
4. Rumours. Deal with these. A few we already know about; for example, that we mean to sack anyone who has been there over five years (though one version I heard said anyone over five feet!)
5. The future. Projections of our sales turnover figures and so on.
6. Concern. Emphasise that we are interested in the business and the employees. Mention the concession on holidays that we have agreed here, namely that both Catholic and Protestant holiday days will be given to all employees regardless of race or religion – and that is in line with our approach to all problems in this area.
7. Any questions. Give assurances, but no promises. Say that you are prepared to see any employee on a one-to-one basis, by appointment, the next day. Give out a sheet at the end, with the information given in this talk in Dutch, for the employees to mull over.

Don finished reading the note. 'You seem to have covered everything, Geoff. Will you let me have the turnover and profit figures you mentioned ... and leave the rest to me. Oh, two points. First, what if everyone wants to come and see me the next day? I can only do so much in 20 hours.'

'They won't Geoff. This is a PR exercise. You've made the offer. That is the point. If quite a few come along, do what my dentist does.'

'What?'

'He gives everyone three minutes to start off with. He then has an x-ray taken, or something, or anything, and makes a later appointment to discuss more fully.'

'OK, Geoff. Now, second, what is all this about the interpreter? I thought we used the man from the local branch of our auditors!'

'Last week, when I was in Enschede, he was not available, and I used a M. Presnic. I got him through the commercial section at the British consulate. I think you should use him.'

'Why not our auditor man? He is English. He got a degree in foreign languages, including Dutch, at Oxford, or some such place, as I recall. I find him easy to get on with.'

'Yes, but do these Dutch? This is their meeting. A lot of them speak the local dialect, half German/half Dutch. Many do not speak any English at all, which is unusual in the Netherlands. We want to be close to them, not distance ourselves with someone who will be seen as a foreigner, an intellectual . . . and not one of them.'

'And Mr Presnic?'

'Is old and dignified, and not at all easy to get on with at first. But he is a local man and speaks the local dialect. Initially I asked him to come along to my hotel for coffee. I found him distinctly sticky when we discussed what I wanted to say at the various government departments which I was visiting. His English was only moderate. The rates he insisted on charging, as a "senior interpreter" for embassy work, were very high.'

'Well go on, give us the good news Geoff.'

'After the meetings, which he handled very well, I pulled out some money to pay him. We had been together for six hours in all. He insisted on charging only for the time at work, and he was pretty conservative even about that.'

'Well?'

'I walked home with him. At our parting of ways he asked me if I would like to come and have a drink at his place. I refused. I had other things to do. I looked at his face. Clearly he wanted me to come along. So I changed my mind.'

'Yes?'

'We had a great time. As a young boy he had been in a local "maquis", and lived in the shrub. He had a great stock of stories. And –

'All right Geoff, so you got drunk and you liked him. Good.'

'Very good indeed, Don. He will be highly respected by the employees at Pelumbo. He will not stand for any nonsense from them. On our side, conversation may be a little difficult, but so what, we can live with that. It's the employees we are concerned about at this meeting.'

'Right, Geoff, you have made your point. Engage him for me, but let me have a little chat first. And I'll give him a cognac with his coffee . . . and don't worry, I'll do my best at the meeting.'

Geoff sat back in his seat. I'm not worried about that, he thought. Don could think very fast on his feet, and he could be very persuasive. He remembered going to see a director of a small business that

Short had eventually taken over. 'Your chairman has just been to see me,' he had said reflectively. 'I'm now definitely in favour of the deal, yet before Mr Dunsinane arrived, do you know, I'm almost certain that, on balance, I was against it. Very strange.'

Short Engineering (B)

Three months after the takeover, Donald has just received a disturbing report from the company's auditors.

Questions

1. What do you think of the report?
2. How many of the problems might be due to 'cultural' differences?
3. What do you think are Geoff's motivations?
4. What do you think of his proposals?

Some while after the takeover of Pelumbo, Geoff walked into Donald's office one Friday for their customary end-of-week chat (referred to as their 'kitchen cabinet meeting' by the staff: certainly many major decisions, later to be presented to the full board, were made there). As soon as he appeared Donald threw down a report on Geoff's seat.

'Look at this,' he said, 'it has just arrived on my desk.' When Geoff began to leaf through it, Donald said almost angrily. 'Just look at the summary [attached] Geoff. It is nothing but criticisms.' When Geoff started to say something he went on, 'I am particularly bothered about the first item on the list, that is lack of motivation in our overseas Dutch staff. That's really bad. We will never get anywhere if we do not have the staff on our side. It is highly critical of the accounts and information, too. You realise this report is from our auditors, with the investigatory work done by their local branch out there. Shakes you, doesn't it? They must have been busy. They must have had a good reason for doing it.'

'Yes, Don, the reason is that I told them to do it.'

'You! ... well good, but what for?'

Geoff paused before replying. 'It had become increasingly obvious to me that something was wrong. I wanted to know what should be done; more accurately I wanted a reason for doing it.'

'So you commissioned the report, you cunning old devil, so that you could act!'

'Yes, the usual reason for calling in consultants. They tell you what you already know, but they give you the lever.'

'Where are you proposing that we apply this lever?'

'To both the accounts manager and the sales manager at Pelumbo. They have got to go, and now is the right time.'

Donald thought a while. 'I see what it is all about,' he said. 'Yes, that will certainly stir things up a bit. But what have you got positively to recommend. Frightening the others is not enough'.

'I'm aiming to frighten them into using responsibility centres, and using them effectively. Each junior manager will be a responsibility centre under my new organisation scheme, and his or her performance will be monitored.'

'How?'

'Using past performance figures and a wide range of measuring methods. Not all of these will be financial, I would like to add. All responsibility centres will be expense centres or profit centres, with the exception of the subsidiary as a whole, which will be an investment centre. Its performance will be checked on by return on net assets.'

'So you sack these two people and put in responsibility centres.'

'No, Don, the other way round. I put in responsibility centres forthwith. Two people do not show up well in the reports on their responsibility centre, and they get the sack.'

'Are you sure it will be these two?'

'Certain. They'll show up badly on any performance appraisal reports.'

'What performance indicators are you using for accounts and sales?'

'Accounts will be based on costs and numbers of staff; also the work done: that is, invoices, statements, payroll calculations and so on. I'm recording all these, and the debtor figures. The delay in debt collection will be costed by putting in a notional interest figure. And as for the writing off of bad debts, I'm going to be ruthless there: anything over a year goes, as you may know. And I'm having complaints from customers logged. Finally I am comparing all these with the figures for our accounts department here.'

'Quite a lot of work in having this done Geoff. It will cost.'

'It will, initially, but the pay-off will be substantial in a year or two.'

'And sales?'

'By sales, and the order-getting costs. I also intend to use bad debts and delay in debtor payments.'

'Bad debts again? This is double counting, Geoff.'

'I want two people out, Don.'

'And you say you have costed all this?'

'Yes, and it will not be much. Most of the costs of collection work will be done in spare time. There will not be any extra salaries or staff costs. The staff at Pelumbo will just see it as part of the long-expected changes: one of the disadvantages of being controlled from overseas.'

'I do not see how you can prove that the accountant is ineffective. Comparing with his own poor past performance figures will not show anything ... Don't you anticipate any trouble with him?'

'No. If it comes to the point I have figures and costs for having all the work of his department done externally; that is, credit factoring, including debt collection and payroll preparation work done by a computerised agency. But I do not anticipate any problems.'

'OK, Geoff. Pour yourself and myself a drink, and go to it!'

Summary of report by the auditors – Short Engineering Co

The problem areas are:

1. Lack of motivation in most of the staff.
2. Lack of a 'professional' managerial approach.
3. Lack of understanding of management accounting procedures. In particular:
    -   Inability to make reasonable forecasts. Forecasts appear to have been made by taking the previous period's figures and adding on a fixed percentage – typically 2.5 per cent for sales and 5 per cent for variable costs – then adding a figure for inflation.
    -   Inexperience of overseas management in preparing reports. No 'workings' are given, and the final figures are suspect. The comparative figures given for the previous month often do not match up with the actual reported figure for that month.
    -   Failure to adhere to timetables, particularly in the presentation of monthly reports.
    -   Not much understanding of the concept of working capital control. The chasing of debtors is spasmodic and lacks any sense of urgency. It appears to be non-existent for those debtors regarded as friends or 'family'.

- Stock control is poor. It almost seems as if large stocks are seen as something of which to be proud. JIT management in ordering occurs more by default than by good control. A 'masterly policy of inactivity', galvanised at the last moment by a panic call for some materials, is their idea of 'just-in-time' management.

4. Language difficulties. We were particularly unimpressed by the accountant who repeatedly stated that he understood 'most of what we had said.' It is now evident that he did not.

These are the main areas where we feel problems exist with your recently acquired overseas unit. However these problems are compounded by the practices of some of the staff at your own HQ. Some of these make requests for information which are not specific. Some requests are made too late for compliance to be reasonably possible.

We have discussed these problems with your finance director, Mr Geoff Pearson, and it has been agreed that in principle, the answer should be:

1. To monitor the staff more effectively by the installation of a system of responsibility centres.
2. To initiate a series of training courses. Some of these courses will be technical. Most will be given by UK staff, a few by external organisations.

Some of the courses will be language courses. Apart from some workers on the shop floor all staff will be required to attend short, in-house, English language courses. Additionally some sales staff will be given the opportunity to attend external language courses in French and possibly German.

Index

Accounting 68–9
East–West differences 202–4
Agency 166–7
Alternative Investment Market
   (AIM) 150
Apple 26, 5

Banks 80, 115–28, 186, 205, 206–7
   service gaps 120–6
Bankruptcy *see* Failure
Bolton Report 3, 95, 199
Break-even 68, 191, 195
British Ventura Capital Association
   (BVCA) 134–6, 138, 141–3, 145,
   152, 158
Business angels 114–15, 138
Business attitudes *see* Social
   attitudes
Business Expansion Scheme 113
Business format franchising 168
Business plan 44, 154, 155, 180–97

Cash flow 68, 191, 95
Centre for Financial Analysis 201–2
Change/denial curve 64–5
Churchill, N. C. and Lewis, V. L.
   61–8
Collateral 118
Companies 8, 35
Companies Acts 3, 199
Competitive advantage 16, 57,
   83–4, 161
Competitive strategy 5
Control 62, 103
Cooperative ownership 35
Corporate venturing 155–7
Customers 77, 183

Debt 68, 115–18, 205
Development capital 146, 206
Differential advantage 43, 55–6
Differentiation 55–6, 82
Distributorship 166–7
Diversification 59–60, 184
Dividend policy 79, 187
Downsizing 16, 17
Due diligence 146

Early stage finance 143, 146
East Europe 202–4, 209
Economies of scale 16, 18, 52–4, 55
English language 207–9
Entrepreneur 21–4, 45, 49, 74,
   94–108
   see also Owner-manager
Entrepreneurial firms 6
Entrepreneurship 74–91
Equity 111–15, 186–8, 205–6
Equity gap 112–13, 132–4, 146, 162,
   206
European Commission (EC) 4,
   198–201, 206, 208, 213–14
European Free Trade Association
   (EFTA) 209
European Observatory for SMEs
   200
European Venture Capital
   Association (EVCA) 137
Eurostat 200
Exhibitions 84
Exit routes 186
Expansion financing 144

Factoring 68, 126–7
Failure 14, 66–70

Family 21, 78–9
Fast growth *see* Supergrowth
Financing 5, 110–28, 180, 182, 191, 194, 204–7
Follow-on finance 144
Forum of Private Business 121
Franchisee 173–5
  characteristics 176–7
Franchising 166–78
Franchisor 172–3
Freud, S. 96

General practitioners 26, 184
Globalisation 16
Greiner, L. E. 61
Growth models 60–8, 86–7, 88–9

Help agencies 35–6

Information asymmetry 113–14
Innovation 80–5, 156
Internal rate of return (IRR) 155–6

Labour Force Survey 11
Leasing 68, 127–8
Loan applications 117
Loan notes 140
Loans *see* Debts; Banks
Location 10–11
Licence 167
Life cycles 14, 15
LIfe-style business 5, 45

Macmillan Committee 112, 131
Management 43–4, 61–7, 85–90, 191, 193–4
Markets 76, 81, 181, 190, 192
Material World 178
MBO/MBIs 133–4, 141, 144–6, 150–2, 155, 161, 162, 188
Mergers *see* Takeovers
Mission statement 183–4
Mezzanine finance 140
Morgan Motor Company 58–9

Networks 16, 18, 30–2, 67, 152, 206
New markets 59
New products 59, 81–2
Niche 15, 58–9

Objectives 181–5
'Over the counter' (OTC) market 113

Owner-manager 5, 25, 45–9, 69–70, 85, 85–6
  see also Entrepreneur

Partners 36–7
Partnership sourcing 17
Partnerships 8, 35
Pencil and paper tests 97–100
Porter, Michael 84
  five forces 50–2, 158
  generic strategies 54–7
Position audit 181–5
Price competition 55–7, 82
Projective tests 97
Psychometric test 97–100
Pull and push factors 18

Quad Electroaccoustics 56

Resources merry-go-round 27–30
Replacement capital *see* Development capital
Risk 88, 155, 188

Sandiford Computer Services Ltd 16
Secondary purchase 144
Sectors 8, 170
Seed capital 145, 148
Segmentation 5, 56–8
Senior debt 140
Shamrock organisation 17
Short-termism 79–80
16 Personality Test (16PF) 98
Small firms
  definition of 3–4, 199
  location 10–11
  statistics 2–3, 6–14, 200–1, 216
Smith, Adam 96
Social attitudes 25–6, 104–6, 135–6, 211
Sole traders 8, 35
Sphinx Ltd 188–9
Stage models *see* Growth models
Start-up 20–39, 46–7, 143
Strategy 42–3, 185–6
  generic 54–8
  growth 49–60
  market entry 34
Subcontractors 77
Success, elements of 44
Succession 214
Supergrowth 41–2, 82, 89–90, 149
SWOT analysis 50, 181–2

Syndication, of financing deals 153
Synergy 60

Takeovers and mergers 59–60,
    212–14
Teams 87–88
3i 42, 56, 112, 135, 142, 146–7, 152,
    160, 215
Trade mark 168
Training 79, 107, 215–16
Training and Enterprise Councils
    (TECs) 215

Triggers 26

Uncertainty 75–80, 90–1
Unlisted Securities Market 113, 150
Unique selling proposition 67

Vendor finance 140
Venture capital 68, 113, 131–62,
    206
Vision 28, 102, 184

Wilson Committee , 112, 119, 205